THE UNITY OF CHRISTIANS

AUGUSTIN CARDINAL BEA

THE
UNITY
OF
CHRISTIANS

EDITED BY BERNARD LEEMING S.J.
INTRODUCTION BY
ARCHBISHOP GERALD P. O'HARA

HERDER AND HERDER

1963
HERDER AND HERDER NEW YORK
232 Madison Avenue, New York 16, N.Y.

Library of Congress Catalog Card Number: 63-11307
© compilation, 1963, Geoffrey Chapman Ltd.
Printed in Great Britain
Imprimatur: Georgius L. Craven, Epus, Sebastopolis, la die martii, 1963.

CONTENTS

Part Two

THE SECRETARIAT FOR THE PROMOTION OF THE UNITY OF CHRISTIANS

Part Three

CONCLUSION

ACKNOWLEDGEMENTS

THIS COLLECTION was first published in Italy, under the title *L'Unione dei Cristiani* by Edizioni 'La Civiltà Cattolica'. It has been translated into English under the general supervision and editorship of Bernard Leeming S.J. Reference to the original publication of each article will be found in a footnote at the beginning of each chapter. Certain slight modifications have been made in the English text, with the approval of the author.

The publishers are grateful to the editors of the following publications for their permission to use material first appearing in translation therein: *The Month*, March 1961 (ch. 5), January 1962 (ch. 10); *The Furrow*, June 1962 (ch. 8, translated I. McQuillan), January 1962 (ch. 9, translated G. Watson); *The Messenger of the Sacred Heart*, January 1961 (ch. 2); to the Apostleship of Prayer in Rome, for their version of ch. 4; to Sheed & Ward, London, for permission to use the lecture given in ch. 6, which first appeared in *Christian Unity: A Catholic View* (ed. J. C. Heenan); to the American Broadcasting Company, who supplied the transcript of the television interview reprinted in ch. 16. The translators of the remaining material were: ch. 1, 16, 18, A. V. Littledale; ch. 3, 11, 13, 20, L. Hughes S.J.; ch. 7, 12, Michael Barry; ch. 14, 17, Geoffrey Stevens; ch. 19, L. C. Sheppard.

ABBREVIATIONS

A.A.S.	*Acta Apostolicæ Sedis*
Acta et Doc.	*Acta et documenta*
C.I.C.	*Codex Iuris Canonici*
C.T.S.	Catholic Truth Society
I.C.I.	*Informations Catholiques Internationales*
K.N.A.	*Katholische Nachrichten Agentur*

INTRODUCTION

POPE JOHN XXIII announced his desire to hold an Ecumenical Council on 25 January, 1959. On Whitsunday 1960, along with other groups of experts charged with the immediate preparations, he set up a Secretariat for the Promotion of Christian Unity. This he described as 'a special sign of esteem and affection for separated Christians'. Its function would be to enable them to follow the work of the Council as closely as possible.

As head of the Secretariat the Pope appointed Augustin Cardinal Bea. A surprising appointment in the opinion of many. The Cardinal was well known as a Bible scholar and lecturer. Some knew of his remarkable authority as a spiritual guide: an authority which won him the confidence of the last two popes. Few were prepared to see him, in his late seventies, emerge on the international plane in a totally new role.

This, in effect, was what the papal appointment invited him to do. He has responded with an astonishing Indian Summer of ecumenical activity. Large audiences in the main cities of Italy, Switzerland, Germany, Austria and France have listened to him. The English Television screen has shown him several times. Leaders and thinkers from all the Christian bodies have met him or corresponded with him. He has published articles which have been translated into every language. All the time he has guided the work of his team of experts in the Secretariat as they prepared draft proposals for the Vatican Council. After long hours of discussion, his mind remains fresh and adventurous, his winning smile encourages the speaker wrestling with new ideas in the Latin tongue. His own Latin is simple and supple. He keeps the debate easily and good-humouredly under control, never making an otiose intervention, never missing a chance to give the discussion a keener edge.

This collection of his public utterances, which I have the honour to introduce, is welcome, first of all, since it makes available in English under one cover much that has hitherto appeared in our tongue only piecemeal and in professional reviews.

A word of caution may be in place. Those who have the cause of Christian Unity at heart know that its interests are served rather by penetrating more deeply into principles than by sensational offers and cut-and-dried schemes. We have come to associate this latter technique with take-over bids. You will find nothing of that kind in this book. Here are the reflections of a mature mind on the most agonizing Christian problem of our times. They challenge in their own right because of their remarkable combination of patient wisdom with youthful freshness and ardent charity. They are supremely valuable as being the expression of the mind in closest contact with Pope John XXIII.

A word of thanks is most certainly necessary. I mean from our side. Bishops, clergy and laity have all, in our own way, struggled with the problems of divided Christendom. However energetically we may have backed schemes for explaining the Faith, there was always a vague realization that more should be done, new approaches should be found, new attitudes should be adopted. Work in the mission fields seemed simpler and more rewarding by comparison. Yet the very fact that we could do something to extend the kingdom of God, where the Gospel has never been preached, made all the more apparent our tardiness in old Christian countries to remove the differences that separated us. Were not those same differences again the reason why the kingdom of God advanced so slowly in the mission fields? Who will listen to discordant voices for long? If there is another voice, clear and coherent, what chance has the Gospel of being heard?

It was necessary for someone in the highest position in the Church to throw light on what many of us must acknowledge to have been our blind spot. We hesitated to cultivate other than purely personal friendships with our non-Catholic brethren. Indeed we were sparing of those. What might our people think? Should we risk compromising the principles of our Holy Faith in their or in any other eyes?

Pope John has given us a lead. In the cause of the unity for which our Lord prayed to his heavenly Father, we must begin by shifting the old emphasis in the phrase 'separated brethren'. The accent must be on the second word—not on the first.

Pope John's own example is an open book in which all can read, but in which we, his own children, are *intended* to read the lesson of a new approach. Formal relations of mutual respect are not enough: they must ripen into friendship. Courtesy must be more than correct; it must be genuinely cordial. Along with the improvement of personal relations must go a better understanding of the mind of non-Catholic Christians: a dialogue, not a monologue, at the deepest level.

The instrument through which Pope John matured and propagated this new approach is the Secretariat of Christian Unity. His chosen right-hand man in the work is Cardinal Bea. It has been his achievement to develop into broad, luminous principles and coherent policies the spontaneous hints and initiatives offered by the Pope on so many different occasions. We on our side cannot be too grateful for his competence, so richly displayed in this present collection.

Non-Catholics will also be grateful. They will find in Cardinal Bea's reflections much to help them to resolve the dilemma felt by all serious students of unity: how to present the changeless Christian faith in a way suitable for the comprehension of the modern world. At times the Cardinal's idiom will be unfamiliar. If they look to the substance of his thought, I should be surprised if they do not find unsuspected meeting points—points which will serve them well in their own task of presenting the ecumenical idea to those who still regard it with suspicion.

This book is the fruit of an apostleship of Christian Unity. The apostle is not a firebrand, though a fire burns within him. He is not an iconoclast, though in a quiet persistent way he has broken many idols erected by ignorance and prejudice on both sides. He is a reformer, yet alert to the danger of scandalizing little ones and convinced that lasting reform cannot be forced but must spring from within—from deep compassion for the sufferings, intolerance, ignorance and suspicion of fallen mankind. He is evangelical, testing attitudes, plans, and hopes by the Word of God as we find it in the scriptures and the teaching magisterium of the Church, which is the mystical Body of Christ. He is penetrating yet simple; so simple, sometimes, that the depth of his thought might easily be missed.

Cardinal Bea's basic conviction is this: the work of reuniting Christians is the work of God and it will be accomplished through the grace of God, no matter how difficult it may seem from a human standpoint. For that reason he makes no forecast about the future. The future is in God's hands; the foolishness of God is wiser than men.

He holds that the truth cannot change but human perception of it can grow in depth and width. No dogmatic definition can be changed but no dogmatic definition exhausts the truth. The truth revealed by Christ has an undiminished power to teach men lessons which we have not yet learned and accents in which we have not yet spoken.

This collection caters for vastly different audiences: simple Catholics, University dons and professors, and 'mixed gatherings' of Catholics and non-Catholics. Some of the chapters were first delivered to Italians and Spaniards, all were written before the Council, and some almost three years ago. The casual reader looking for items of 'news interest' may perhaps find nothing startling. Wisdom seldom startles, though it makes thoughtful those who will listen.

One point of great importance is the Cardinal's insistence upon the effect of baptism in relating all the baptized to the mystical Body. This is the basis of a brotherhood which is truly Christian and does not exist between Christians and the unbaptized, even though all men are children of a common Father. Christian baptism is the basis of a union already existing which must be developed to its natural completion. In these addresses the reader will find the Cardinal insisting on the need, not only for charity towards non-Catholic Christians, but also respect and esteem for them; he will find the Cardinal stressing the need for a deeper attention to sacred scripture on the part of scholars, the clergy and the faithful. Theological 'dialogue' is definitely not a monologue. Catholic theologians must listen as well as speak so that they can the better understand the thought and mind of their separated brethren.

As I write, the Second Vatican Council has actually begun. The Basilica of St Peter's is witnessing a sight which is unique in all the history of the Church. Each meeting of the General Congregations begins with the celebration of a low Mass; it is a dialogue Mass between the celebrant and the more than two thousand five hundred Fathers of the Council gathered from the four corners of the earth. At each Mass we are vividly reminded of the universality of the Church in the persons of those who are the celebrants of the Congregation Masses. Our minds leap from country to country and even from continent to continent as we see each day's celebrant approach the altar. Saragossa and Mexico City; Rotterdam and Nagasaki; Florence and Philadelphia; South America and Africa: all are represented in the persons of the Archbishops or Bishops who are the celebrants of the General Congregation Masses. One of the Masses was celebrated by the Negro Bishop of Koupela in Africa. There has also been Mass in the Byzantine Rite and it was a most beautiful ceremony to witness. To-day the anniversary of the Coronation of Pope John XXIII a solemn Mass will be celebrated in the Ambrosian Rite by the Cardinal Archbishop of Milan. One cannot assist at these Masses without being profoundly moved by a sense of authentic universality and unity. Another interesting and striking element of the General Congregations is the presence of some thirty-eight Observers, representing non-Catholic Churches. They occupy, one can say, a privileged place in the Basilica, on the floor level close to the Papal Altar. It was the desire of Pope John XXIII that they should be present. Two days after the Council opened the Observers were received in special audience by the Pope. At the end of his address the Holy Father confided the heartfelt desire he has to work and to suffer for the hour to come when the prayer of our Lord at the Last Supper may be realized.

On 15 October, Cardinal Bea, as President of the Secretariat for the Promotion of Christian Unity, gave a reception for the Observers. Surrounded by the members and consultors of the Secretariat, he echoed the theme of the addresses contained in the present volume by his first words 'My dear Brothers in Christ', a title based on the grace of baptism which has established indestructible bonds, stronger than 'all our divisions'. Cardinal Bea reminded his hearers 'that our faith in the irresistible efficacy of the grace of Christ and in the work of the Holy Spirit among the baptized must not be weak'.

Professor Edmond Schlink of the University of Heidelberg replied on behalf of the Observers. After expressing his thanks to the Holy Father for his initiative in creating a new atmosphere of friendly approach and serenity towards the non-Catholic Churches, Professor Schlink concluded his speech with the assurance 'that the solemn invocation of the Holy Spirit at the opening of the Council has also been the prayer of all of the Observers and guests for the happy outcome of the Council'.

May the reading of these writings and addresses of Cardinal Bea prompt us to join in that invocation of the Holy Spirit for the promotion of Christian Unity. 'This is the Lord's doing and it is marvellous in our eyes' (Mt 21:42).

Gerald P. O'Hara
Apostolic Delegate in Great Britain.

Rome,
Feast of St Charles Borromeo,
4 November, 1962.

PART ONE

PROBLEMS, PRINCIPLES AND MEANS

I

THE CATHOLIC ATTITUDE TOWARDS THE PROBLEM[1]

His Holiness Pope John XXIII, in announcing the Ecumenical Council, assigned to it, among other tasks, that of furthering Christian unity. For those who, though baptized, are separated from the Apostolic See, he hoped the Council would be an 'inspiration to seek out that unity which Jesus Christ prayed for so ardently from his heavenly Father'.[2] So the Council should make a serious effort towards the unity which our Lord himself desires and prays for. It is in this context of striving for unity that we should read also the memorable and solemn words uttered by the Holy Father in his address of 14 December 1960: '. . . it is a command and a sacred duty to place holiness, both of clergy and laity, at the base of every effort to develop the energies of the Church . . . We do not hesitate to say that all our care and zeal to make the Council productive of great results could remain useless if this collective effort towards holiness were to lack unanimity and resolution. Nothing can further the purpose of the Council so much as the pursuit and attainment of holiness.'[3]

One may say, then, that the whole Church has been mobilized in the great cause of union. We have heard an impressive call to the fold of Christ.

This mobilization of the Church is for each of us a summons to holiness, to prayer and to sacrifice. It also invites us to reflect on the attitude of the Church towards our separated brothers and to

[1] Original text: 'Il cattolico di fronte al problema dell' unione dei cristiani', in *La Civiltà Cattolica*, 1961, I, pp. 113-129.

[2] Encyclical *Ad Petri Cathedram*, in *A.A.S.* LI (1959), p. 511. English translation, C.T.S., London, 1959, para. 14.

[3] *Osservatore Romano*, 14-15 Nov. 1960, p. 2.

consider our own attitude towards them and the doctrinal principles
involved.

I

Our attitude towards separated brethren

In this matter, the right *via media* is not easy to discover. Looking
at the facts, we find two attitudes almost diametrically opposed.

The first is adopted by those who are most impressed by the
existence of heresy or schism: separated Christians either adhere to a
doctrine or doctrinal system declared by the Roman Catholic
Church to be heretical, or belong to a schismatical body which
refuses obedience to the Bishop of Rome as visible head of the whole
Church of Christ. Now heresy and schism are of their own nature
most serious and whoever adheres to them by his teaching and
example creates dangers to the faith of other members of the Church.
It is this that leads to the first attitude, one of extreme reserve,
defensiveness, severity and even the avoidance of contact.

The other attitude is almost diametrically opposed to this. It is
inclined to condemn outright the severe attitude I have described,
to look on it as a survival of the ill-famed 'Inquisition', or at least
as outdated, suited to the Old Testament and not to the New, and
certainly not to the charity of Christ. Nowadays—so it runs—we
must be 'open to all', try to understand and recognize what is true
and good in the position of others, taking account above all of their
sincere intentions and realizing our own shortcomings. We ought
to learn from them and draw upon the riches to be found in other
Christian bodies as well as in our own. This attitude could end in
making the Catholic Church merely one among equal Christian
bodies; there is much talk of the real or alleged defects, of the mis-
takes, the pettiness, and the narrow-mindedness of our Church.
Demands are made for a spirit of charitable conciliation, ready to
make concessions even at the cost of some sacrifice, so long as unity
is furthered. Sometimes people go as far as asking for such 'understanding' of separated brethren as to demand of them acceptance
only of dogmas judged 'essential'.

What is to be said of these two attitudes?

The mere description of them brings into focus the main elements of the problem. It is not hard to see that both attitudes are extreme, each containing some truth and some falsehood or, at least, something exaggerated or incomplete. A more careful analysis of them is therefore necessary, so as to distinguish what is true and right from what is mistaken or exaggerated.

As to the first attitude, I consider it important to recall the well known distinction made by St Augustine: *Odisse errores, diligere errantes*—hate error, love those who err. Distinguish, therefore, between heresy and schism as such, and the people who, in one way or another, adhere to them.

'Hate error'

Let us consider, first of all, heresy and schism in themselves. It is a fact that the Church, from the very first pages of the New Testament, displays great severity in matters of discipline, of obedience to her authority, of faithfulness in doctrine. It is true that this severity surprises modern man (and perhaps us as well), and sometimes even jars upon him as counter to his sense of humanity, of understanding, broadmindedness and tolerance. He regards it as axiomatic nowadays that human relationships should be regulated mainly, even exclusively, by a 'civilized' outlook.

Nevertheless both Holy Scripture and the history of the Church show definite severity. To try to ignore this would be cowardly; the words of scripture, which are the words of God himself, must be taken seriously.

To simplify it, I will leave out the evidence of the Fathers of the Church and of the Councils, and deal only with the New Testament, which is the rule of faith and life for all who call themselves Christians.

Now it is beyond dispute that the New Testament uses severe language about right conduct and true doctrine. St Paul, to whom we owe the sublime hymn to charity, nevertheless sometimes seems harsh. He writes to the Corinthians: 'Choose, then; am I to come

to you rod in hand, or lovingly, in a spirit of forbearance?' (1 Cor
4:21). As to the Cretans, he cites one of their poets, who calls them
'always liars, evil beasts, slothful bellies', and he orders Titus to 'be
strict, then, in taking them to task, so that they may be soundly
established in the faith' (Tit 1:13). Moreover, severity is not limited
to words, but is to be shown in action. To the Corinthians he writes:
'If anyone who is counted among the brethren is debauched, or a
miser, or an idolater, or bitter of speech, or a drunkard, or an
extortioner, you must avoid his company; you must not even sit at
table with him' (1 Cor 5:11). The apostle's severity can be sometimes really terrible. With regard to the incestuous Corinthian, he
lays down uncompromisingly: 'Call an assembly at which I will be
present in spirit, with all the power of the Lord Jesus Christ, and so,
in the name of our Lord Jesus Christ hand over the person named to
Satan for the overthrow of his corrupt nature, so that his spirit may
find salvation in the day of our Lord Jesus Christ' (1 Cor 5:4-5).
Whatever the interpretation of this 'handing-over' to Satan, there
can be no doubt that it meant a punishment of extreme severity.

As regards St Paul's attitude to heresy, certain words of his might
sound as if he were resigned to it: '. . . Parties there must needs be
among you, so that those who are true metal may be distinguished
from the rest' (1 Cor 11:19). Yet, though admitting the inevitability
of heresies and schisms, Paul speaks of them in most forceful terms
in his famous farewell discourse at Miletus: 'I know well that
ravening wolves will come among you when I am gone, and will
not spare the flock; there will be men among your own number
who will come forward with a false message, and find disciples to
follow them. Be on the watch, then . . .' (Acts 20:29). And his
condemnation of the incestuous Corinthian for evil conduct is
matched by condemnation of perversions of doctrine. He exhorts
Timothy always to keep the faith and a good conscience, and
continues: 'Some through refusing this duty, have made shipwreck
of the faith; among them, Hymenaeus and Alexander, whom I have
made over to Satan, till they are cured of their blasphemy' (1 Tim
1:19-20).

St Paul's attitude does no more than echo that of Jesus: 'Woe to the world for the hurt done to consciences! It must needs be that such hurt should come, but woe to the man through whom it comes!' (Mt 18:7). 'Better for him to have had a mill-stone tied about his neck, and to be cast into the sea, than to have hurt the conscience of one of these little ones' (Luke 17:2). In particular, regarding submission to the Church, the Lord said: 'If he will not even listen to the Church, then count him all one with the heathen and the publican . . .' (Mt 18:17), that is, excluded from the community of the faithful. These words of his, like the others quoted, are severe enough to disconcert many of us. Let us therefore try to discover on what this strict attitude is based. It will then seem less startling.

Strange as it may seem, the cause of this severity, when all is said and done, is love. The apostles felt themselves bound by a very strict obligation to their divine Master. What they preached was no invention of their own, resulting from their own personal reflection, but a sacred deposit entrusted to them by Christ. They were authorized witnesses, 'whom God had appointed beforehand' (Acts 10:41), conscious of their mission as witnesses and of their corresponding responsibility for the preservation and faithful transmission of the truth to which they witnessed (Luke 24:48; Acts 1:8; 2:32; 3:15; 5:32; 10:39; cf. 1 Cor 15:11). Not only did they transmit it faithfully, but they took means to make sure that in its transmission it should be kept unaltered (Acts 10:15 etc.; 1 Thess 2:13; 1 Cor 11:23-25; 15:1-11; Gal 1:11-12; Col 2:6ff.). What Jesus said of the law of the Old Testament applies, in a true sense, to the fidelity of his apostles: 'Heaven and earth must disappear sooner than one jot, one flourish disappear from the law . . . whoever then sets aside one of these commandments . . . and teaches men to do the like, will be of least account in the kingdom of heaven' (Mt 5:18-19). These words of Christ were echoed by St Peter: 'Yet always you must remember this, that no prophecy in scripture is the subject of private interpretation. It was never man's impulse, after all, that gave us prophecy; men gave it utterance, but they were men whom God had sanctified, carried away as they spoke, by the Holy Spirit' (2 Pet 1:20-21).

The apostles and the heads of the Church, then, are bound by a most grave obligation to keep and to transmit intact and unchanged the teaching entrusted to them. Upon this depends the precious gift of unity in faith. The faithful, in turn, are equally bound to follow the leaders of the Church, to accept their teaching and to follow their direction.

Love of Christ then means love, also, for the faith, and conviction that this faith must be maintained unchanged and unsullied. The heads of the Church, consequently, feel an ever-jealous love for unity in faith among the souls whom God has entrusted to them, and feel their conscience weighted by the heavy obligation to preserve their flock from all contagion of false ideas or doctrine; for they know that unity and faith are the means for the salvation of their souls. Here they cannot give ground.

Thus this very severity springs from love for the wanderers and from concern for their eternal salvation. To his strict injunctions to the Corinthians St Paul adds: 'I write this in absence, in the hope that, when I come, I may not have to deal severely with you in the exercise of that authority which the Lord has given me to build up your faith, not to crush your spirits' (2 Cor 13:10). And he explains to the Thessalonians the reason for avoiding association with those who cause scandal: 'If anybody refuses to listen to what we have said in our letter, he is to be a marked man; avoid his company till he is ashamed of himself . . .' (2 Thess 3:14). Even 'handing-over' to Satan, harsh as it is, is done 'so that his spirit may find salvation in the day of our Lord Jesus Christ' (1 Cor 5:5).

In all this the main thing to be borne in mind is the spirit of zealous love: love of truth, of unity, of the souls of the faithful, and also of those of the wanderers. Love of the faithful and of those who go astray does not, perhaps, cause us any difficulty; but it is not so with this zealous love of truth and purity of doctrine. Living, as we do, in a world teeming with ideas, and with all kinds of philosophical and religious systems at variance with one another, we are perhaps too inclined to acquiesce, to adopt an attitude of indifference, to be ashamed of the intransigence of Catholic dogma, as of something niggardly, unmodern, out of touch with reality and almost fanatical.

Furthermore, an ill-informed love for unity and for our separated brethren may drive us, at times, to a false kind of 'eirenicism'.

All the texts we have cited above show how foreign is such an outlook to the letter and spirit of the New Testament, and hence it is inspired by a less enlightened zeal and charity. With good reason the authority of the Church is vigilant about correct doctrine and about the protection of the faithful from dangerous influences. Rightly too, the Church regulates meetings and conversations with those of other communions on doctrinal questions. Even in discussions and collaboration with non-Catholics in matters not directly religious, as, for example, in questions of social work and relief, the faithful are warned not to do anything that would compromise revealed doctrine or the general outlook of the Church.[1] Consequently, no work for union should lead to neglect of the soundness of one's own faith or of the integrity of Catholic dogma. The aim must be that noble one set before us by the apostle, that all may arrive at the:

'Common unity through faith in the Son of God, and fuller knowledge of him. So we shall reach perfect manhood, that maturity which is proportioned to the completed growth of Christ; we are no longer to be children, no longer to be like storm-tossed sailors, driven before the wind of each new doctrine that human subtlety, human skill in fabricating lies, may propound. We are to follow the truth in a spirit of charity, and so grow up, in everything, into a due proportion with Christ, who is our head' (Eph 4:13-15).

'To love those who err'

So much for hatred of error. It remains to speak of love of those who err. But I repeat, it is charity that inspired the New Testament severity in face of heresy and schism. There is no contradiction in hating the error and loving those who are in error; these attitudes are different expressions of a single charity, which mingles severity and gentleness, both rooted in charity and growing out of charity.

Of this charity the Pope has spoken often. Immediately after his

[1] Cf. *Instructio de motione oecumenica*, 20 Dec. 1949, in *A.A.S.* XLII (1950), p. 145.

election, in a broadcast message of 29 October 1958, John XXIII spoke of his sincere desire for the union of all Christians: 'As we greet the Western Church so we greet the Eastern Church and open our arms and our heart to all those who are separated from this Apostolic See, where St Peter himself lives in his successors "until the consummation of the world" (Mt 28:20) and fulfils Christ's command to bind and loose on earth (Mt 16:19) and to feed the Lord's flock (John 21:15-17) ... May all return; with full and tender longing we beseech them to return ... They will not enter a strange or unfriendly home but their own home.'[1]

Again, in his first encyclical, *Ad Petri Cathedram*, he addressed separated Christians in the following words: 'Allow us to express our affection for you and to call you sons and brothers... We address you, then, as brothers even though you are separated from us. For as St Augustine said: "Whether they like it or not, they are our brothers. They will only cease to be our brothers when they cease to say: Our Father".'[2]

Let us notice here that, according to the words of the Holy Father, the Catholic Church is, for baptized non-Catholics, not 'a strange or unfriendly home but their own home', and that he calls them brothers and sons. Leaving aside, for later discussion, the precise doctrinal import of these words, let us underline the fact: the charity he has in mind is the charity that exists among brothers, the charity that a father, the Pope, has for all the faithful, the mother's love that the Church has for Christians who are not Catholics.

Now let us examine in greater detail the reasons for this attitude of charity.

In the first place, we must say that the severity shown in the New Testament texts we have cited above is directed to those who, *individually and consciously*, *withdraw themselves* from the true faith and obedience to the Church of Christ. This is certainly not the case of all those now separated from us. The great majority of them inherit their position from their forebears who, in many cases, were

[1] *A.A.S.* I (1958), pp. 839f. English translation, *Catholic Documents*, IV, no. 26, p. 9, Thomas Nelson & Sons Ltd., Edinburgh.
[2] *A.A.S.* LI (1959), pp. 515f.

torn from the Church by force or deception. We have only to recall the celebrated adage: *Cujus regio, ejus religio*. As it is no merit of ours to have been born and brought up in a family belonging to the Catholic Church, so it is no fault of theirs that they are sons of parents separated from our Church. Accepting in good faith the inheritance handed on by their parents, these non-Catholics can sincerely believe that they are on the right path.

Nor should we forget that, in spite of all the differences in doctrine and worship, our separated brethren still have much in common with us. The Oriental Church still preserves unbroken the succession of their bishops from the apostles and, along with that, valid sacraments, above all the Holy Eucharist. The liturgy of the Mass is the centre of their religious life, is considered 'the true sacrifice atoning for the living and the dead'[1], and is celebrated with great solemnity. In doctrine the Orientals retain the ancient apostolic and patristic tradition, and differ from the faith of the Latin Church only in a few points, particularly in their denial of the dogmas defined by Councils since their separation, such as the primacy and infallibility of the Pope. Although they have not accepted the definitions of the Immaculate Conception and the Assumption, devotion to our Lady remains strong among them, and these dogmas are found in their liturgical books and generally admitted by their members.

The Protestant inheritance from the Mother Church is not as rich as the Oriental, unfortunately, but they too have preserved precious elements of Catholic doctrine and worship, although the amount varies with the different forms of Protestantism. Above all, one notices in many Protestants, particularly in the ordinary faithful, a sincere piety, a great veneration for the Word of God contained in holy scripture, and a real effort to observe the commandments of God in their daily life. We can certainly presume that the Lord grants to these men, who publicly bear witness to the name of Christ, the graces necessary to lead a Christian life.

The longing for unity displayed by whole groups, not to speak

[1] C. Algermissen, *The Christian Denominations*, English translation, Konrad W. Grunder, B. Herder Book Co., New York, 1945, p. 650.

of individuals, shows how powerfully this divine grace is working today. The private letters I have received from Protestants often bear witness to the power of the grace which has made them aware of the good things the Catholic Church offers her members, and which awakens a keen desire to share in these benefits. This grace is also the explanation of the many individual conversions in various countries, as, for example, in England (an average of ten thousand each year), and in the United States (more than a hundred thousand). The mention of only a few names is enough to show the high intellectual and cultural calibre of some of these converts—Newman, Thomas Merton, Sigrid Undset, G. K. Chesterton, Johannes Jörgensen, Gertrud von le Fort, Edward Schaper, Bruce Marshall, Graham Greene.

Furthermore, in whole groups and communities we observe 'tendencies towards a restoration of the ancient liturgies in public worship'[1], and 'exchanges between the churches, which, for so long, were of a polemical nature only, have become genuine dialogues, in which both parties together strive towards the truth'.[2] Another sign of the desire for unity of all Christians is the World Council of Churches (Geneva), which brings together about 180 religious groups recognizing, as the condition for membership, 'Jesus Christ as God and Saviour'.[3]

These facts certainly show that we are witnessing a great change and this change is due not to mere human and natural motives, but to supernatural influences. The Holy See itself says, in a document of supreme importance: 'The present time has witnessed in different parts of the world a growing desire amongst many persons outside the Church for the reunion of all who believe in Christ. This may be attributed, under the inspiration of the Holy Ghost, to external factors and the changing attitude of men's minds but above all to the united prayers of the faithful. To all children of the true Church

---

[1] Cf. *Weltkirchenlexicon, Handbuch der Oekumene* (a non-Catholic dictionary of all the Christian communities throughout the world), ed. Franklin H. Littell and H. Hermann Walz, Stuttgart, 1960, p. 18.

[2] Ibid., p. 1039.

[3] This was written in 1961. The World Council of Churches now includes 201 such 'groups', and has a trinitarian as well as a christological basis.   Ed

this is a cause for holy joy in the Lord; it urges them to extend a helping hand to all those sincerely seeking after the truth by praying fervently that God will enlighten them and give them strength.'[1]

Since, then, our Lord himself bestows such graces on so many of our separated brethren who are in good faith, and since the Church exhorts us to help them by heartfelt prayers, ought we not feel an obligation to hold them dear with that true and sincere supernatural charity of which the Holy Father gives us so magnificent an example?

This charity must show itself in a zeal for union based on intellectual and heartfelt conviction. It will support unfailing prayer for union. It will lead us to that understanding which is so necessary if we are to rise above hostility and groundless prejudices and are to have an overriding respect for the convictions of separated brethren.

The limit, and the sole limit, to this charity we have already made clear. It is our own Catholic belief and the absolute integrity of dogma. But perhaps here we should not talk of any limit. Perhaps it is better to say that the only point of caution is this: that our charity must remain, in every sense, authentic, that is, absolutely faithful to the integral truth taught by Christ and his Spouse, the Church, remembering the saying of St Paul: 'The powers we have are used in support of the truth not against it' (2 Cor 13:8). For once the firmness of our faith and the integrity of dogma are attacked, an attack likewise is made on our union with Christ and his Church, and so on our capacity to help our separated brethren, the capacity to work effectively for unity. Our motto, then, is 'Truth in a spirit of charity', according to the words of St Paul: '*Veritatem facientes in caritate . . .*' (Eph 4:15).

II

The ultimate basis for the attitude of charity

These considerations amply justify the attitude of charity we should have towards our separated brethren, but it is clear we have

[1] *Instructio de motione oecumenica*, loc. cit. p. 142.

not yet gone to the root of the matter. Why do we call these Christians, separated from the Church, 'brothers', 'sons of the Church'? I shall try to give an exact answer to this question, though I know that not every aspect of it is fully clear. Let us, then, select certain matters which can be held with reasonable assurance.

As a point of departure, we will take the doctrine of Pius XII's encyclical *Mediator Dei*. There, speaking of the effects of baptism, he says that the baptized become 'by a common title members of Christ the Priest'[1]. This is the crystallization of the teaching of St Paul that Christ, though he has many members, is 'a single body', and this because of baptism. Paul actually says: 'All you who have been baptized in Christ's name have put on the person of Christ; no more Jew or Gentile, no more slave and freeman' (1 Cor 12:13). With baptism, he writes to the Galatians (3:27), we have 'put on Christ', we are all only one in Christ Jesus. The Code of Canon Law reproduces this teaching in legal terms (can. 87): 'By baptism man is constituted a person in the Church of Christ with all the rights and duties of Christians, unless, in the case of rights, there is some obstacle which prevents their exercise.'

Now notice that the teaching of *Mediator Dei* and St Paul is unqualified; it states what is always effected by the actual reception of baptism, provided, of course, that it is valid. So this must somehow hold good for our separated brethren also, even though they are separated from the Holy See as a result of heresy or schism inherited from their ancestors.

What difference then, do heresy or schism make to what has been effected by baptism? Pius XII in his encyclical *Mystici Corporis* declares explicitly that 'schism, heresy or apostasy are such of their very nature, that they sever a man from the body of the Church'[2], and continues: 'Only those are to be accounted really members of the Church who have been regenerated in the waters of baptism and profess the true faith, and have not cut themselves off from the structure of the Body by their own unhappy act or been severed therefrom for very grave crimes, by the legitimate authority . . . It

[1] *A.A.S.* XXXIX (1947), p. 555. English translation, C.T.S., London, 1961, para. 92.
[2] *A.A.S.* XXXV (1943), p. 203. English translation, C.T.S., London, 1960, para. 22.

follows that those who are divided from one another in faith or government cannot be living in the one Body so described, and by its one divine Spirit.'[1]

These statements are obviously in the same severe tones that we have already found at the very beginnings of the Church, in the New Testament: they reiterate, most impressively, what a terrible thing is the cleavage caused by heresy and schism.

The question now arises: do these statements apply unreservedly to all the separated brethren, both those separated from the Catholic Church as a result of their own deliberate act and those separated on account of some heresy or schism in which they were born and which they inherited? Those familiar with the terminology of the Church, the Fathers and the Code of Canon Law, know that the Church means by 'heretic' and 'schismatic' those who, formally and consciously and so with full knowledge of the case and full liberty of decision, are such or should be held to be such.[2] Who would be so bold as to assert that all separated brethren are in this condition? The demands of Christian justice and charity and the necessity for a realistic approach are better satisfied, as we have said before, by admitting their good faith, leaving the judgement of each case to God alone, and making no attempt to draw up neat little lists and statistics.

But even leaving aside the important question of good faith, further accuracy is needed: the encyclical *Mystici Corporis* denies that heretics and schismatics belong to the mystical Body, which is the Church, *only in the full sense* in which Catholics are said to belong to it. That is, it denies full sharing in the life which Christ communicates to his Church, and in the divine Spirit of Christ which is the soul and life of the Church. Our separated brethren are, indeed, deprived of the enjoyment of so many privileges and graces which are *special* to the members visibly united with the Catholic Church,[3] but the encyclical does not by any means exclude all

---

[1] *A.A.S.* xxxv (1943), pp. 202f. English translation, C.T.S., London, 1960, para. 21.

[2] Cf. *C.I.C.*, can. 1325, 2; cf. texts of the Fathers cited in S. Tromp S.J., *Corpus Christi quod est Ecclesia*, iii; *De spiritu Christi anima*, Rome, 1960, pp. 185-190.

[3] Cf. encyclical *Mystici Corporis*, in *A.A.S.* xxxv (1943), p. 243; English translation, C.T.S., London, 1960, para. 102.

forms of membership of the Church or deny all influence of the grace of Christ. This is a highly important conclusion imposed by the very terms of the text, and we shall see its meaning more clearly in what follows.

The position of separated brethren in the Church of Christ

Bringing together all these points from the official teaching which we have explained so far, we may outline the position of separated brethren in the one true Church of Christ in some such terms as the following:

(a) Of fundamental importance is the conclusion just drawn from *Mystici Corporis*. We must, therefore, emphasize the fact that heresy and schism, even when they are formally such, do not completely destroy that membership in the Church of Christ which, as *Mediator Dei* and St Paul teach, is created by baptism. Non-Catholic Christians must not, therefore, be put on the same plane as the non-baptized; for they always bear, not only the name of Christ on their foreheads, but his actual image in their souls, deeply and indelibly imprinted there by baptism.

(b) From a more positive point of view, in virtue of baptism, they are subjects and members of the Church. And this effect of baptism is not removed by heresy or schism. Such a link is the minimum required to justify the language used by the Church, for how otherwise could they be called 'brothers', and be invited to 'return' to her, if they have never visibly belonged to the Church? How could it be said that, for them, she is not a strange home but their own, words which show that the Church considers them objects of her maternal love? How could the Holy Father call them his 'sons'? And this link with the Church is confirmed by the jurisdiction she exercises over them in various cases.

In this connection it is interesting to notice the Holy Father's words in the recent discourse at the opening of the preparatory work of the Council. He says that 'one great point to be held firmly by *every baptized person*' is that 'the Church remains for ever his mystical Body (Christ's). He is the Head, to it each of us believers is related, to it we belong'.[1] Why should this point have to be held firmly by *every* baptized person, and consequently by separated brethren, if they do not belong there in any way whatever?

(c) For their part, separated brethren, according to the teaching of *Mystici Corporis*, are related to the mystical Body of the Redeemer 'by some unconscious yearning and desire'.[2]

(d) Because fundamentally, even if not fully, they belong to the Church, they also have the benefit of the influence of God's grace. If Christ loves souls and is good and merciful towards them, it would be hard to understand or even to conceive that he could completely abandon these souls which bear his image engraved in them, or that he could treat them in just the same way as he treats those not yet endowed with this special relationship to him. It would be harder still to think of Christ acting so if we recall that for the most part these souls are in good faith. And looking at the facts, how are we to explain all the good we have recognized earlier in our separated brethren except by the influence of such grace? Furthermore, the *Instruction* of the Holy Office which we have cited says explicitly that the ever-increasing desire for unity to be observed among separated brethren is the work of the Holy Spirit.[3] The Holy Spirit, then, works in a special and powerful way in them too, although, as we have said, not in such a full manner as in the members visibly united with the Catholic Church. Pius XII, in the encyclical *Mystici Corporis*, is referring to this when he states that 'by the inspiration and help of divine grace they will be drawn to share in that unity and charity' of the Church,[4] and addresses to them, 'with most loving heart', the invitation 'to yield their free consent to the inner stirrings of God's grace'.[5]

(e) Because of their position, separated brethren are the object of deep and tender affection on the part of Holy Mother Church.

[1] *Osservatore Romano*, 14-15 Nov. 1960, p. 2.
[2] Cf. encyclical *Mystici Corporis*, in *A.A.S.* XXXV (1943), p. 243. English translation, C.T.S., London, 1960, para. 102.
[3] Cf. *Instructio de motione oecumenica*, loc. cit., p. 142.
[4] Encyclical *Mystici Corporis*, in *A.A.S.*, XXXV (1943), p. 195. English translation, C.T.S., London, 1960, para. 5.
[5] Encyclical *Mystici Corporis*, in *A.A.S.*, loc. cit., p. 243. English translation, op. cit., para. 102.

This is evident when Pius XII speaks of 'a heart overflowing with love' for them, and it is even more evident in the words of Pope John XXIII cited in the first part of this study. It is indeed a love that feels grief and sadness, the love of a heart wounded by estrangement, because the estrangement prevents our brethren from enjoying so many privileges and rights, and makes them lose so much grace. But perhaps for this very reason it is all the deeper and more burning, a love to which God's words in Scripture apply: 'What, can a woman forget her child that is still unweaned, pity no longer the son she bore in her womb? Let her forget; I will not be forgetful of thee' (Is 49:15).

Catholic Ecumenicism

Some very important conclusions follow from what we have said.

(a) The Church can never be unconcerned about separated brethren. They are, as we have said, her members, though not in the full sense, they are her sons and so necessarily the object of her maternal care. She has a strict duty, then, to do everything in her power to bring them back to her, so that they may have life in its fullness and enjoy in full all the rights and privileges of sons. The Church has always been conscious of this duty. Lyons (1274) and Florence (1439-1442) were Councils for union. The decrees of reform in the Council of Trent and its negotiations with separated brethren are evidence of the same effort. The same is even evident in the many works of controversy that appeared after the Council, like those of St Peter Canisius, St Robert Bellarmine, Baronius and others. The Church's efforts towards union have not always taken the same path nor proceeded at the same pace, since the state of the Church and the general religious situation changes from century to century. But today such efforts are particularly necessary and pressing. The Church of Christ is faced with a secularized, technological and materialistic world; in the countries which used to be called missionary, the past few years have seen the development of a situation decisive for the future of Christianity in those lands. The

Church of Christ, today more than ever, needs to be strong, and its strength will depend on its unity.

(b) The same pressing obligation of working for the unity of Christians is laid on all the sons of the Church, whether they are members of the hierarchy or laymen, in accordance with each man's opportunities.

(c) The unity of the Church desired by her divine Founder is, like holiness and catholicity, one of her essential aspects; but, in reality, *unity is not yet complete and perfect.* It needs our work in order to become ever fuller and to surmount victoriously all obstacles and difficulties. And it is not just any kind of unity but, according to the will of her Founder, a unity in doctrine, in government and in the means of salvation which are the sacraments, and it is founded on the rock chosen by Christ himself, St Peter and his successors.

(d) What we have said makes clear how the Catholic Church understands the ecumenical movement. Briefly, it can be set out in three propositions. The first: that essential unity already exists in the Catholic Church and is the unity which Christ willed and achieved in Peter and his successors, the bishops of Rome: unity of doctrine, sacraments and rule. The second: that there is a further unity still to be achieved, the unity of the members unhappily separated from the Apostolic See. The third: that this unity of the separated members is not to be brought about by force but by the free acceptance of union with the Catholic Church, it being 'absolutely necessary that this should come about by their free choice since no man believes unless he is willing'.[1] We must, then, help to prepare for it by patient labour, full of understanding and charity, according to the capacity of each son of the Church. In the last analysis, it will be the work of the Holy Ghost, for he alone can give separated brethren light and strength to overcome all the difficulties which delay the decisive step.

(e) Prayer is a means which enables all the faithful to contribute towards unity. On the necessity of prayer Pius XII has a stirring

---

[1] Encyclical *Mystici Corporis*, in *A.A.S.*, loc. cit., p. 243. English translation, op. cit., para. 103.

passage in the encyclical *Mystici Corporis*: 'If there are still many, as unhappily there are, who wander outside the path of Catholic truth and fail to give their free consent to the inspiration of divine grace, this is due to the fact that not only they themselves, but the faithful also, fail to offer to God more fervent prayers for this intention.We therefore earnestly and insistently exhort all lovers of the Church to follow the example of the divine Redeemer and to offer such petitions without ceasing.'[1]

Let us, then, join in the prayer that the Church daily repeats through her priest in the Mass:We offer (these gifts) for the holy Catholic Church, that thou mayest grant that she be united . . . throughout the whole world.' 'Lord, look not on my sins, but on the faith of thy Church; grant her peace and unity according to thy will.' In the earliest days of the Church, the Lord was pictured as gathering together his scattered people as the grains of wheat are gathered to become the Bread of the Eucharist. The present context shows the imagery in all its deep significance.

Conclusion

The three great movements in the life of the Church during the last fifty years have been the liturgical movement, the lay apostolate, and the missions. At the same time the movement in favour of separated brethren has steadily grown and has now reached vast proportions. One can almost speak of a general mobilization of all ranks in the Catholic Church in favour of these brethren. The plain fact is that the Holy Father has definitely designated union as the ultimate aim of the Council, even if it is not the immediate aim, and has asked the whole Church to make a united effort for prayer and purification in preparation for it. But the Council cannot reach the finishing point even if it is a point of departure. The concern is to foster more frequent and wider contacts with separated brethren, inspired by the greatest possible frankness and charity. Only in this way will it be possible, by slow and hard work, to attain a real

[1] Encyclical *Mystici Corporis*, in *A.A.S.*, loc. cit., p. 245. English translation, op. cit., para. 103.

meeting of minds, to eliminate prejudices, to enlighten and deepen faith and charity, and to achieve closer and closer collaboration in fields not directly concerned with the faith. The Holy Father himself, speaking of union with brethren of the Eastern Church, has defined the stages of this persevering work as, 'first of all, an approach, a drawing together and only then complete union'.[1] It is clear then that at the moment there is no question of spectacular results, nor of successes in the near future, but of long, patient preparation, to which can be applied the proverb quoted by our Lord himself: 'One man sows, another reaps' (John 4:37). This preparatory work obviously requires, in those engaged on it, a sound knowledge of their own beliefs, clarity of ideas, firm adherence to their own faith and, above all, the holiness which comes from humility, charity, prayer and sacrifice, and the example of a good Catholic life.

Since this work of preparation has joined to it the grace of the Holy Spirit which our Lord implored on the night of his death, and which he himself implores each day through the celebrant of each Holy Mass, we may have serene confidence that the day draws ever nearer when there will be 'one fold and one shepherd' (John 10:16) for all who bear witness to the name of Jesus.

[1] 'Esortazione al clero veneto', 21 April 1959, in *A.A.S.*, LI, (1959), p. 380.

2

THE OBSTACLES TO CHRISTIAN UNITY[1]

OUR PRAYER for January is that the truth and charity of Christ may remove the obstacles that still stand in the way of the reunion of all Christians in the one Church of Christ. It is a very far-reaching intention, embracing all the Christians who are scattered throughout the world. It is an intention which is dear to Christ's Vicar on earth; the unity of Christians is very close to the Pope's heart and he talks about it frequently, prays for it, and asks others to pray for it. As an indication of his fatherly concern for this reunion, he has created a special Secretariat with the task of promoting the union of all Christians and giving effective aid to all efforts to achieve this same great purpose.

The union of all those who bear the name of Christ is, after all, the great desire of our Lord himself. In the last hours of his life he prayed for all those whom the Father had given him, that is for all those who believe or will believe that the Father had sent him: 'Holy Father, keep them true to thy name, thy gift to me, that they may be one, as we are one' (John 17:11). And returning to the same request, he prays: 'That they may all be one . . . that they too may be one in us as thou, Father, art in me, and I in thee' (John 17:21).

This desire of our Lord is unhappily still very far from fulfilment. The Catholic Church has indeed spread in a marvellous way in the world during the last few decades and it now numbers about 500 million. But there are about another 400 million who, although they have been baptized, yet live separated from it (238 million Protestants split into many groups and 165 million Orthodox). All

---

[1] Original text: 'Gli ostacoli all'unione dei cristiani', in *Messaggero del S. Cuore*, 96 (Dec. 1960), pp. 577-586; republished under the same title in *Oikoumenikon*, a. 1, vol. 1, quad. 2 (15 April, 1961), pp. 155-162.

those who are validly baptized, from the fact of their baptism, have
the status of 'persons in the Church of Christ', and have the full
rights and duties of Christians except where an obstacle prevents
the exercise of rights, as laid down in Canon Law (cf. Canon 87).
Basically, this is the same doctrine as the apostle St Paul taught (cf.
I Cor 12:13; Gal 3:25ff.; Eph 1:5ff.). The encyclical *Mediator Dei*[1]
on the sacred liturgy explicitly and categorically affirms this: by
reason of their baptism, Christians are in the mystical Body and
become by a common title members of Christ the Priest. If, therefore, we wish to be loyal to the will of Christ, we ought to pray
and work for the removal of all obstacles, so that every single
baptized person may enjoy to the full all the privileges and rights
conferred on him by baptism, in the unity of the one holy and
visible Church. And this naturally suggests that we should appraise
the number and the weight of the obstacles which still block the
way to universal union. Make no mistake; the obstacles are formidable. Yet they should not dismay or discourage us, but, rather, stir
us to more confident prayer, in the faith which, as Jesus said, can
move mountains: 'I promise you, if you have faith, though it be
but like a grain of mustard seed, you have only to say to this
mountain, remove from this place to that, and it will remove;
nothing will be impossible to you' (Matt 17:19).

Let us speak of the obstacles with truth and charity

In speaking of obstacles to union, I do not want you to think that
I paint too dark a picture or exaggerate. The sad realities of the
situation make that quite needless. Nor must you think that I mean
to deny the good—the very great good—that exists among the
separated brethren, still less to pass judgement on their responsibility,
either with regard to the historical fact of separation or the individual situation which exists for each of them. The historical fact is too
complicated to be the object of human judgement—God alone can
unravel the threads of that tangled skein of history. And when we
look at the individual situation of our separated brethren we find

[1] *A.A.S.* xxxix, 1947. English translation, C.T.S., London, 1961, para. 46.

that the vast majority only accept the legacy handed down to them from their ancestors. Just as it is no merit of us Catholics that we were born in a family already belonging to the Catholic Church, so it is no fault of theirs to be sons of parents separated from our Church. And so, in accepting the legacy handed down to them, these non-Catholics, in good faith, are convinced that they are on the right path. So when we speak of the obstacles to union, we do not wish to deny the deep longing for union that exists today among all classes of our separated brethren. This longing is certainly the work of the Holy Spirit, something to gladden all of us who are children of the Church and also to stimulate us to give our help to all those who sincerely seek the truth.[1] We know, too, that various groups among our separated brethren have made and are still making immense efforts to achieve the union for which they long, and for that too we should be very grateful. But all this is only further cause for investigating and calmly evaluating the obstacles to unity that still remain, to enable us to give the greatest possible assistance towards the realization of the great desire of our Lord.

The obstacles as regards the Orthodox

The obstacles are not everywhere the same, but differ mainly according to the history and the nationality of the various groups. The group longest separated from communion with the See of Rome is the Eastern Churches. The Church of the East had very early (from the fourth century) lost the fullness of unity, mainly from the numerous controversies about the Incarnation. In this way there sprang up the Nestorian Churches which in the Middle Ages spread to the most distant parts of China but today are of comparatively less importance. The other great heresy, however, Monophysism, is still alive today in the Coptic, Jacobite and separated Armenian Churches. The Church of Constantinople maintained the true faith (therefore she took the name 'Orthodox', i.e. 'of the true doctrine') and remained, although with some weakening, in communion with the Church of Rome until the eleventh century. The formal

[1] Cf. *Instruction of the Holy Office*, 20 December, 1949, *A.A.S.* XLII (1950), p. 142.

rupture came in 1054 and, in spite of several attempts at union, has lasted till the present day. To this Church there were united for several centuries before the break with Rome the Christian communities of various Slav countries—of Bulgaria, of Serbia and above all of what was then called Greater Russia—for Constantinople exercised over them a certain patriarchial primacy. As a result of this, little by little these communities also were cut off from Rome and form today the world of the 'Orthodox Churches'.

These Churches have certain great advantages when compared with the various groups that cut themselves off in the sixteenth century. The Orthodox Churches have preserved unbroken the succession of their bishops from the apostles and, along with that, valid sacraments, above all, the Eucharist. In doctrine they retain the ancient apostolic and patristic tradition, and differ from the faith of the Latin Church only in a few points, particularly in their denial of the dogmas defined by Councils since their separation, such as the primacy and infallibility of the Roman Pontiff. Although they have not accepted the definitions of the Immaculate Conception and the Assumption, devotion to our Lady remains strong among them, and the substance of these dogmas can be found in their liturgical books and is generally accepted by their faithful. Objection to them lies mainly in their definition after the breach with Rome.

In the course of the centuries, however, the concept of the unity of the Church among these churches has changed. According to the doctrine that prevails among the Orthodox today, this unity does not demand the subordination and submission of each single church or group of churches to a single head, who would be the Successor of Peter, the Vicar of Christ, the Roman Pontiff. Rather, they say, it is established by the mutual 'communion' of the individual local church, that is, by agreement in faith and in the 'mysteries' (sacraments) and in a certain feeling of brotherhood. The individual churches do not recognize among themselves a head who would have authority over all. At the time of the Byzantine Empire the Patriarch of Constantinople had a certain pre-eminence, but with the collapse of the Empire he has lost this position and the churches are grouped on a basis mainly national. So the 165 million Orthodox are today, for practical purposes, divided into sixteen national patriarchates independent of each other, and frequently involved in mutual disagreements, sometimes acrimonious. The authority of the bishops and patriarchs has little by little lessened and today, besides these, in every national group there is a 'Holy Synod' including the laity, which makes decisions on ecclesiastical questions together with the Bishop. It is obvious that this complex situation causes difficulties in every attempt at union with the See of Peter.

Union is further hindered by unfortunate incidents in the past like the seizure of Constantinople in the Fourth Crusade (1204) and by the difference of mentality between the East and West, which is a matter weighty and important. It will definitely not be easy to overcome all these difficulties and we need much light and many graces to heal such painful wounds and find a way of reconciliation which takes into account all the factors in question. But the divine grace which has already inspired in so many of our Orthodox brethren a deep longing for unity, will show us the right way, even though it may be a way slow and hard, on condition that we beg with earnestness and fervour for this grace and duly co-operate with it.

The obstacles as regards the Protestants

Even more difficult is the question of union with respect to all those groups which take their origin from the unhappy events of the sixteenth century, which split the Latin church in two. These groups are usually—though indeed not very accurately—given the common name of 'Protestants'. Even in their separation they have kept, in varying degrees, much of the rich inheritance of truth and devotion which derives from the Mother Church, and indeed, in many cases they were originally cut off from this Church, not of their own choosing, but on account of the absolute power of prince or the bad example of wordly prelate. Those among them who hold faithfully to the doctrines inherited from their Catholic ancestors and try to live according to them, easily come to recognize that they do not possess the whole truth and that they lack many aids which our Lord has promised to his faithful. This is the explanation of the longing for a deeper religious life which many Protestants feel today and of the desire to share, by union with their Catholic brethren, in the spiritual benefits which they see them enjoy.[1] Although the exact nature of the unity has not yet been defined so as to exclude all vagueness and disagreements about details, the strength of the desire among Protestants is shown by the start towards unity which was made by the creation, in 1948, of the 'World Council of Churches' with its headquarters at Geneva. Today this is made up of 180[2] groups in which are included a certain number of Orthodox churches. The doctrinal point chosen as a basis and admitted by all the members was this: Jesus Christ is recognized as God and our Saviour. A broadening of this basis, which is obviously too limited, so as to include the Incarnation, the revelation of the Father in the Son, and the testimony of the Holy Spirit who leads us into all truth—therefore a Trinitarian formula —a broadening desired above all by the Orthodox churches, had not been accepted up to a few months ago. Only last August, the Central Committee of the Council decided to refer this matter to the next General Assembly of the Council at New Delhi in 1961. We must remember that even with the acceptance of this extension, there will not yet be full unity of faith. Nevertheless one must recognize that an excellent start has been made.[3]

[1] This may be seen, for instance, in the Sammlung group among the Lutherans of Germany, cf. *The Unfinished Reformation*, by Hans Amussen, Ernst Finckle, Max Lachmann, Wolfgang Lehmann and Richard Baumann, translated by Robert J. Olsen, Fowler Wright Books, Tenbury, Worcs. 1961; among the French Reformed in the monastery at Taizé in France, and in the books of Max Thurian, *Confession* and *Marriage and Celibacy*, SCM Press, London, 1960 and 1961; and, in general, by the liturgical movement in many churches.

[2] At the end of the year 1961, the number was 201.—ED.

[3] At New Delhi in December 1961 the following basis was adopted: 'The World Council of Churches is a fellowship of Churches which confess the Lord Jesus Christ as God and Saviour according to the scriptures, and therefore endeavour to follow their common calling to the glory of the one God, Father, Son and Holy Spirit.'

This definition of the goal of the movement was submitted to the churches for their reflection and comment by the New Delhi Assembly:

'We believe that the unity which is both God's will and his gift to his Church is being made visible as all in each place who are baptized into Jesus Christ and confess him as Lord and Saviour are brought by the Holy Spirit into one fully committed fellowship, holding the one apostolic faith, preaching the one Gospel, breaking the

There is another outstanding and most serious difficulty, namely that, as many ordinary Protestant people understand their own teaching, there is not, and almost cannot be, any real doctrinal authority in the Church, but each individual is free to make his own decisions about religion and to follow the guidance he receives from the Holy Spirit. It is true that there are many Protestant 'confessions of faith' such as the Augsburg Confession, the West-minster Confession and many others; but in modern times few regard such 'confessions' as still binding. It is true, also, that in almost all the groups there are Synods, Assemblies, Conventions and that through them decisions are made even about doctrinal matters, as is clear from the establishment of 'united' Churches like the Church of South India and the United Church of Christ in the United States. Yet few, if any, of these Synods, Assemblies or Conventions have, or even claim to have, an authority which can bind the consciences of the faithful to follow decisions made; reliance must be placed upon the influence of outstanding persons, and upon persuasion, to win acceptance of proposals or decisions. Moreover there are in the English-speaking world over 250 groups, each auto-nomous and independent, and many differing radically from others. Many of our separated brethren, in all denominations, deplore this state of affairs, and are working zealously to remedy it. Meantime, the lack of authority and cohesion among Protestants presents formidable, if not insuperable, difficulties in anything like immediate discussions about union on the part of the Catholic Church.

Obstacles of a more general nature

Finally there are obstacles with respect to all the separated brethren, whether Orthodox or Protestant. Above all else, there is an immense lack of sympathy, and prejudices, misunderstanding, and unhappy historical memories. These have built up among many

one bread, joining in common prayer, and having a corporate life reaching out in witness and service to all, and who at the same time are united with the whole Christian fellowship in all places and all ages in such wise that ministry and members are acknowledged by all, and that all can act and speak together as occasion requires for the tasks to which God calls his people.'—ED.

non-Catholics, and some Catholics too, an atmosphere of distrust and sometimes of positive aversion. Often, too, there is great ignorance of Catholic truth among our separated brethren; there are even completely mistaken ideas, nurtured, in part, by century-old prejudice passed on from one generation to another.

A further obstacle to union is, unfortunately, the kind of lives which some Catholics lead. One often hears it said: 'Why become Catholic if the Catholics are no better than us?' To those Catholics who are so faithless to their religious and moral duties, one can apply the words spoken by St Paul to his fellow countrymen: 'The name of God has become a reproach among the Gentiles, because of you' (Rom 2:24). On the other hand, a good Catholic life illustrates what Jesus means when he says that our good works are a light by which we shine before the eyes of men, so that seeing them they glorify our Father who is in heaven (cf. Mt 5:16).

An attitude of charity

One especially good work is the practice of true, deep and active Christian charity towards our separated brethren. About Catholic dogma we are obliged to be uncompromising. Yet this intransigence, joined to memories of the struggles of the past and of the injuries inflicted during them, has too often tended to narrow and harden the minds and hearts of separated brethren and to lead them, if not to hatred, at least to lack of any real interest. Nevertheless, they are still brethren, and must be treated as brethren. Rightly did the Holy Father recall to us the striking words of St Augustine: 'Whether they will it or not, they are our brethren. They will cease to be our brethren only when they cease to say: Our Father.'[1]

Pray with great humility and faith

There are many obstacles, then, in the path towards union, and the obstacles are large, in fact almost mountainous. But this situation will frighten only those who trust in their own strength and not in

[1] *Enarr. in Ps.* 32, II, 29 (*PL* XXXVI, 299); *A.A.S.* LI (1959), p. 515.

the omnipotence of God and in the invincible might of the action of Christ and his Holy Spirit. As regards our poor co-operation with this irresistible might of Christ—a co-operation absolutely required by God—let us humbly acknowledge how poverty-stricken and ineffectual we are, and yet let us also stir up and nourish in ourselves the deepest trust in the omnipotence of God and Christ. Strengthened, then, with this humility and this trust, we gird ourselves for prayer, sacrifice and charity. January, the month of the Church Unity Octave, should be a special stimulus to prayer, for during it Catholics and separated brethren intercede for union. The daily contemplation of the pierced heart of Jesus, to whom we offer every day our prayers, works and sufferings, urges us to sacrifice. The love of him who has loved us and given himself for us (cf Gal 2:20), impels us to charity. True and active charity towards our separated brethren will be an example of conduct truly Christian. It will also be a powerful means of obtaining from our Lord graces ever more abundant and efficacious for the difficult work of union and for those to whom the Vicar of Christ has in a special way entrusted the task of promoting the union of all the baptized. It is a noble directive for our prayer, this union of all Christians. It is a directive which should rouse a response from the depths of our hearts, to keep us faithful to our Christian ideals, faithful even to sacrifice, faithful even unto death. Only in heaven will we see what immense value our life has, in this way, acquired; value for ourselves, for the Church, for humanity, for God.

3

THE MEANS OF ACHIEVING CHRISTIAN UNITY, AND ITS PROSPECTS.[1]

1. I MAY take for granted among you the resolution to do everything in your power to further the cause of unity: what, then, in practice is it possible for us to do to help promote the union of the baptized?

(a) The first means is prayer. This is at once a necessary means and a completely reliable one. It is not easy for one of our separated brethren to find the way to the flock of Christ; he needs a good deal of light and, when the way has been found, he needs a great deal of courage to follow it in spite of all the difficulties, which sometimes seem insuperable. And when a whole group is envisaged, the difficulties may increase almost immeasurably. A special occasion for prayer is the *Octave of Prayer for Christian Unity*, as it is called, which in our time is observed equally by Catholics and their separated brethren from 18–25 January, between the feast of the Chair of St Peter and that of the Conversion of St Paul. This Octave was most strongly commended by St Pius x and Benedict xv and again most recently by our present Pope, who insists that the Octave of Prayer for union should be spread throughout the whole world. 'We gladly apply to ourselves the words of our immediate predecessor Pope Pius xii, of happy memory, expressing the holy desire that this practice should be spread to every part of the world, as widely as possible . . . especially in view of the Ecumenical Council.'[2]

(b) Our prayer is the more certain to be heard the more we com-

[1] Original text: 'Mezzi e prospettive del lavoro per l'unione dei cristiani', in *Annali dei Sacerdoti Adorati*, 66 (April 1961), pp. 225-229. A summary of a conference given at Ferrara, to the Instituto di Cultura Religiosa, Casa G. Cini, 9 November, 1960.

[2] To the Superior General of the Franciscans of the Atonement, 28 October, 1959. *Acta et doc.*, I, 55 A.

bine it with real work, as far as conditions and opportunities allow.

One kind of real work is to give the example of a true Catholic life, an example which all the faithful can and should give. A distinguished convert recently wrote:

'In my many devious wanderings on my way to the Church, I had repeated proofs that the missionary power of the Church and the most persuasive and cogent evidence of her real nature are to be found among humble folk, among simple people and not among the famous or the prominent. It was "the little ones", not "the great ones" who gave me the help I needed to go on to the end in my journey towards the Church.'[1]

The First Vatican Council said that the Church is a beacon lifted up among the people.[2] But this should apply to each individual Catholic: he, too, by his attitude to life and by his conduct, must be a beacon, attracting everyone to give his service to the one true Church of Christ. Now, you may perhaps feel a difficulty here. You may ask: 'What use is our good example as regard the unity of Christians since we do not live among non-Catholics?' All the same, we do in plain fact have contact with non-Catholics. Recent statistics show that some seventeen million tourists visit Italy every year. Judging by the countries from which they come, probably a half, or more, of them are non-Catholics; and these eight or nine million non-Catholics see at least something of Catholic life in Italy. And what do they see? Is everything they see the reflection and the evidence of the riches of truth, grace and holiness which dwell in the Catholic Church? So a great deal does depend upon the example we give of a really Catholic life.

(c) Another kind of real work, possible to everyone, is some daily sacrifice either offered or, at least, accepted, for the intention of helping the cause of union.

(d) In some cases, one's profession or social position may afford opportunities for more direct work. What we say in social conversation or even what we write, may help mutual understanding, and

---

[1] J. Schwitzke, in K. Hardt, *Wege der Gnade zur Fülle der Wahrheit*, Heidelberg 1959, p. 159f.
[2] Cf. Is 11:12; Denz n. 1994.

can dispel some of the prejudices, antagonisms, misconceptions, and ignorance, which too often are an obstacle to union. And, finally, there are fields open to our co-operation with our separated brethren which are not directly connected with faith: various social and charitable organizations; the defence of the human rights and human values so often disregarded and denied today: the rights of religious liberty, respect for human life, concern for world peace and the means of safeguarding it, and so on.

It is clear that this sort of active collaboration always requires due prudence and caution. Such work can endanger one's own faith, and for this reason one must observe the wise rules which the Church has laid down, and work under the direction of the immediate ecclesiastical authority, which in this case is the diocese.

2. The principal part in the work of union falls to the hierarchy of the *Church herself.* The hierarchy must pave the way for union, on their side doing what they can to remove obstacles and dealing officially with our separated brethren or their authorized representatives.

(a) The *means* used by the Church for such relations was usually an Ecumenical Council, in which all the bishops of the Church were present united with their visible head, the Vicar of Christ. So it was with the Council of Lyons, and the Council that started at Ferrara and continued at Florence. The Council of Trent, too, was planned as a Council for union. Does the coming Council plan to be a Council of union of this sort? No! That is not the Pope's intention. In his first encyclical *Ad Petri Cathedram* (20 June 1959), the Pope made his mind about the Council more explicit: 'the evidence of sincerity, concord and charity' to be found in the Council would make it for separated brethren 'an inspiration to seek out that unity which Jesus Christ prayed for so ardently from his heavenly Father'. And the Holy Father begs and exhorts us to pray that the Council may bring 'this unity in harmony, this true, active, fighting peace' to those who are his children and equally to all those 'who, though separated from us, yet cannot do other than love truth, unity and harmony'.[1]

[1] *A.A.S.* II (1959).

(b) The Council, then, although not envisaging the immediate realization of union among all Christians, can prepare for it and intends to prepare for it, on a *long-term policy*, by improving the atmosphere between Catholics and non-Catholics, by creating conditions more favourable to union, and by solving some of the problems connected with it. To speak in more general terms, one may perhaps describe this long-term policy, together with the stages which must successively be covered before arrival at the desired goal, in the words the Pope used with reference to union with the Orientals: 'an approach, a drawing together, and only then union. . . .'[1] And the Pope himself took a most important and practical step. On 30 May 1960, he invited the Cardinals to his private library, and announced the setting up of the Preparatory Commissions for the Council; and then he added: 'We have also in mind a special Secretariat which will make it possible for separated brethren to follow the work of the Council, and thus to make easier their reunion in the one fold of Christ.'[2] The setting up of the Secretariat, he said, was meant to be greater evidence of 'the love of the Holy Father and his good will towards those who are called Christians, but who are separated from this Apostolic See'.[3] In the homily delivered on the feast of Pentecost (5 June 1960) the Pope again revealed his magnanimity and breadth of outlook, saying: 'What a striking event it might be, and what a full-flowering of human and heavenly charity, a definite move towards the gathering again of separated brethren of the East and of the West, into the one fold of Christ, the eternal Shepherd. This must be regarded as one of the most valuable achievements which could be made by the Second Ecumenical Council of the Vatican.'[4]

The satisfaction and gratitude with which the setting up of the Secretariat for Christian Unity was welcomed are attested by the many letters which came to the Secretariat from Catholics and their separated brethren, by the numerous articles published in newspapers and magazines, and above all by the frequent dis-

[1] *Acta et doc.* I, 19.
[2] Ibid., p. 92.
[3] Ibid., pp. 95-98.
[4] Ibid., p. 108.

cussions between non-Catholics and the President or the Secretary of the Secretariat. At the reunion of the Central Committee of the World Council of Churches which was held at St Andrews, Scotland, in August of this year, it was said that 'the fact that dialogue with the Roman Catholic Church becomes possible is to be welcomed'. But these letters and conversations also make plain how difficult and delicate the task of the Secretariat still is and how much need, therefore, there is for prayer that the work may be helped and sustained by the light of divine grace.

3. And what are the prospects of union? Certainly it is difficult, not to say impossible, to answer this anxious query. The outcome depends not only upon us, but also upon a large measure of co-operation on the part of separated brethren. There is good reason to hope that this will be given. The Holy Spirit has aroused in many of them, both individuals and entire groups, a great yearning for unity, as we have already seen. Moreover, both in doctrine and in worship there is an approach which brings them closer to the Catholic position. The existence of the World Council of Churches itself, of which we have spoken earlier, and its commission called *Faith and Order*—a section devoted to study of the biblical teaching about the nature of the church—are evidence that the desire for unity is alive and at work. Many notable professors and prominent members of separated Churches voice the same feeling. The needs, and one can say even the agony, of our time inspire all men of good will to seek aid and remedy in the strength that the religion of Christ promises and gives for the good of humanity. Dialogue is proceeding at high levels; Catholic and non-Catholic professors are discussing in sincerity and mutual esteem controversial points of the faith, conversations which a half century ago would have been inconceivable . . . all this gives good grounds for Christian hope. But the best ground of all is that our Lord himself has prayed for this desired unity. On the eve of his death on the cross, he said to his Father: 'Holy Father, keep them true to thy name, thy gift to me, that they may be one, as we are one . . . that they too may be one in us as thou, Father, art in me, and I in thee . . . and I have given them the privilege which thou gavest to me, that they

should all be one, as we are one; that while thou art in me, I may be in them, and so they may be perfectly made one' (John 17:11, 21-23). In the Preface of the Feast of Christ the King, his kingdom is described as 'a kingdom of truth and of life, kingdom of holiness and grace, kingdom of justice, of love and peace'. Now the kingdom is his Church in all her fullness: the Church of all time and of eternity, the Church militant and triumphant. What is true of his Kingdom is true of his Church, and more particularly of the unity of the Church. Unity in the full sense is then unity in truth, unity in holiness and grace, unity in justice, love and peace. Here, then, is the full and deepest significance of our problem of the union of Christians. Let him who wishes to work for the union of Christians in the first place keep intact his own union with Christ and with his immaculate spouse, the Church, united in faith, in charity, in sanctity and grace. Unity in faith means, as we have seen, personal constancy in the faith and a zealous vigilance to preserve the integrity of Catholic dogma. Unity in charity means an attitude of charity towards separated brethren, a charity which is understanding, delicate, active to the point of sacrifice. Unity in holiness and grace means our exemplary personal life, preserving and increasing the holiness which we receive in baptism, and encouraging it in others: it also means prayer and sacrifice to obtain for our separated brethren the graces needed to find and achieve the one true unity in the one true Church.

Let us try to imagine what it would mean for the great task of union if all the members of the Catholic Church were to achieve this threefold unity to an outstanding extent. What persuasive, irresistible force the Church would then have in her work for the union of all the children of God, of all the members of Christ! What power, above all, she would have to conquer the heart of God and to obtain from heaven a new Pentecost, a Pentecost of light, of grace and of strength for our separated brethren! We must also take into account here the far-reaching consideration that the Council, while being bound to follow the intentions of the Pope and to work before all for a renewal of the Catholic Church in herself, will at the same time also make the greatest possible contribution to that longed-for goal, the union of Christians. The work of the Church for union will be the more fruitful and powerful the more she herself and all and each of her individual members are firm in unity of faith, charity, holiness and grace; that is to say, the more closely she is united with her divine spouse and Head. For this reason prayer for a happy outcome to the Council is also a powerful prayer for the union of Christians, and this is the greatest desire of our Lord himself and of all the children of his holy Church.

4

MUTUAL RESPECT AND CHARITY BETWEEN CHRISTIANS[1]

I BELIEVE I am right in thinking that a number of Catholics, especially in countries where Catholicism is virtually the only religion, will feel hesitant, embarrassed, or completely nonplussed when confronted with the need for charity and mutual respect in preparing the way for unity. They ask: must we ignore the fact that non-Catholics are heretics or schismatics? Must we forget St Paul's strongly worded condemnation of heretics as those who have made 'a shipweck of the faith' (1 Tim 1:19), forget how bluntly the Fathers and the Councils have spoken out against heresy? Do you want us to fall in with the idea that the really important thing is for the individual to live his own faith and serve God honestly according to that faith, whatever it may be? The answer to all this must be 'no'! Then, they say, let the bishops, priests and theologians do their proper work, and convert our separated brethren; our work is to pray and do penance for their conversion. For the rest, it is safer to keep well out of it

1. The basic position of Catholics: complete adherence to the truth of our faith

This uncertainty and perplexity is understandable. And it serves to underline a point of fundamental and essential importance, which no contact with our separated brethren must let us forget: *our adherence to the truth of our faith*, as contained in Holy Scripture and

[1] Original text: 'Preparare la via nella stima e nella carita', in *Messagere del S. Cuore* (April 1962), pp. 193-203. Reprinted in *Oikumenikon*, a.2, vol. 2, quad. 23 (15 April 1962) pp. 130-137.

Catholic tradition and presented to us by the teaching authority of the Church must be *complete and unconditional*. No approach to our separated brethren, no work for union must ever weaken that absolute adherence. So when we talk of greater respect and understanding between Catholics and non-Catholics there is no question at all of adopting their outlook or their faith.

2. *The need of love and respect towards separated Christians*

By baptism they are made our brothers

Having established this essential point once and for all, the next question arises: would it not be better as far as possible to keep simple Catholics away from non-Catholics? Surely we have really nothing in common with them, there is no link between them and us? But there is a link. Remember baptism. In virtue of baptism— provided it is validly conferred—every baptized person becomes a member of the mystical Body of Christ, a brother of Christ and hence our brother also (cf Rom 12:4f; 1 Cor 12; Eph 1:23; 4:4; 5:28ff; Col 1:18, 24). Moreover, baptism confers on him the help and grace he needs to live as a Christian and a son of God. And so the Holy Spirit of God is at work in his soul, helping and guiding him. Proof of this is to be seen in the intense longing for unity which is growing stronger and stronger in the non-Catholic Christian world. The Holy Office, in its notable instruction on the Ecumenical Movement,[1] explicitly attributed this to the working of the Holy Spirit in the hearts of our separated brethren. The general intention for which we pray next month is 'that all those baptized in Christ may more generously obey the promptings of the Holy Spirit'.[2] Note the significant use of 'all the baptized'. The Holy Spirit, then, is at work in the souls of all the baptized.

---

[1] *A.A.S.* XLII (1950), p. 142.
[2] The word 'intention' merely specifies the object of intercession for a month, in exactly the same way as, during the Week of Prayer for Christian Unity, on each day intercession is made for particular groups or purposes. Cf the leaflet of the Faith and Order Commission of the World Council of Churches.

The vast majority are in good faith, born and brought up in separation

But for some a serious misgiving will remain. Granted that what has been said about baptism is true. Nevertheless, what happens to the effects of this baptism when the baptized person, having attained responsible years and greater or less education, denies various truths of our faith and refuses to accept the authority of the church? Has he not then made himself personally responsible for the sin of heresy or schism? This question is certainly not to be taken lightly. He who knowingly and with full consent accepts heresy and refuses obedience to the Church certainly commits a very grave sin and is not freed from it until he shows that he has repented of it. But is this really the case with all our separated brethren? The great majority of them have inherited their religion from their ancestors. They accept this inheritance conscientiously and believe, in good faith, that they are on the right path. Who would dare deny this good faith and set himself up as judge of them and their responsibility? It certainly accords better with the facts, and with justice and Christian charity, to admit their good faith, and in particular cases to leave the judgement to God alone, without probing into details or making classifications.

If anyone possibly finds difficulty in admitting this good faith, let him turn to the New Testament and learn there the proper attitude of meekness and humility. The New Testament is so aware of the unfathomable depths of the human heart that St Peter, for example, had no difficulty in saying to men who had collaborated in so dreadful a crime as the killing of the Son of God—so grievous a thing: 'I know that you, like your rulers, acted in ignorance' (Acts 3:17). Note that he does not excuse the ordinary people only, but also 'your rulers'. And St Paul explains his own furious persecution of the Christians, which caused him to brand himself as a 'blasphemer, a persecutor, a man of violence', by saying 'I was acting in the ignorance of unbelief' and adds immediately the significant words, 'and yet he had mercy on me' (1 Tim 1:13). That is, says Paul, God, by his mercy, showed that he himself ratified this compassionate and lenient judgement. All this simply mirrors the divine meekness of Jesus on the Cross: 'Father, forgive them for they know not what they do.' This is the Christian teaching about judgement even in such cases of utmost gravity; how much more should this teaching apply in the case of those who simply accept the faith of their ancestors, the faith in which they were brought up! We are on the sure path, a divine path, when we follow the example given us by Christ and his saints and make this teaching our rule in our attitude to our separated brethren. St Augustine put it in a nutshell: 'We must hate error but love those who err.'

So nothing forbids us to practise in their regard *the sublime and profound teaching of the New Testament on mutual respect*. St Paul's command: '(Be) eager to give one another precedence' (Rom 12:10), applies to our attitude towards them. Paul wrote to the Philippians also, exhorting them: 'Yours is to be the same mind which Jesus Christ showed.' He meant that incomprehensible humility through which 'he dispossessed himself, and took the nature of a slave, fashioned in the likeness of men . . . accepted an obedience which brought him to death, on a cross'; and this mutual respect should be such 'that each of you . . . have the humility to think other men better than himself' (Phil 2:5-8, 3). Paul's teaching here is a faithful echo of our Lord's: 'With you it shall be otherwise; whoever would be a great man among you, must be your servant, and whoever has a mind to be first among you, must be your slave.' And he confirms his teaching with his example: 'So it is that the Son of Man did not come to have service done him; he came to serve others', so much so that he will 'give his life as a ransom for the lives of many' (Matt 20:26-28).

3. *Failure in this brought lamentable consequences*

Let us compare this magnanimous teaching of the New Testament with the facts, especially the facts of history. Daniel-Rops, the well-known historian of the Church, spoke of the 'infinitely painful situation at the beginning of the seventeenth century, which stabilized the break in Western Christianity we have seen develop gradually since the fourteenth. The baptized no longer feel that they are brothers, despite the generous efforts of some exceptional men, like St Peter Canisius, who try to see in their enemies only separated brethren.'[1] Let us look at some details of this sad situation. It is unfortunately true, for example, that in virtue of the motto, *cuius regio illius religio* (the religion of the ruler must be the religion of the people) the conscience of very many of the faithful was violated; they were compelled to accept the religion of their master, forgetting that faith is essentially a free act, as St Augustine said: 'It is not possible to believe, if one does not will to.'[2] Christians of different denominations have too often believed that to defend the truth of their own faith they must generalize about the defects, excesses and sins (actual or presumed) of others. They felt they could admit nothing good, or practically nothing, where there was not the fullness of the truth of the faith. Here was a sin against truth, justice and charity in the name of a false love of the truth and of Christ. And so calumny, distrust, and hatred were sown between the baptized in the name of loyalty to Christ. Even where things did not come to this pass, people took it on themselves to judge the good faith of the other side instead of leaving this to the judgement of God alone, as Christ had taught. And so they harmed the Gospel, in the name of the Gospel! At other times, while professing personal humility, they indulged in a kind of social pride, attributing everything good to their own group—not, of course, in theory, but in practice—and to the other group all the evil and all the blame. So often they thought that in order to convince the 'adversary' it was first of all necessary to humiliate him. In fact the contrary is true: the more humility, the more respect you show your neighbour, the more easily will you win him.

We have looked to history for these examples instead of to the present day, in order to avoid judging any of our present brethren in Christ and wounding feelings.

These examples serve as a *concrete warning* and illustrate what we

---

[1] Daniel-Rops, quoted by Cardinal Bea from the Italian version, *Storia della Chiesa*, v, 2, Torino-Roma, 1958, p. 230ff.
[2] *In Joann Ev. tract.* 26:2; *P.L.* xxx, 1607.

mean by those words in the title of this chapter: 'Mutual Respect and Charity between Christians.' When, in the light of these historical examples, we consider the relations in all their manifestations between Catholics and separated brethren—books and publications of all kinds, especially in apologetics and history, lectures, sermons, teaching in schools, right down to the everyday contacts of each individual Christian—then the extent of what remains to be done and the magnitude of the tasks entrusted to our prayer and penance are very obvious.

4. *Results of mutual respect. What of Italy?*

To avoid any misunderstanding, let me repeat that we are not calling into question in any way at all our attitude to the truth of our own faith—that is and must remain absolutely sacrosanct. What I am discussing is our attitude towards Christians of other faiths. This attitude must be formed by the teaching of the New Testament; it must be marked with such humility and deep respect for our neighbour that we even acclaim him a better Christian than ourselves. History shows us clearly enough how damaging this lack of respect can be and, on the other hand, how important mutual esteem can be in preparing the way towards the unity willed by God. An attitude of deep respect will open the hearts of Christians to contacts which are free from prejudice and mistrust and are serene and understanding, instinct with mutual trust. In this way each party can come to appreciate the good possessed by the other and the two can gradually draw closer together, in the sphere of human relations and then also of Christian with Christian.

All we have said applies not only to the countries in which there are many Christian denominations but to those also in which most of the people are Catholics. Take, for example, a country like Italy. Each year about seventeen million tourists come to Italy. We know the countries from which these tourists come, and so we can safely say that at least half of them are not Catholics. Other Catholic countries may not have so many tourists but the number is always rising and in consequence the opportunity for contacts is always growing. More and more frequently, Catholics and non-Catholics will be meeting each other, so it is very important for these meetings to be marked by a spirit of deep mutual esteem. What a different opinion of Catholicism those non-Catholics will take away with them if the Catholics they come into contact with have a deep and real religious life and, most important, are men of real humility and have respect for others, even those outside their own faith. Such encounters will dissolve very many of those prejudices which are either inherited or acquired from upbringing. This improved attitude will bear its own fruit and spread its effects when the tourists return to their own country. As a result of their personal experience, they will be able to soften many prejudices and lessen much mistrust.

5. A special instance: dialogue between experts

We have been talking about increased understanding between Catholics and their separated brethren. There remains one particular form of contact which deserves and needs great help from our prayers. This is the conversations between theological experts of both sides. These conversations have now been going on for some time in different countries and their success is encouraging. These are not disputes, such as we had in the sixteenth century and later, but friendly conversations within a restricted circle of theologians. Their purpose and aim clearly is not, as in a political conference, to work out some compromise on the points at issue—our fidelity to Christ and his teaching would not permit that—but rather to understand the other's point of view and show him our own, in order to see more clearly where there is agreement and where there is not. Then we are able to concentrate our own studies on these particular points at a deeper level. In fact, during the long separation—for the Oriental church, nearly a thousand years, and for the reformed churches, four centuries—the different denominations have taken different paths and undergone very varied influences; so the differences in outlook have grown ever wider. Naturally enormous difficulties stand in the way of mutual understanding: the very terminology used often differs or else the same words are used with different meanings. These profound mental differences are the root cause of separation and of so many of our difficulties in making contact with each other. Only very gradually, through long and patient discussion, with a calm, respectful, and even affectionate readiness to hear the other man's point of view, can they be removed.

The value of such discussions is heightened by the fact that they are highly appreciated by our separated brethren. For example, the Central Committee of the World Council of Churches, in a resolution of August 1960, explicitly expressed the desire that such unofficial discussions between theologians should continue and that their number should even be increased. There is another reason for their importance: these discussions are held between university professors who by virtue of their position enjoy great prestige, and it is also they who educate and instruct the new generation of ministers of religion who, in turn, may pass on the fruits of such discussion to their people.

6. *What each of us can do*

Only a few can participate in these discussions. But *everyone can help by prayer* and sacrifice, asking the Holy Spirit to assist all those who do take part. Man's helplessness in the face of obstacles and his consequent need of grace is seldom so obvious. For this reason everyone who prays for the 'dialogues' makes real contribution towards the good fruits which may slowly but surely grow from them. We pray also for the many Institutes in different countries both of the East and the West whose purpose is to help mutual understanding between Catholics and other Christians. We pray too that all theological research may be carried on in a spirit of dialogue with our brethren, which means taking into account their opinions, problems and difficulties. In this way students of theology will become priests truly prepared to help souls who seek the truth.

7. Conclusions.

Mutual respect the best way of overcoming obstacles

History tells us of two attempts or, rather, of two actual unions with the Eastern Church. The first was in the thirteenth century in the General Council of Lyons and the other in the fifteenth century in the Council of Florence. Neither of the two was satisfactory, still less lasting. Why? The reason, as far as we can judge, was that agreement was reached by the authorities without the main body of the clergy and the faithful being adequately prepared for union. Now the best method of preparation, to begin with at least, is the one we have been discussing: the increase of mutual respect and understanding between Catholics and non-Catholics. There must be no delusion about the prospects of union. There are mountains to be scaled. A long preparation is indispensable. In addition to the work of the divine Spirit of union, we must have the co-operation of all the baptized in a long and patient effort gradually to draw closer together and to understand each other. The primary and most important element in this work is deep mutual respect.

The call upon us all

These are the great and essential graces we must ask for during this month—and afterwards as well—for the 900 million Christians in the world today. This is not a mere exhortation. It is a demand. It is a demand made upon us by the New Testament teaching about mutual love and respect. It is a demand made by the imperative need to work for the union of all the baptized, which we know is the absolute will of Jesus Christ and our heavenly Father. It is a demand made by the example and the explicit words of the Vicar of Christ: and a demand made by holy Church in blessing this prayer and setting it before us. It is a demand implicit in the gentle but effective action of divine providence in stirring all Christians to long for unity. It is a demand made by the need of humanity itself: Christ is the sole salvation of humanity; but, that it may acknowledge

Christ, it is necessary that we become one, according to the prayer of Jesus, 'that they may all be one: that they too may be one in us, as thou, Father, art in me, and I in thee; so that the world may come to believe that it is thou who hast sent me' (John 17:21). It is a demand, finally, made for the peace and happiness of humanity, and hence a supreme demand for the glory of God among men.

5

ARCHBISHOP FISHER'S VISIT TO POPE JOHN XXIII[1]

THE RECENT visit of Dr Geoffrey Francis Fisher, Anglican Archbishop of Canterbury and Primate of all England, to His Holiness
Pope John XXIII has aroused a great deal of attention in the Press.
As inevitably happens with affairs of this sort, the nature and
purpose of the meeting was interpreted in many different ways,
both before and immediately after the event. The Pope himself
was quite frank when he said that 'it has been the occasion not only
of great interest but also of many fanciful stories'. Some commentators imagined that they were witnessing the preliminary
steps to important discussions on union. Others, more realistically,
stressed the profound differences in matters of faith which separate
the Christians of the Anglican communion from the Roman
Catholic Church. A third group refused to be excited, in the belief
that a visit of this sort could achieve little or nothing.[2]

We are not concerned to pass judgement on the statements and
forecasts of various newspapers, or to decide how well-informed
they are. It is sufficient to remark that one outcome of the meeting
has been for 'the thoughts of many hearts to be made manifest'
(Luke 2:35). In the reactions of the Press one can observe different
currents of thought, Anglican as well as Catholic, with eminent
spokesmen for each one. Some were motivated and directed
primarily by their concern for dogmatic truth, anxious that there
should be no giving way to compromise in matters of doctrine and

[1] Original text: 'A proposito della visita di S.G. il dott. G. Fisher', in *La Civiltà
Cattolica* IV, 1960, pp. 561-568. Reprinted under the same title in *Oikoumenikon*, a.I.,
vol. 1, quad. 3 (1 May 1961), pp. 277-284.

[2] *La Civiltà Cattolica* discussed the varying views expressed about the visit, cf. IV,
1960, pp. 337-353.

that no dangerous confusion should arise. On the other hand, those who were moved primarily by their earnest desires for union felt that they could interpret the event as opening wide the doors to understanding, as a substantial breach in the barriers, and a promise of mutual *rapprochement* in the future. Others again have tried to steer a middle course, without betraying the truth in matters of doctrine or failing in charity, and taking care not to compromise what might possibly be the first steps on the long road towards union. Further, some sections of the Press, each according to their own lights, have presumed to observe in Vatican circles either an attitude of prudent reserve, even coldness, or one of friendly understanding and warm goodwill.

It is not entirely a waste of time to recall these various opinions and observations, despite their ephemeral nature. For they reveal how complex is the subject under discussion and show how different points of view can influence the various attitudes we adopt. Unfortunately newspapers frequently publish superficial and hasty opinions, because they do not take these differing points of view into consideration and are therefore unable to make balanced judgements. It seems worthwhile, therefore, to analyse, at least briefly, some of the opinions that have been expressed about Dr Fisher's visit. For this kind of meeting could easily be a frequent occurrence; and, in fact, it does often happen in our world that Christians of different faiths come into frequent and prolonged contact with one another. We need a clear understanding of the theological principles which should govern such contacts: one which would enable us rightly to judge the behaviour of the principals in an event of this sort, and which would help us to regulate our own conduct in similar circumstances according to the dictates of our faith.

1. The first principle is not merely personal integrity in matters affecting the faith, but also the duty of safeguarding Catholic dogma in its entirety. The reason for this is clear: the unity of Christians cannot be built on the betrayal of truth. Unity is above all 'unity through faith in the Son of God, and fuller knowledge of him' (Eph 4: 13). This love of truth, which is indeed an obligation imposed

on all, in the eyes of the Catholic Church carries with it a special mark of loyalty to the person of Christ, her divine Founder. It is not the Church's task to preach her own discoveries, the fruit of her own reflections, but to propound what Jesus has taught her; her office is to bear witness to him, to hand on the sacred deposit of faith confided to her by her divine Master.[1] This serious obligation explains her inflexible attitude, one which appears in the New Testament itself in matters touching this fidelity to the divine teaching.[2]

This inflexibility may surprise and even antagonize people of today. But if it is examined closely enough, one can see it, even in its austerity, as loving concern both for the faithful and for those who stray, as well as a desire to safeguard the truth and the unity of the faith.

2. The second principle, equally essential, is that of charity. This is too obvious to require explanation; here it is more a question of pointing out the particular aspect of charity which concerns us, namely, charity towards our separated brethren. This is clearly not just the charity we owe all men—a charity so magnificently described by St Paul in the thirteenth chapter of his epistle to the Corinthians, and possessed by him to such an heroic degree that he was willing to be separated from Christ for the sake of non-believing Jews, 'his own kinsmen by race' (Rom 9:3). We are more nearly concerned with charity towards Christians or, as the Holy Father prefers to express it, towards 'our brothers', for they are our brothers, even though separated from the Catholic faith. In fact Pius XII's encyclical on the sacred liturgy, *Mediator Dei*, states explicitly that those validly baptized 'are in the mystical Body and become by common title members of Christ the Priest':[3] a precise summary of Pauline teaching.[4] Canon law, in its turn, echoes this doctrine when it declares that a person, validly baptized, becomes a member of the Church of Christ, with all the rights and duties of a Christian, save only in those cases where an obstacle prevents a person enjoying the use of these rights.[5] Sufficient attention has not always been paid to

---

[1] Cf. Luke 24:48; Acts 1:8; 2:32; 3:15; 5:32; 10:39; 1 Cor 11:23; 15:11.
[2] Cf. Mt 18:17; Acts 20:39; 1 Cor 4:21; 5:4-11; Tit 1:13; 1 Tim 1:19.
[3] *A.A.S.* (1947), p. 555. English translation, C.T.S., London, 1961, para. 92.
[4] Cf. 1 Cor 12:13; Gal 3:26ff.
[5] *C.I.C.*, can. 87.

the fact that the Holy Father does not hesitate to call all separated Christians brothers—and even sons; and the doctrine of the mystical Body enables us to understand why he does so. In the encyclical *Ad Petri Cathedram* which outlines the programme of the future Ecumenical Council he turns to them and says: 'Allow us to express our affection for you and to call you sons and brothers ... address you, then, as brothers, even though you are separated from us. For as St Augustine said: "Whether they like it or not, they are our brothers. They will only cease to be our brothers when they cease to say: Our Father".'[1] It is a question, then, of the charity which must exist between brothers, and a love which the Holy Father, the father of all, feels for his children. This love is correlative to the maternal love of holy mother Church for her children. And hence it follows that it is the duty of the Church not only to preserve intact the integrity of the Catholic faith but also to show a mother's love for all her children. By baptism they have become members of the mystical Body of Christ and, by that very fact, the Church's children: even though some are deprived of the full use of their rights because they are visibly separated from her.[2] The love of the Church for them is a love full of deep sorrow and grief, and of a heartfelt affliction because of the separation which prevents them enjoying so many privileges and rights, and makes them lose so many graces.[3] The words of God in Holy Scripture, 'Can a woman forget her child that is still unweaned, pity no longer the son she bore in her womb' (Is 49:15), refers to this love. The Church cannot possibly forget these children of hers, because her motherhood is of supernatural origin, inspired by the infinite love of the blessed Trinity itself. So she has the right to say, using the words of God: 'Let her forget; I will not be forgetful of thee' (ibid.). If for any reason a child does not know and hence does not recognize his own mother, she nevertheless does not cease to be his mother nor he the fruit of her womb; it is impossible for her not to have for her child a mother's love and tenderness. In the same way the Church

[1] *A.A.S.* LI (1959), p. 515ff. English translation, C.T.S., London, 1959 paras. 57–59.
[2] Cf. the encyclical *Mystici Corporis Christi*, *A.A.S.* XXXV (1943), p. 243. English translation, C.T.S., London, 1960, para. 102.
[3] Cf. *Osservatore Romano*, 4 December 1960.

never fails to have a deep and tender affection for all her children, though they may be visibly separated from her, and this affection can never be belied.

3. These two essential principles, outlined above, enable us to understand how delicate a situation arises for those responsible for the welfare of the Church on the occasion of a visit of the head of a separated communion. The mission confided to the Church by her divine Head and Master requires her to hand on to all men the sacred deposit of the faith which he has committed to her, in all its purity, and to safeguard its unity. Thus she cannot compromise in matters of dogma and must avoid any equivocation which might endanger the faith of any of her children—either those visibly united to her or separated from her. She must carefully avoid any attitude which might engender doubts about the faith taught by her, give rise to obscurities which would detract from the clarity and purity of the faith or seem to encourage a certain false eirenicism or indifferentism which, while stressing points of similarity between the Catholic faith and the beliefs held by other Christian communions, would fail to point out the differences. These are her obligations if she is to remain loyal to Christ, her Spouse, and avoid compromising her genuine love for her separated brethren.

On the other hand, if this solicitude of the Church to protect the integrity of dogma and the faith of her children leads her sometimes to act with a just severity, it does not follow that she should act without courtesy, suspiciously or in any way which might offend against her character as a mother or against her charity towards her separated brethren. This charity must inspire all 'to act with the most perfect courtesy', as Pope John recently expressed it.[1] It is only thus that she can combine the duty of preserving the purity and unity of the faith with the duty of a mother; acting always with that supernatural love taught by the divine Head of the Church and inspired by the blessed Trinity which is Love itself.

We can see then, how much the prudence and light of the Holy Spirit are required on occasions such as this visit if the Church is to meet the demands of loyalty to the faith and of maternal love. It is

[1] Cf. *Osservatore Romano*, 4 December 1960.

obvious that in so delicate a matter one can stress now one point of view, now the other, according to the circumstances. And who could presume to know better than those most closely concerned what is exactly the right attitude to adopt, the perfect balance? No wonder the Pope revealed recently that 'he had prepared himself for this meeting with earnest prayer'.[1]

4. There are other factors which must obviously influence the Church's attitude in these matters, besides the two essential principles mentioned above. Discretion, to name only one, is a necessary prerequisite when one enters the very thorny field of religious relationships; and this is particularly true of the Church's situation vis-à-vis her separated brethren. When, therefore, we are treating of a meeting between heads of Christian communions, one inspired not only by friendship or purely human charity but, more than that, by an essentially Christian spirit, i.e. loyalty to the person of Christ, we must realize that we are treading on most holy ground. Such sacred matters should not be offered in the open market-place to the casual passer-by like merchandise to the gaze of profane eyes, nor considered as a means to satisfy men's curiosity or to amuse them. They cannot even be compared to diplomatic negotiations, however important these may be. The utmost discretion is also necessary because of the danger of confusing so sacred a thing as the authentic union of faith with superficial and spectacular gestures. The result of such confusion would be the belief that unity can be achieved by external demonstrations, whereas it can only spring from a life of union with Christ, from a truly Christian life permeated by profound humility, charity, prayer and sacrifice.

The unique character of the meeting between the Holy Father and the Anglican Primate of all England makes this discretion all the more necessary. This meeting took place after four centuries of complete separation and while separation is still a sorrowful reality. For the Catholic Church, as we have seen above, it is a separation of the children from their mother the Church. We are, as it were, gazing in upon the private sorrow of a mother and her shame for a

[1] Cf. *Osservatore Romano*, ibid.

stigma which has brought disgrace and dishonour to her great Christian family. How could one expect a mother to give wide publicity to these first steps towards a new *rapprochement* after so long and so sorrowful a separation?

Furthermore, we are well aware of this mother's firm faith that she is the only true Church of Christ, and of the duty of all her children to follow her. Responsibility for the past is known only to God, and this question comes unbidden to the mind: what sorrowing mother, in similar circumstances, would not ask herself anxiously whether sufficient patience, prudence and charity had always been shown in the guidance and education of her children; and whether, with greater holiness, prayer and sacrifice, it would not have been possible to avoid the terrible rupture which has existed for centuries? Our holy mother the Church, like any true mother, must ask herself these questions when she sees the broken link in the chain of supernatural love which binds her to her children. Undoubtedly this most loving mother welcomes with joy a meeting such as this, and sees in it a sign of a widely experienced nostalgia for union. She also recognizes that it is the work of the Holy Spirit and an answer to the united prayers of the faithful.[1] But since she must exercise due discretion and treat the situation with a delicate reserve, her joy cannot be without restraint.

5. These considerations should help us to appreciate the nature of the problem with which the Church is faced on such occasions as this. It is a question of combining genuine prudence with the real necessity of satisfying the legitimate curiosity of world opinion. Because of the ever-growing strength of the ecumenical movement, both amongst Catholics and non-Catholics, reunion has become one of the vital factors for the peace and unity of the modern world. It is impossible, then, for the world not to take an interest in it. We are thus presented with a practical problem of the utmost delicacy, and one which does not permit of easy solution: how far can we satisfy the public's desire to know all the details of a meeting of this sort, and where should a prudent silence begin? It is a problem requiring tact, discretion and good judgement; one that can be

---

[1] Cf. *Instructio de motione oecumenica*, 20 December 1949, in *A.A.S.* XLII (1950).

solved only by those who have full knowledge of every aspect of the case. All the interested parties should be able to say with the Pope that they have fulfilled their respective duties with a tranquil mind.[1]

The fact that we have stressed at length the precautions which the Church must necessarily take by no means implies that we wish to minimize the importance of the visit. On the contrary, we attach the highest possible import to it. For us, its deep significance is to be found chiefly in what it reveals and symbolizes: the new atmosphere now shared by the Roman Catholic Church and Anglicanism. The initiative was wholly from the Anglican side, and particularly from Dr Fisher himself, after consultation with responsible and important members of the Anglican communion.[2] And the announcement of the visit was, with a few exceptions, favourably received. The essential point to bear in mind is that the very idea of such a visit, which was approved officially both by the Anglican communion and then by public opinion, would have been inconceivable a few decades ago. This in itself indicates a remarkable change of atmosphere, which we dare hope will continue to grow still more favourable as a result of the visit.

Far from wishing to underestimate the merits of the man to whose initiative we owe this visit, we would, on the contrary, point out that the importance of his action can best be appreciated in the light of the principles outlined above. It was Dr Fisher who sensed the change of atmosphere; pointed it out; realized the obligations entailed and took the necessary steps to bring the public to a greater awareness of the new atmosphere and to foster their interest.

We are sincerely convinced that this visit of last December will bear fruit, though we have no wish to specify its nature. We prefer to follow the Pope's example, his confidence and supernatural prudence when he said that we must always trust in the grace of God and not be in a hurry with judgements and forecasts.[3] This

[1] Cf. *Osservatore Romano* 4 December 1960.
[2] Cf. *La Civiltà Cattolica* IV, 1960, p. 345.
[3] Cf. *La Civiltà Cattolica*, IV, 1960, p. 345.

trust in the grace of God does not preclude our co-operation; rather it requires from us that we do our part by living a truly Christian life of humility, charity, prayer and sacrifice, so that Jesus Christ, the Founder and Head of His Church, 'who has inspired this generosity in you will bring it to perfection' (Phil 1:6).

6

THE PRIEST: MINISTER OF UNITY[1]

IT WAS announced that this Conference would be in Latin, but I thought it would be easier to express these modern matters in a modern language, and I only hope that my English is not too offensive to your ears. It is a great joy for me to be able to address you today as priests who represent the secular and regular clergy of almost every diocese and congregation of the country—this country once so rightly called 'the Island of Saints'. Today, due to events for which we do not wish to blame anyone, the Christians of Britain are divided into many sects. The total population is about 51,600,000: of these some 4·8 million (9 per cent, approximately) are Catholics, and together with them is the Church of England, with 27 million baptized members, of whom some 6·2 million are practising, about 800,000 Methodists, 380,000 Congregationalists, 325,000 Baptists, 130,000 in the Salvation Army, and considerable numbers either in smaller groups or completely indifferent.[2] This deplorable state of affairs reflects what prevails in the world at large: the division of the nine hundred million Christians scattered all over the world. Of these Christians, 32 per cent of the world population, about 52 per cent, a little less than five hundred millions, are Roman

[1] Original text: a conference given in English at Heythrop College, Oxon, 7 August 1962. First published in J. C. Heenan, ed., *Christian Unity*, London 1962. Archbishop Heenan of Liverpool organized this ecumenical meeting of clergy from all the dioceses and religious orders and congregations.

The text of this chapter is a revision of a conference given at Saint-Odile, France, 'Mouvement Jeunes Séminaristes' (2 September 1961), published as 'Le prêtre, ministre de l'union des chrétiens' in *La Documentation Catholique*, 50 (1961), 1345-1354, and in *Vocations sacerdotales et religieuses*, January 1962, pp. 7-16.

[2] There is considerable variation in the numbers given in different publications. Here I follow those given in *Lexikon für Theologie und Kirche*, III, Freiburg i. B., 1959, col. 888, and in *Bilan du monde*, II, Paris-Tournai, 1960, p. 655ff.

Catholics; 27·8 per cent, or about two hundred and fifty million, belong to the communities originating from the Reformation; and 16·7 per cent, equal to about a hundred and fifty million, are Orthodox or, in any case, separated Eastern Christians.[1]

To complete the picture, let us add that communities deriving from the Reformation are subdivided into more than two hundred groups. In the United States one can count two hundred and twenty-seven denominations officially recognized by the State. Nevertheless the whole world today is tormented by a deep longing for unity in its public, social, and economic life. This is not only on a national and international level, but on a world-wide scale. Moreover, the longing for unity among Christians, which is steadily growing, is all the more powerful since it does not arise from a merely human desire but from a divine command of God and of the divine Founder of the Church. It is, in addition, the result of a special inspiration of the Holy Spirit, as is declared in the Instruction of the Holy Office regarding the ecumenical movement.[2]

The unity of all who believe in Christ and who have been baptized in his name is, one can say, the strongest and the deepest desire of the divine heart of our High Priest. The priestly hearts of those who, by an infinite mystery of grace and of mercy, share the character and the mission of Christ the High Priest, must also have the same ardent desire, must suffer from division and long for the advancement of unity. We who are gathered together here are certainly convinced about this deep love for unity that has brought us together. Therefore, in this spirit we ask: how must the priest act to be in accord with Christ's own idea and the will of the Church, in order to become an authentic minister of unity among Christians? How must he prepare himself? What can he do to promote unity in the ministry entrusted to him? How should he proceed?

---

[1] The various sources of statistics differ considerably. We have chosen to follow the more balanced estimates. One may consult *Bilan du monde*, Paris and Tournai (1, 1958-9, 2, 1960) 1, 119-22, 140-42, 175-81; *Atlantino Missioni* (Venice, 1960) p. 25; K. L. Franklin and H. H. Walz, *Weltkirchenlexikon, Handbuch der Ökumene*, Stuttgart, 1960.

[1] Cf. *A.A.S.*, XLII (1950), p. 142.

I

General Preparation

In speaking of 'general preparation', I mean merely to invite you to consider with me those elements in our priestly calling which have a special bearing on efforts for unity. It is clear that in large measure we have already made this 'general preparation'. Yet the Church's legislation obliges us to continue what we call 'our formation' and in doing so, by continuing it and bringing ourselves up to date, we ought to have a special eye upon everything that relates to our apostolate for unity. It can be summarized under two headings: intellectual formation, and religious formation or holiness.

1. Intellectual and theological formation

The apostle of union must not only know his own faith thoroughly, so as to be able to move without danger among the many ideologies, religious systems and subtle reasonings which confront him every day; he must also keep always up-to-date. By rethinking religious truths he must find solutions to those ancient problems which constantly present themselves anew, in new forms and under new aspects. Only in this way will he be able to move with security and find his way in the midst of so many new ideas. He will also be able to guide others, by providing explanations, solving their problems and giving advice.

In this field, philosophy is of particular importance, both as regards philosophical tenets and as regards the history of philosophy, that is, the growth of different systems of philosophy. We know, in fact, that philosophical systems both express a particular mentality and, in turn, contribute towards moulding the mentality of men. It is inevitable, therefore, that philosophical systems have an influence on religious thought. This phenomenon affects our separated brethren all the more, since their theology is not bound to tradition and admits no control by a teaching authority. For this reason their language and mentality are largely dominated by the different modern philosophies. Only the priest familiar with different philosophical currents will be able to understand and sympathize with them in their search for the truth.

Philosophy, however, only prepares the way to understanding. The proper field for activity of the apostles of unity is the field of faith and of religious science, that is, of theology. It is here above all that the priest must be outstanding, must have a wide and profound knowledge, so as to be able to give adequate answers and solutions to the problems which exercise the minds of our separated brethren. Neither should we delude ourselves by thinking that it might be enough simply to repeat the traditional proofs and the old distinctions. In the theological field—and here, perhaps, more than anywhere—there is a continuous tendency to evolve. The mentality of our separated brethren at the present time is not simply that of the sixteenth century, nor even of the nineteenth century. Our answers to their questions must therefore be relevant to the present situation. This presupposes further and continuous study and a deepening of our own theological knowledge. It is not enough merely to know the actual problems of our separated brethren. We must also have explored the possible points of contact. Those acquainted with the situation know how very useful and promising are the trends to be noted in contemporary Protestant theology, which lend themselves to extensive development. These can be of immense help to us and can help them more easily to grasp Catholic truth.

In a particular way, we must advance more and more in a sound and extensive knowledge of holy scripture. While hundreds of millions of separated brethren take their stand exclusively on holy scripture, living spiritually by it and taking it as the rule for their religious life, the priest coming in contact with them will not be able to understand them or convince them unless he is equally, or even more, imbued with biblical doctrine and a love for holy scripture. Continual reading of the scriptures—of the holy Gospels, of the letters of St Paul, of the Psalms, the Books of Wisdom and of the Prophets—and the deepening of the theological doctrine contained in the different passages and books—this, for the apostle of unity, is the indispensable preparation for his apostolate.

We must take note, moreover, of the spirit in which all this work has to be done. It is not a matter of preparing ourselves for polemics, but rather a serene study inspired by a great love for the truth, together with a great love for our separated brethren. This twofold love will help us discover many ecumenical aspects in those problems where we probably never would have suspected them. Where, according to the earlier mentality, one could see only 'adversaries', the priestly view, guided by the love for unity and for separated brethren, will reveal to us brothers in Christ, errant indeed, but still brothers. We must love them if we want to understand them and to help them on the way to a full knowledge of the truth of Christ and of his Church. I developed this thought in a talk given last November at the Catholic University of Fribourg in Switzerland, illustrating it with examples drawn from philosophy, from the history of dogma, from dogmatic theology, canon law and Church history.[1] After this talk, several professors told me of their joy, but also of their regret in not having noticed such obvious facts before.

2. Priestly Holiness

Surely we need not insist here on the necessity of holiness. We know very well that sanctity is not only the indispensable condition and the soul of the priestly apostolate, but—insofar as it depends on us—is its very source. The aim of the priestly apostolate is to communicate (in subordination to Christ and in co-operation with him and the Church) the supernatural life of grace. It is axiomatic that life can be communicated only by those who possess it and only in the measure that it is possessed; the life communicated can only have vitality equal to the life of him from whom it has come. In the supernatural order of grace this means that the more intimately one is united to the source of grace—to the Holy Trinity, to Christ and to his Church, the mother of all the living—the better one can serve as an instrument in communicating grace.[2] Since unity is the

[1] Cf. ch. 7 below, 'How university research and teaching can further Christian Unity'.

[2] Cf. A. Bea, 'San Paolo sull'essenza e l'importanza della vita interiore', in A.L.A. (Rivista delle religiose d' Italia) nos. 9-10, September-October, 1961, pp. 8ff.

work of grace, and even the work of grace *par excellence*, those who want to cooperate must possess the life of grace, and therefore holiness, in an eminent degree. So, the holier they are, the better they can share in this work.

It is useful to specify in more detail which particular aspects of holiness are more necessary to and bear directly on the apostolate of unity. One word embraces them all; that word that indicates the essence of all holiness: 'charity'. First of all, love of God and of Christ which leads us (in consistent adherence to the faith and in unity of intellect and will) to accept the whole doctrine, the whole truth of Christ which he teaches us through our holy mother the Church. The same charity moves us to do what we can to let our separated brethren partake in the fullness of truth and of grace. This charity will make our own the words of St Paul: 'With us, Christ's love is a compelling motive' (2 Cor 5:14).

We shall speak more specifically later on about love of our neighbour. Now we wish to stress only one aspect which is of great importance for the priest in his work for unity, namely, humility and the high esteem and respect we should bear towards our separated brethren. This springs from charity, according to the words of St Paul: 'Charity is patient, is kind; charity feels no envy, charity is never perverse or proud' (1 Cor 13:4). Why are these virtues so important for the apostolate of unity? For this reason: our separated brethren simply cannot understand the real meaning of our assertion that the Catholic Church is the only true Church of Christ. Consequently, they reproach us with being proud, with thirsting for power—a reproach and a prejudice which has been strengthened by centuries of controversial propaganda, as I must call it. How can this antecedent difficulty be dealt with? Prudent and helpful explanations are, of course, in order; but this granted, no better means of countering this feeling among our separated brethren can be imagined than to make the greatest effort to behave with true Christian humility, to strive to hide ourselves behind the truth and sincerely to regard ourselves as 'worthless servants' (Luke 17:10) of Christ. In our contacts with our separated brethren we shall not seek anything other than the truth. We shall not try to make them surrender by force of argument but by force of truth. We shall not seek to be triumphant ourselves, but look only and always for the triumph of Christ and his truth. Have not the saints always taken the greatest care to accompany their preaching by an intense and continuous exercise of humility? 'God thwarts the proud' (1 Peter 5:5; James 4:6), says holy scripture, and men do the same. We must imitate the Pope who with great simplicity speaks sincerely of his 'humble person' and describes himself as 'the humble successor of St Peter'.

To humility must be joined the greatest respect towards our separated brethren, according to the saying of St Paul: 'Think others better men than yourselves' (Phil 2:3). This respect was warmly recommended to us in the general intention of the Apostleship of Prayer, approved by the Holy Father for the month of May of last year. It will teach us also the right way to put the truth forward. Conviction in proposing the truth is proper, but this should not tempt us to despise the convictions of our brethren. These convictions have been inherited from their ancestors, deepened through their education, and are considered by them as a sacred trust. Of course, we may not, through a false eirenicism, abandon the doctrine of our holy faith or fall back into indifferentism, as if all confessions or religions were equally true. But neither may we despise those who belong to other denominations. Much less should we argue with such insistence as to give the impression that at all costs we want to force others to give up their faith and to accept ours. Such methods do not take into consideration the difference between the evidence for a truth and the objective certainty of it and the difficulty a man has in understanding it and realizing it. We must respect the secrets of the human heart and the freedom of man. Faith must necessarily be free: 'One cannot believe unless one wills to', says St Augustine, and Pius XII, of holy memory, makes these solemn words his own in the encyclical on the Church as the mystical Body of Christ.[1] If God, who is the absolute Master of man and whose scrutiny no thought or desire of man can escape, nevertheless respects the freedom of man and does not force him,

[1] Cf. *A.A.S.* XXXII (1943), p. 234; translation, C.T.S., London, 1960, para. 103

how much more should we poor creatures do likewise in our relations with our own brothers!

The Specific Preparation

In broaching the question of specific preparation, we might start thinking at once of the study of those denominations with which we most frequently come into contact. We must make a study of the ecumenical movement, of the initiatives of both Protestants and Catholics, in order to draw inspiration for our own activity. All these approaches are necessary and indispensable. That is why several competent speakers will discuss them during this conference. Nevertheless, there are more fundamental aspects and questions. Many questions of principle arise which are equally valid for all ecumenical work, in whatever field it may be done. I would like to lay stress upon this. To be brief, what we must do is to appraise the general situation and go on enlarging our vision of it in the light of our faith. We must see clearly the goal to be reached, the human factors involved, the obstacles and the means. This vision has to be precise and clear, realistic and balanced but, above all, deeply supernatural.

1. First of all, *a vision of the final goal*, of the unity we desire and for which we strive.

(a) *Unity of faith* stands paramount: that is, the profession of the same faith by all who are baptized. Man today is surrounded by a veritable chaos of ideas, and of philosophical and religious systems. It is easy to understand the temptation to yield to a certain scepticism, to be ashamed of the intransigence of Catholic dogma as narrow, hardly modern, not realistic, rather akin to fanaticism. A misunderstood love for our separated brethren could also lead to a certain levelling, to a false eirenicism, which would assert that all that is required for reunion is the recognition of those truths considered to be 'essential', of the fundamental dogmas, omitting all the rest or deferring them to some future date.

It is evident that this cannot be the way to true and authentic unity. There are surely among our separated brethren many elements of truth and piety, and we must recognize and acknowledge them with sincere joy. But, in spite of these, we may not ignore the differences and the deficiencies, particularly on essential points. Sound work for unity must first of all safeguard the integrity of Catholic dogma, constantly aiming at the sublime goal proposed by the Apostle: '. . . common unity through faith in the Son of God and fuller knowledge of him. So we shall reach perfect manhood, that maturity which is proportioned to the completed growth of Christ: we are no longer to be children . . . driven before the wind of each new doctrine that human subtlety, human skill in fabricating lies, may propound. We are to follow the truth in a spirit of charity, and so grow up, in everything, into a due proportion with Christ, who is our head' (Eph 4:13-15). We must always keep intact this clear vision in all our work for unity, ever deepening it, and fervently desiring to share this precious treasure with all those with whom we have to deal.

(b) As well as belief, Christian unity is concerned also with unity in the use of *the means of grace* which are the sacraments. There is already a certain unity in virtue of baptism, as we shall see later on. A baptized person, whoever he may be, is not for us the same as a Moslem, a Buddhist, or a Brahmin. A baptized person is our brother in Christ, and we must strive to let him share, not only the graces the Lord gives him in virtue of baptism, but also all the other great graces which Jesus has placed in the hands of the Church, especially in the sacraments, and above all in the great sacrifice of the Holy Mass and of Holy Communion. Now, these separated brethren do not recognize many of these sacraments as such, and so they deprive themselves of their salutary effects. In order to be an apostle of unity, the priest must first of all imbue himself with a great esteem and veneration of the holy sacraments and all the liturgical adornment that surrounds them. The liturgical movement, fostered with unity in mind, is a precious help; this is particularly so today, because the desire for a liturgical life is alive in the hearts of many of our separated brethren who are no longer satisfied with the sole ministry of the work of a preacher in a place without any sacred character.

(c) Unity would not be perfect, however, unless it included *submissiveness* to those commissioned by God to guide and rule us in matters of faith and of practice, that is, to the shepherds of the flock, successors of the apostles, united among themselves and united with the chief shepherd, the successor of St Peter, the Bishop of Rome. And this probably is the hardest among the requests we will have to make of our beloved Protestant brethren, who for many centuries have been taught that in the Church of Christ there is no authority that could bind the individual conscience of each of the faithful. The democratic idea which is today dominant in a great part of the free world stresses and strengthens this feeling of religious autonomy. The apostle of unity must therefore have a clear and concrete view of the hierarchical structure of the Church, founded by Christ, and of the great benefits coming from this hierarchical structure, willed by Christ. He will, above all, make it clear that this is certainly a question of the definite will of God, of the divine Founder of the Church, to which we have to submit ourselves. But, on the other hand, this mandate, and the hierarchical structure deriving from it, are sources of great graces. Through it the Hierarchy gives us directions in matters of doctrine and of religious practice. In fact, it is precisely this desire to have an authoritative guidance in religious life that has led and is still leading not a few non-Catholics to the Catholic Church. The apostle of unity must have an accurate idea of this prerogative of Christ's Church and be acquainted with the blessings it brings to souls.

2. We must have a clear idea of the people with whom we have to work, that is, our separated brethren. I repeat that by 'separated brethren' I do not mean any particular group, but all in as much as they are separated from us. What is the teaching of our faith with regard to all such separated brethren?

(a) The first aspect is the relation of these brethren to Christ, to his mystical Body and, therefore, to the Catholic Church.[1]

---

[1] For a longer exposition of this question cf. Chapter 1 above.

Concerning this relation, the Catholic Church affirms resolutely the general doctrine of the New Testament that, through valid baptism, even though it is conferred outside the Roman Catholic Church, the baptized person is organically united with Christ and his mystical Body. By grace he becomes the adopted child of God and, for this reason, all who are validly baptized are brothers. Now, since the Catholic Church teaches that she is the true Church of Christ, she necessarily considers also these baptized persons, who live separated from her, as somehow belonging to her. They are 'sons' of the Church and our 'brothers'; the Pope calls these 'separated brethren' also his 'sons'. This he does not say and could never say about those who are not baptized, who are not Christian. It is true, of course, that these separated brethren do not recognize the Catholic Church as the true Church of Christ, consequently they are also somehow separated from her and are not her sons and members in the full sense, as Catholics are. They are separated from Catholics by differences in faith, differences in the use of the means of the life of grace, in the sacraments, and also by the fact that they do not recognize the authority of the Church and of the Bishop of Rome. These differences are certainly very serious, but yet they do not destroy nor take away that kind of fundamental belonging to Christ and to his mystical Body and the Church, of which I have spoken.[1]

From what we have said, the situation of our separated brethren regarding the salvation of their souls is clear. Having been baptized, remaining in the good faith in which they were born and have been educated, they receive, in virtue of their belonging to Christ, the help necessary for an authentic religious life, for the observance of the law of God and, therefore, for their salvation. They are thus on the way of salvation and this in virtue of that fundamental belonging to Christ and to the Church of which we have spoken.

(b) The next consideration concerns *obstacles* to union with separated brethren.[2] Here, too, we must have a realistic vision, not deluding ourselves, but having the courage to face facts. On the

---

[1] Cf. Chapter 1 above.
[2] The subject has been treated more extensively in Chapter 2 above.

other hand, we must not allow ourselves to be drawn to pessimism or to exaggeration. The facts are depressing enough and need no exaggeration. Nothing is more obvious than that on the road to union mountainous impediments still bar the way. Indeed, a whole mountain range of resentments, misunderstandings, prejudices, suspicions and mistrust has grown up through the centuries—and on both sides. There is an almost instinctive hostility, which is the more dangerous and harmful because people are scarcely conscious of it. Perhaps this is why we are so often accused of pride, imperialism and of claiming a monopoly of truth.

And so we come to the principal and most fundamental issues: doctrine about the Church, her nature and hierarchical constitution, the authority of the Church in matters of doctrine and discipline, by which she can really bind in conscience. On all these points there are divergences even more profound especially with regard to the communities originating with the Reformation, but partly also with regard to Oriental Christians in general and the Orthodox in particular. This is where the deepest chasm divides us.[1]

(c) But let us mention at once the more encouraging aspects, the flashes of light, though faint, that are starting to illuminate the horizon, and the small beginnings of approach to the Catholic doctrinal position regarding the threefold unity of the Church about which we have spoken above. In fact, more and more voices and appeals are heard asking for a clarification of the quality and the authority of the 'ministers' of the Church and of their 'ministry'. There is a demand that this authority should have the opportunity and the courage to explain the doctrine of faith authoritatively enough to bind the consciences of its own faithful. They have begun moreover to affirm that, regarding holy scripture, it essentially belongs to and is committed to the Church and to her interpretation. It cannot, therefore, simply be interpreted by anyone according to a presumed or real inspiration received from the Holy Spirit. Finally, on account of this trend, there is an increasing number of exegetes and of learned theologians who recognize that Jesus really conferred 'the primacy' upon Peter. They admit that he had the

---

[1] For more particulars cf. Chapter 9 below.

authority of the true head of the college of apostles, though they contend that this primacy constituted only a personal privilege given to St Peter and not a permanent institution which would pass on to the whole Church.[1]

Besides the flashes of light concerning doctrine, we must also emphasize the efforts made by our separated brethren, above all in the ecumenical field. This is a fact which we ought to understand and appreciate rightly—it is always the clear and balanced vision that matters! Right from the beginning we have emphasized the most painful state of division prevailing among our separated brethren, especially among those springing from the Reformation. Let us underline now what with good reason can be called a gigantic effort, to come at least in some measure nearer to that unity which is so eagerly desired.[2] I am speaking about 'ecumenicism', the 'ecumenical movement' which at the present time is of such great importance.

This movement originated outside the Catholic Church, but it started because of the desire of our separated brethren, divided in many groups, big and small, to find a way towards unity and towards fraternal collaboration, especially in the missionary field. The movement tries to promote unity by means of international conferences, studies, scientific and theological research, reciprocal assistance and help, mutual endeavour to defend religious freedom, and in charitable and social activities. The most concrete expression of this movement is found today in the World Council of Churches, which includes 201 member-Churches, most of them Protestant of different denominations, but with a certain number of Orthodox communities. Next to the World Council of Churches there is the International Missionary Council, founded forty years ago, and since last November 'integrated' in the above-mentioned World Council of Churches. Catholic Christians can rejoice about all this for it is a powerful expression of the desire for unity. It is a phenome-

[1] For some examples cf. A. Bea, 'Die Bedeutung des 2. Vatikanischen Konzils fur die Einheit der Christen', *Stimmen der Zeit*, vol. 170, no. 87 (1962), pp. 241-58, esp. pp. 250ff.

[2] See for example J. P. Michael, *Die Christen suchen eine Kirche*, Freiburg i.B., 1959 (the same work appeared in Italian with a good bibliography, Brescia, 1961).

non which fifty years ago was still impossible, and regarding which
the well-known Holy Office Instruction on the Ecumenical Movement says that it is 'the work of the Holy Spirit and the fruit of
much prayer'.[1]

We must realize that this unity of the World Council of Churches
is not yet the threefold unity described above, which Christ has
willed and implored from the Father. Some have desired that the
Catholic Church become a member of this organization. This is not
possible, since the structure given by Christ to his Church must stand
clear and unmistakable before all the world; and there is, it must be
said, still much ignorance and confusion of mind about the nature of
the World Council. But at the same time we must fully appreciate
the real achievements of such bodies and pray that they may prosper
more and more, and not stop short at a half-way point, in a purely
practical unity. May they proceed courageously and help to prepare
little by little for that full and perfect unity willed by Christ.

III

Means of Action

Now we must go on to describe in concrete terms what action
the priest can take to foster Christian unity. Since we are speaking of
priests in general, and not of those who may be specially appointed
by their superiors, the question is this: what can the priest do for
unity in the course of his ordinary priestly ministry? It is not a
matter of deserting one's own duty, or of fulfilling it hastily and
carelessly, in order to devote oneself to work for unity. It would be
wrong to want to work for God in this way, disregarding God's will
in one's own daily life. What possibilities, then, does the ordinary
priestly ministry offer for work for unity?

1. The first and most important means is to preach untiringly
the great duty of all the faithful to work for unity. We cannot say
that the consciousness of this duty is very much alive among all
Catholics, in every country. There is hope that the Council will

[1] *A.A.S.*, XLII (1950), p. 142.

awaken consciences in this respect also. It is not necessary to repeat here at length the reasons and the motives for this apostolate. The fact is that our separated brethren, in virtue of baptism, already belong in some way to the Church. But, at the same time, they are deprived of many graces which would come to them if they belonged fully to the visible organism of the Church. The most elementary charity requires us to do what we can to bring them to full membership of the Church. There is, moreover, the absolute will of God and of the divine Founder of the Church that all those who believe in him and are baptized 'may be one'. There is, at the same time, the importance of this unity for the world. It is, in fact, seeing the unity of those who believe in Jesus that can lead the world to believe of Jesus that the Father has sent him (John 17:21). The world can find its salvation only in him.

Our century has received the immense grace of three great movements that have entered deeply into the consciousness of wide strata of the faithful. There is, first of all the consciousness of the duty on the part of the laity to collaborate in the apostolate of the Church. Hence the movement called the lay apostolate. There is likewise the love of the Word of God, and for the holy liturgy, in the biblical and the liturgical movements. There is, finally, the sense of responsibility, incumbent on all Catholics, for the non-Christian nations, realized in the missionary movement. Nowdays, a fourth movement has to rise, to assert itself and to spread: the movement towards unity. There is needed a sense of the serious responsibility of each Catholic for the brethren separated from us and for the reunion of all those who are baptized in Christ.

2. The second means is to teach the faithful how to put this duty into practice and how to make practical a personal interest in all those who are baptized in Christ.

(a) The first, the very first, way to take an interest in unity is by prayer. The popes, especially since the time of Leo XIII, have constantly insisted upon the necessity of prayer for unity. A special occasion for this prayer is the Octave of Prayer for Christian Unity, which is observed now both by Catholics and non-Catholics, from

18-25 January. Not long ago Pope John XXIII, in recommending the Octave, said: 'With pleasure we make ours the words of our immediate predecessor of happy memory, expressing the pious wish that this practice may be spread in every region of the world, and, as widely as possible, especially in view of the Ecumenical Council.'[1] For an individual to return to the Church great graces are needed to enlighten the mind, strengthen the will and overcome all the many obstacles. If such great graces are needed for an individual conversion, how much greater must the graces be, in order that a group or a whole community may find the way to reunion. Now this grace must be implored with humble, confident, persevering, and insistent prayer.

(b) In the second place comes the example of an authentic Christian life, to be given by all the faithful. This always makes a greater impression than words. The First Vatican Council said in one place that the Church is, according to the image used by the prophet Isaiah, a sign lifted on high among the nations, which calls them to assemble.[2] Pope John XXIII, in his turn, does not tire of repeating that the next Council should constitute—by the sincerity, the concord and love which will prevail—a gentle invitation to separated brethren to seek and rediscover that unity willed by Christ.[3] Both these affirmations are true, too, in due proportion, for individual Catholics. They too should be in their own environment a sign that points to the true Church and an invitation to join her. And this applies in a quite particular way in an environment where Catholics live every day amongst a majority of their separated brethren, for whom they should be, by their exemplary Catholic life, apostles of unity.

We can perhaps insist once more on what separated brethren expect particularly from us and what is the most efficacious means for promoting unity. It is that attitude of humility about which we spoke above. Our affirmation that the Catholic Church is the

---

[1] A letter to the Superior General of the Franciscans of the Atonement (28 October 1959) in *Acta et doc. Concilio Oecumenico Vaticano II apparando*, ser. I, vol.I, Citta del Vaticano, 1960, p. 54f.

[2] Cf. Denzinger, *Enchir. Symb.*, no. 1794.

[3] Cf. *Acta et doc.*, loc. cit., ser. I, vol. I, p. 15.

only true Church of Christ will be accepted much more easily if it is accompanied by the virtue which is the 'innate' character of Christ's disciples: 'Learn from me; I am gentle and humble of heart' (Mat 11:29).

Charity, a great love for all the separated brethren we meet on our way—it is that charity which, although holding firm and unwaveringly to its own faith without compromise or weakening, at the same time is faithful to the warning of the Apostle of the Gentiles: 'Charity is patient, is kind; charity feels no envy; charity is never perverse or proud, never insolent, does not claim its rights, cannot be provoked, does not brood over an injury; takes no pleasure in wrongdoing, but rejoices at the victory of truth; sustains, believes, hopes, endures, to the last.' (1 Cor 13:4-7). Pius XI once said to a group of Italian university students: 'It is almost unbelievable how many mistaken notions and misconceptions are current among our separated brethren of the East, and how constantly they are repeated against the Catholic Church. But Catholics also are sometimes lacking in a due appreciation of these separated brethren; sometimes brotherly kindness is missing, because knowledge is missing. No one knows all that is good and precious and truly Christian in these broken parts of the ancient catholic truth. Pieces broken off from gold-bearing rock are themselves gold-bearing as well. The venerable Churches of the East have preserved a heritage so holy, so worthy of veneration, that they deserve not only the fullness of respect but also the fullness of sympathy.'[1] We cannot say that these words refer only to Italy and to the relations between Catholics and Orientals. We must confess loyally and honestly that in many other countries also, and among Catholics and Protestants, there are on both sides many prejudices, many resentments and much mistrust. All this can be gradually overcome only by the effort to know each other and, above all, by true and authentic charity.

(c) One final way to put our interest in our separated brethren into practice is to co-operate in fields where questions of faith are not directly concerned, especially in matters of social co-operation, of

[1] Address of 8 January 1927, cit. D. Bertetto, *Discorsi di Pio XI*, Turin, 1959, I, p. 671.

defending Christian principles in public, social and cultural life, in charitable undertakings and especially in international relations.

Such co-operation would follow the constant line of teaching given us by Pius XII, and has been explicitly approved, since 1959, by the Congregation of the Holy Office.[1] Pope John XXIII, in his first Christmas broadcast, made a moving appeal that 'all the goodwill among men should foster order, justice and brotherhood among the Christian nations united in a common desire for understanding and for sincere respect for the sacred freedom of the common life which embraces the religious, civil and social spheres'.[2] Here, too, comes that great preoccupation, the preservation of world peace. What could it mean for humanity, if the whole Christian world, nearly a billion men, a third of the human race, were to act in complete unanimity on the momentous questions of nuclear arms, disarmament and peace!

3. After this indication of the means of priestly activity, let me briefly emphasize once more how important it is that all our activity be deeply supernatural. Today, a certain naturalism and activism continually lie in ambush, which too easily lead us to forget the importance of grace and the supernatural. This would deprive priestly action of its true content and therefore of its efficacy. Remember what we have said above, the more vital one's own life, the more one can communicate it to others. The closer one is united to the Blessed Trinity, to Christ, and to the Church, bride of Christ, the more efficaciously will one be able to work with others for unity. This holds good for the priest himself as well as for all the faithful. Let us then, above all, inculcate the supernatural means that have the great advantage of being within the reach of every one of the faithful.

IV

Method of Procedure

Here we are dealing not with the way of proceeding in general—

[1] Cf. *A.A.S.*, XLII (1950), p. 145.
[2] Christmas Broadcast 1958, cf. *A.A.S.*, LI (1959), pp. 10f. English translation in *Catholic Documents*, vol. IV, no. 26, p. 21.

in this sense much that we have already said, e.g. regarding humility and charity, is relevant—but more specifically with how to proceed to action. This can be summed up under three headings: prudence, dependence on one's superiors, supernatural confidence.

(a) To be *prudent and cautious*. Work for unity can present dangers even for him who is engaged in it. We have already noted that we should be well grounded in doctrine, constant and firm in our own faith and in its applications. It is all too easy to let onself be carried away by enthusiasm, under the pretence of its being a good and holy matter, and to disregard all caution and prudence. In undertakings that are most holy, prudence is most needed, since it is natural that Satan should have an interest in them, and, 'passing for an angel of light' (2 Cor 11:14), turn them to his own purposes. Thus he tries to spoil noble characters, causing waste of time and effort and compromising the good cause. Today when the nostalgia for unity is spreading more and more, even among that strata of the faithful called 'the masses', we must remember that mass psychoses exist, fraught with illusions which lead to most dangerous delusions. An example of such a dangerous illusion was noticed in several public opinion polls, which revealed that many people expect the Council actually to achieve reunion.[1] That is certainly utopian. This is an instance of how important it is that priests, who guide the people spiritually, should be well-informed and should have an intelligent and balanced outlook, neither too optimistic nor too pessimistic.

(b) The best guarantee, then, of not taking the wrong path, is close attachment to the Church's hierarchy, both with the diocesan hierarchy of one's own bishop and the organs appointed by him, and with the universal hierarchy, the Pope and the Sacred Congregations. It is this close attachment which will save and preserve us from doubts about our right course, from enterprises too venturesome and risky, and from imprudent retirement or advance. The directives from the Holy See are wise, the fruit of long and

[1] One enquiry was made by the Bavarian Catholic Action, another in France; cf. A. Bea, 'Die Bedeutung...' cf. above p. 85 n. 1; *La Documentation Catholique*, 15 April 1962, vol. 59, pp. 502ff.

wide experience, and are given in virtue of the assistance of the Holy Ghost, promised by Christ to his Church. These directives will help us to overcome all obstacles and to achieve solid results for the salvation of souls and the welfare of Christ's Church.

Yet here too there is the mean of sweet reason. We must be open to the directives of the Holy See and of the Council, but this must be so in dependence upon and under the guidance of our immediate shepherds. Recall what I have already said: this dependence, besides being God's will and a guarantee of right courses, is also a source of blessing and of grace for our efforts. God leads us through the authority set up by himself, and blesses obedience to it.

(c) We need a confidence which is supernatural, a faith that can move mountains (Mat 17:19). The mountains certainly exist, as we all know: and it is no overstatement of the facts, and no exaggeration, to say so plainly. Positions entrenched over the centuries and strengthened from generation to generation cannot be changed in a short time, even with the most intense effort. Courage, then, to see the difficulties and the obstacles clearly: but courage also to see equally clearly the work that the Holy Spirit is already achieving. Awareness, too, of the need of patience, for with the Lord 'a thousand years count as a day' (2 Peter 3:8); but awareness, also, that the action of Christ and of his Holy Spirit, with which we unite our weak powers, is irresistible. It is this thought which will give us an unshakeable confidence and an invincible courage. Let us remember the words St Paul addressed to the Corinthians, speaking of his apostolic work: 'It was for me to plant the seed, for Apollo to water it, but it was God who gave the increase' (1 Cor 3:6). The result, the increase, is God's concern. Prudence, dependence on one's superiors, supernatural confidence: this is our great task, which we must again and again call to mind ourselves and teach to the faithful. They too are in great need of this in order to be able to proceed with balance and according to the Spirit of God.

Conclusion

'God wills it': this is the decisive phrase in the question of unity. We know that God wants it, not only from the words of the Vicar of Christ and from other ecclesiastical superiors. It is God himself who makes this manifest through many circumstances, which during these last decades have all converged so wonderfully towards the great goal of unity. Twelve years ago the Holy Office in its Instruction on the ecumenical movement (20 December 1949), was able to write: 'In many parts of the world . . . under the inspiration of the Holy Spirit . . . a desire has awakened and is growing daily in the hearts of many, who are separated from the Catholic Church, that unity may be achieved among all who believe in Christ the Lord.'[1] This is still more true today. It is proved by the wonderful reception by non-Catholic Christians of the announcement of the Council, whose friendly interest goes on increasing. Even twenty years ago such reactions would have been inconceivable.

It would be a great pity, even a sin, to close one's ears to this clear call sounded by circumstances and situations which have come about through the infinitely wise and fatherly providence of God. Christ himself, a few hours before his passion and death, implored from his Father the everlasting unity of his Church: 'I pray for those who are to find faith in me, that they may all be one . . . as thou, Father, art in me, and I in thee', and he added a reason particularly memorable: '. . . so that the world may come to believe that it is thou who hast sent me' (John 17:20-21). The heart of the priest must beat in perfect harmony with the heart of our High Priest.

The unity of all believers in Christ is meant to be a witness to Jesus' divine mission. This witness is sorely needed in the world today. A large part of the world is abandoning more and more not only Christianity but God himself, professing a formal atheism. Many sections of humanity are being tempted, with almost diabolic methods, to forsake faith and all religion. This unbelieving world must be met by a world united in Christ and with Christ in the 'one, holy, catholic and apostolic Church'. To attain this high goal, all Catholics, and first of all we priests, must work together in faith and trust. Let us, then, offer ourselves for labour in this noble cause and do our part in the realization of Christ's desire that 'there may be one fold and one shepherd' (John 10:16).

[1] Cf. *A.A.S.*, LII (1950), p. 142.

7

HOW UNIVERSITY RESEARCH AND TEACHING CAN FURTHER CHRISTIAN UNITY[1]

LET ME begin with a personal reminiscence. Twenty-six years ago the Pontifical Biblical Institute, of which I was then Rector, received an invitation to take part in a congress of Old Testament scholars at Göttingen organized by two non-Catholic scholars, Professors Volz and Hempel. An invitation to a Pontifical Institute to take part in a congress organized by Protestant Old Testament scholars was something so new and unexpected that I thought I should refer it to Pius XI. Significantly, Pius XI gave his immediate approval.

At Göttingen we received a most friendly welcome. We contributed to the congress a report on the excavation work done by the Institute, and took part in the discussions. In recognition of our participation, the Rector of the Pontifical Biblical Institute was requested to give the concluding address.

This event was a sign of the times. It showed that in the field of biblical research the time for polemics was passed. An exchange of ideas, rising above denominational standpoints in order to remove differences of opinion by calm and frank discussion, was being sought. Congresses like this, in which Catholics and non-Catholics meet to work together and for discussion have since taken place on many occasions; at Strasbourg and Oxford, for example, both in the field of Old and New Testament scholarship, and of patristic studies. Historical problems have also been dealt with at several international and inter-denominational congresses. Similarly, at

[1] Original text: 'Akademische Forschungs- und Lehrtätigkeit im Dienst der Einheit der Christen', an address given at the opening of the academic year at the University of Fribourg, Switzerland, 15 November 1961, and published in *Freiburger Universitätsreden*, no. 24.

congresses on orientalism and comparative religion Catholics and non-Catholics have been working closely together for about thirty years. The specialist journals *Old Testament Studies* and *New Testament Studies* publish the work of both Catholics and non-Catholics.

These facts—and we could cite many others—show that collaboration by scholars of different denominations, even in fields closely connected with religious problems, is not only a possibility today but a reality. Such friendly co-operation has done valuable service for the cause of Christian unity, for which every true disciple of Christ is bound to work. Every Catholic University's activities in teaching and research must be drawn into this task. In what they write and what they teach, scholars must endeavour to keep 'ecumenical' interests in view and to promote them; scholarship and learning, while remaining disinterested and objective, can still produce results valuable to ecumenical work as a whole.

In this spirit, I should like to quote St Paul, the Apostle of the Gentiles: 'I long to see you, in the hope that I may have some spiritual gift to share with you, so as to strengthen your resolve; or rather, so that the faith we find in each other, you and I, may be an encouragement to you and to me as well' (Rom 1:11-12). On this important occasion then, I take it that we are all agreed that a Catholic University has a serious responsibility for the cause of Christian unity; let us therefore consider together the various ways in which it can meet the responsibility.[1]

I

Research and Teaching

In their later careers Catholic university students will encounter this problem of Christian divisions; it is a live issue, met with in academic, professional or business life. They must be prepared to meet it and to make some contribution towards its solution. But if they are going to do this, their outlook must be ecumenical and

[1] The text of this address has been expanded for its printed version. It develops certain themes which, because of shortage of time during the actual address, were only referred to in passing or not dealt with at all.

they will need a correct approach. In saying this, I am not suggesting that everyone should specialize in academic ecumenism. It is, of course, true that ecumenism has already become a branch of learning in its own right. Special Institutes or Faculties are wholly devoted to it, for instance on the Catholic side, the Johann-Adam-Mohler Institute at Paderborn, the Centre attached to the Catholic University of Louvain, and on the Protestant side, the Institute founded at Copenhagen by Professor Skydsgaard and others like it. But here I am thinking rather of the general ecumenical education it is possible to give laymen and future priests within the framework of the ordinary courses in the various Faculties. And I am thinking, too, of the principles and methods to be accepted by university teachers in their research, writings and lectures.

1. *Philosophy and the history of philosophy*

Let us start with philosophy and the history of philosophy. It is well known that current philosophical systems both form the mentality of their age and at the same time express it. It is therefore inevitable that the theology of a given age and its doctrinal expression are influenced, consciously or unconsciously, by philosophy, and this influence is stronger when theology is less bound to a particular tradition. Hence philosophy, by clarifying concepts and modes of expression, can also contribute towards an understanding of the theology of a given period and thus towards interdenominational understanding. I am thinking, for example, of such key terms as church, unity, faith, worship and the like. The Aristotelian and scholastic modes of thought and expression used in our Catholic theology are often altogether foreign to non-Catholic theologians and students of comparative religion. This being so, a professor of philosophy or of the history of philosophy has an important role: in dealing with various systems and their terminology, to set them in their historical context, to suggest points of contact with different systems and, perhaps most important, to translate terminology into language of current usage. This will help to clear up misunderstandings and misinterpretations and will foster mutual understanding—not, of course, that philosophy should encroach upon theology; it can, however render theology a great service if in its own philosophical domain it deals objectively and thoroughly with questions of this sort, thus laying a foundation on which the theologian can build.

Moreover, this way of dealing with philosophical problems will also directly serve the ecumenical cause by directing attention to present-day intellectual trends and making possible a sympathetic and promising dialogue between Catholic and non-Catholic philosophers. To attain this goal, the philosophical treatment of a divergent opinion must not content itself with establishing—the expression is Karl Barth's—what is 'said', but will go beyond the words and make clear what is 'meant', that is, the content and real significance of the words. There is much to be done here in the history of philosophy and in systematic philosophy, both in teaching and in research.

The task is not easy: it will require much painstaking labour. But the labour will be rewarded. Intellectual relationships and points of contact will come to light which are not obvious to us at present. The influence of outlooks inherited from a more or less distant past has deeply affected the modern religious thinking of our separated brethren. This is often not fully appreciated; but recognition of it can also further mutual understanding and unity.

2. The History of Dogma

The same outlook and approach is applicable to the history of dogma. The theologian must never forget that very many of our theological formulations, which do indeed express timeless and definite truths, must nevertheless be understood and appraised with reference to the ideological background of the times in which they developed. Historical circumstances frequently caused particular questions to be raised and only one particular aspect of a timeless truth to be emphasized in the answer and thus the truth did not yield the fullness and depth of its meaning.

An example of this is found in the concept of the Church as the

4

Corpus Christi Mysticum, as found in Pius XII's encyclical *Mystici Corporis Christi*. This concept, which is quite clear in St Paul's letters (Rom 12:4; 1 Cor 12; Eph 1: 23; 4:4; 5:28ff; Col 1:18, 24) and has been expounded by many Greek and Latin Fathers, struck many readers of the encyclical as something altogether new. The actual historical difficulties of the time led the Council of Trent and the First Vatican Council to lay special stress upon the juridical and organizational aspects of the Church. These Councils did not explain the whole reality of the Church and left somewhat in the background the living supernatural functions and relationships implicated in the 'Body of Christ' concept. In studying the history of dogma, therefore, it is always necessary to bear in mind on the one hand the limitations placed in dogmatic formulations by historical circumstances and on the other the inexhaustible treasure hidden in every truth of faith. Various recent statements of the Church's teaching authority are a reminder that we should pay attention to this aspect also: to the fullness of the Catholic truth. Pius XII's encyclical *Humani Generis* says: 'This twofold spring of doctrine divinely made known to us (scripture and tradition) contains, in any case, treasures so varied and so rich that it must ever prove inexhaustible'[1], and the encyclical *Divino Afflante Spiritu* (para. 44) emphasizes that many apparently insoluble difficulties in biblical exegesis, after having been the subject of full discussion, have only been solved recently as a result of scientific advance (*Enchiridion Biblicum* 563). Speaking of the mystery of Redemption, Leo the Great long ago told us that this truth of faith is so profound that 'human weakness . . . will always find itself incapable of giving an adequate account of the works of God's mercy'.[2]

The history of dogma must show that at certain times only *one* aspect of a truth of faith was given prominence, and explain why this happened; such is part of its function and task. This dependence of dogmatic formulations on the historical situations and upon the

[1] '*Uterque doctrinae divinitus revelatae fons* (i.e. scripture and tradition) *tot tantosque continet thesauros veritatis, ut nunquam reapse exhauriatur,*' *A.A.S.* XLII, 1950, 568. English translation, C.T.S., London, 1961, para. 21.

[2] '*Humana infirmitas .¹ . . in explicandis operibus misericordiae ejus (Dei) imparem se semper inveniat*', Sermo 62, de Pass. Domini, 11; *P.L.* 54, pp. 349f.

intellectual climate of the times must be given its full weight; and only when this is done will people today, and especially separated brethren, come to realize that the Church is living in a changed intellectual climate and is stressing aspects of the truth which in times past were not stressed. Out of the fullness of the timeless truth revealed by God and proclaimed by the Church aspects are coming to light which were not emphasized in times when the situation to be met and the problems to be solved were quite different. Such contributions from the history of dogma can be most valuable for mutual understanding and can give a university student an outlook which will be of definite help to him in his future career.

3. Dogmatic theology

What has been said about the history of dogma naturally leads to the ecumenical tasks set for dogmatic theology today: it must strive to bring out the truth contained in a dogma *in all its fullness*, and at the same time point out the perspectives which are *at present* of particular importance for fruitful dialogue with separated Christians. The first task of the dogmatic theologian is to grasp accurately, deeply and in its different bearings the content of the truths of faith, as they are contained in scripture and tradition and authoritatively taught by the Church. Next he must distinguish and determine the timeless and eternal content amid the historically conditioned interpretations and formulations of past centuries; and, in doing this, he must avoid both any dilution of the truth and any over-emphasizing of the non-essential.

The dogmatic theologian must also be sensitive to the particular problems and questions being posed at the *present time:* how are these problems to be assessed and solved in the full light of the unchanging, timeless treasure of revelation? The Fathers and the great theologians of the past explained the truths of faith to the minds of their contemporaries, using the intellectual tools of their day. Think, for example, of St Augustine, St Albert the Great, St Peter Canisius. The modern theologian must do likewise in the completely changed intellectual world of today.

The questions which are now of concern to our separated brethren are different from those of the sixteenth century, and different even from those of the nineteenth. No doubt some essential traits remain constant, but many different influences and factors have brought modifications and changed outlooks. An attentive hearing given to separated brethren of today will convince any dogmatic theologian that they are ready for serious and sympathetic discussion of all modern problems. An openness of mind on our side may bring to light valuable and useful data, which in turn can help them to an easier understanding of Catholic truth.

These brief pointers show the immense tasks which face theology because of the problem of *rapprochement* and the ecumenical question. Here the modern interest in looking at ideas from the point of view of their historical development comes to our aid. The individualism which for so long dominated Protestant thinking has long since given way—under the influence of secular science—to interests far more social and historical. The modern scientific approach is to inquire into the origin of ideas, the environment from which they spring, their historical evolution and the influence which they underwent in coming down to us. In theology this approach raises various questions in relation to religious truths: in each case, their conformity with scripture, the history of their transmission (i.e. the question of tradition, at least of historical tradition) and the present relevance of each truth of faith. The main duty of the ecumenical theologian is to give our separated brethren clear explanations drawn from the sources by scholarly and verifiable methods. The wealth of material provided by the controversial theology of the sixteenth and seventeenth centuries can no doubt still be of use to him; but he will have to examine it carefully, think it out afresh and adapt it to the present situation. And above all he must never imagine he is dealing with an 'adversary', but with a sincere partner in dialogue who is seeking the truth and, who expects from the Catholic scholar, a clear, solidly-based and frank exposition of it. Keeping all our love of truth and our loyalty to the faith, we must today force ourselves, in teaching, writing and discussion, to enter into the concerns, the difficulties and the outlooks of our separated brethren. We must be sincerely anxious to discover ways in which to help them recognize the full truth. In this way theology, through its own intrinsic value, will become almost of itself one of the main instruments of ecumenical work.

4. Holy Scripture

In this work holy scripture is of primary importance, for it is the common ground on which we and our separated brethren stand. It will be impossible for the coming Council to give answers to every single question; it will have to limit itself to basic statements. Then after the Council the detailed work of scholarship will play its part and this must to a large extent consist in expounding scripture. Separated Christians must be convinced from biblical sources that the doctrine, the sacramental outlook and the organization of the Church are rooted in holy scripture.

All who take part in the ecumenical movement or come into contact with it will need knowledge of sacred scripture. This knowledge should be wide, exact and based upon a sound, methodical analysis. It should not be confined to exegesis in the narrow sense but should include true biblical theology, which is a synthesis of detailed exegetical work. Publications dealing with problems of unity should be grounded on a real scholarly knowledge of the Bible. The teaching of exegesis must be thorough but it must also take sufficient account of ecumenical questions. It is providential that Pius XII, in his encyclical *Divino Afflante Spiritu*, attached such great importance to *biblical theology*. 'But commentators must have as their chief object to show what is the theological doctrine touching faith and morals of each book and text, so that their commentary may not only assist teachers in expounding and corroborating the dogmas of faith, but also be useful to priests in their work of explaining Christian doctrine to the people and help all the faithful to lead a holy and Christian life.'[1] This requirement applies in general to the work of exegetes; but it is especially important for sound preparation of theological discussions with

[1] *Enchiridion Biblicum* 551. English translation, C.T.S. London, 1959 para. 29.

those of other faiths. In his choice of texts for treatment, the professor of scripture should therefore pay special attention to the passages which bear on the question of unity: his biblical theology will be based first of all on a textual exegesis capable of standing up to any reasonable criticism. Such a course of scripture will provide a student with an invaluable tool for theological discussion with separated Christians. It can, too, help to replace, by a gradual acceptance of correct meaning, the too frequent misinterpretations of scripture and the resultant misunderstandings.

And now a brief indication of a task common to both theology and philosophy. The well-known Instruction of the Holy Office (20 Dec. 1949)[1] about the ecumenical movement, lists among the possible areas of harmonious co-operation with non-Catholic Christians, *the joint vindication of ideas based on the natural law and the heritage common to all Christians.* This, however, presupposes that these areas of agreement have been carefully worked out beforehand. What is involved in questions of the natural law is the concern of philosophy, and especially of philosophical ethics. What concerns the common Christian heritage falls within the competence of the various branches of theology. It is well known that there are dangers inherent in an attempt to find a common substratum beneath different denominational convictions. It is easy to succumb to the temptation of underlining the common elements and suppressing the differences. This would be a mistaken eirenicism. The danger, however, is no reason for recoiling from a task which in itself is so valuable and so necessary. The task can be carried out with full regard for justice and truth. The Holy Father recently said that he always prefers to underline what unites men and to go along with them as far as he can without being unfaithful to justice or truth.[2]

5. *Church history and Canon Law*

A few words ought to be said here about Church history. An exact knowledge and a correct interpretation of this is of great

[1] *A.A.S.* XLII, 1950, pp. 142–7.
[2] To the 'Pax Christi' pilgrimage, *Osservatore Romano*, 27 July 1961, p. 1.

importance for the work of the ecumenical movement, particularly in regard to the rise and expansion of the different communities of separated Christians. Many prejudices and misunderstandings among Christians rest upon an historically inaccurate presentation of events and the people involved, and they can only be put right by historical re-assessments based on the sources. A very significant example of the good done by such writing of history is to be found in the popular history of the Church by Daniel-Rops. The success and the good results it has achieved are well known. Important, too, is accurate knowledge of conciliar history, not only that of Trent, on which Professor Hubert Jedin has recently published his first volumes, but also of the earlier councils which dealt with questions of faith. Just as important is a scholarly and well-documented history of religious life both before and during the time of the Reformation and, in particular, a thorough exposition of the political influences which gave definitive form to the religious life of European countries and, partly through colonialism, of African and Asian territories. Every university teacher and research worker who produces an objective historical study, in a spirit of charity, does the ecumenical movement an eminent and meritorious service.

Much the same could be said about canon law as well, but a few indications will suffice. Apart from an occasional dogmatic norm, ecclesiastical legislation has grown out of particular needs and historical situations and cannot in any way be treated as absolute. A series of lectures on the disciplinary measures of the councils, penitential practice in various periods, a survey of differences in marriage law or ecclesiastical administration—to name only a few —would give a good opportunity to show how legal regulations are historically conditioned. It will be very important to point this out explicitly, since non-Catholics are often inclined to see in ecclesiastical legislation an expression of the 'power politics' of the Roman Church and of its excessive juridical structure. It is usual for them to point to the contrast between the 'Church of law' and the 'Church of love'. To counter this the teacher of canon law must constantly draw attention to the pastoral requirements which lie behind so many legal definitions, and point out that different periods demand different solutions, as has been demonstrated by the many new regulations which have come into force since Pius x. Non-Catholics will feel relieved by the realization that so many juridical and liturgical regulations were conditioned by the historical situation, and that the Church herself is now taking steps to adapt its laws to the mentality and circumstances of the present times. Such adaptation Pope John xxiii has declared to be one of the purposes of the council and of the process of revising canon law which is to follow on it.

6. *Legal Sciences—Literature—History of Art—Natural Sciences.*

So far I have been mainly concerned with the various branches of theology and the sciences most closely connected with theology. The reason for this lies in the nature of the task which faces the ecumenical movement. The branches just mentioned do indeed stand in a very direct relationship to immediate ecumenical requirements. This however should not be taken to mean that nothing can be done to promote the cause of unity in other spheres of learning, e.g. legal sciences, literature, the history of art and natural sciences. The possibilities offered in all these spheres can be grouped under three aspects, one or other of which will obviously be more relevant to a particular sphere.

(a) One aspect is suggested to us by the possibility, already referred to, of harmonious co-operation with non-Catholic Christians in the *joint vindication of ideas based on the natural law and the heritage common to all Christians.* It is not difficult to see how this possibility can be of interest to the various branches of learning. We have already seen that philosophical ethics may clarify, confirm, and deepen ideas based on the natural law, and that theology may do very valuable work by bringing to light the ideological substratum in the common Christian heritage possessed by different denominations. When this valuable preliminary work has been done, other sciences can help the results to be recognized and accepted, the legal sciences, for instance, the philosophy of law and international law. Further, literature and the history and philosophy of art, without abandoning their own fields, can help towards the application and realization of these common ideas on the concrete level of everyday life. This is no longer the age of 'art for art's sake', and dissociation of art from the moral order has very few partisans today.

(b) Another aspect is the *co-operation* of the various profane sciences *with the branches of knowledge already mentioned, theology, the history of dogma etc.* One thinks of the valuable services and the indispensable data which history in general provides for Church history. One thinks also of the collaboration of the natural sciences with theology in the development of a Christian anthropology. A splendid example of this co-operation is the International Institute for the correlation of theology and science, set up at this University (Fribourg) and attached to the *Görresgesellschaft*, under the presidency of Professor Joseph Kalin. As everyone knows this Institute provides a meeting-ground between theologians and scientists, and it is worth remarking that Pius XII sent his blessing when it was founded.[1] In his encyclical *Divino Afflante Spiritu* Pius XII drew attention to another field of fruitful co-operation. He first reminds biblical scholars not to leave out of account anything which archaeology, ancient history and the history of ancient literature have brought to light and which may help us to understand exactly what the ancient biblical authors intended to convey and their ways of thinking, narrating and writing. He then turns to the Catholic laity reminding them that, by their scientific investigations, they will be performing 'a very great service to the Christian cause by assisting in the measure of their power towards the elucidation of cognate questions hitherto not fully solved'. The dignity and nobility of all branches of science will, by this co-operation take on 'an added and nobler dignity, a consecration as it were'.[2]

A still wider field open to nearly all the sciences is indicated by the French hierarchy. In a profound observation recently made in

---

[1] Cf. *A.A.S.* XLIX, 1957, p. 931.
[2] In *A.A.S.* XXXV, 1943, p. 317. English translation, C.T.S., London, 1959, para. 43.

a joint pastoral letter, the bishops declare that the natural sciences and technology have unfortunately been completely dissociated from the moral order and because of this are threatening the world with the destruction of millions of human lives and with unimaginable disasters. It is therefore a supremely urgent task 'to discover the spiritual significance of science and technology, and the possibilities they offer for the achievement of God's creative design and of brotherly harmony among men'.[1] The task outlined here is primarily incumbent on the Church and its theology; but certainly not exclusively on them. It can be fully accomplished only by the co-operation of scientists, theologians and philosophers.

(c) A third, very general, possibility is to be found in the common obligation for all Christians of whatever denomination *to serve the truth*. A notable instance of such co-operation is the Academy of Sciences, founded twenty-five years ago, thanks to the breadth of vision of Pius XI. This academy brings together scholars of completely different religions, even non-Christians. The only bond which unites them is that each of them, in his own special field, works exclusively for the truth. The Church's love of the truth has recently been forcefully emphasized once more by the present Holy Father on the occasion of this Academy's jubilee.[2]

This instance, however, prompts the question as to how far there is any service rendered to Christian unity here, since even non-Christians are admitted to this Academy and the service of truth is a duty of humanity in general. But the answer is not difficult. Disinterested service to truth is service to unity also, because Christians are conscious of a special obligation to the truth, since Christ is himself the Truth, and thus Christians meet one another on a very special common ground. But even more than this, Christians know that they have a duty to a common heritage of the truths affirmed in holy scripture. Since it is a sound principle that one truth cannot contradict another, this attachment to the truths in the scriptures means that the Christian scholar, whatever line of study he is pursuing, must necessarily be hesitant to accept

---

[1] *La Documentation Catholique*, XLIII, 1961, 58, p. 1344.
[2] Cf. *Osservatore Romano*, 29 October 1961, p. 2.

any result suggested by his research which seems to contradict a truth clearly stated in holy scripture. This attitude of mind is not a dictate of a prejudiced outlook, but arises from love of truth, a love which forbids him to offend against any truth. We can, perhaps, add another reason why scientific devotion to truth makes a contribution to Christian unity. The disinterested love for truth which it inculcates and produces is the safest way and the most effective means of bringing men gradually to overcome the gravest obstacles to unity: prejudices, misunderstandings, emotional attitudes, susceptibilities etc. Search for truth will lead men to make themselves ready for the truth of Christ and for acceptance of it.

It is difficult to generalize. Nevertheless I should like to point to a twofold character in scholarship's contribution to Christianity. In the first place scholarship makes valuable contributions through the results of its research and teaching. Over and above this, harmonious and brotherly co-operation among Christians of different denominations creates an atmosphere of mutual understanding and trust, a genuine Christian charity, which is of vital importance for the movement towards unity. I shall say more of this in what follows.

II

The Main Inspiration for the Task.

1. The programme which has been set out in these preceding considerations is certainly far-reaching and difficult; nevertheless we must accept it. For if there is an obligation today to work for Christian unity, this obligation falls above all upon those whose academic, scientific or professional functions gives them the vocation of forming the future intellectual élite of the nation, by inspiring them to their future labours in a fitting and a worthy spirit. It is not only the voice of the Vicar of Christ which is calling for this; it is above all the breath and movement of the Holy Spirit himself, which today reveals itself more powerfully than ever before in the longing and striving after religious unity. Our Catholic Universities and Faculties cannot remain deaf to this moving appeal for unity. They must equip the present and future apostles of unity,

priests and laymen, not only with the requisite knowledge but also with the true ecumenical spirit.

2. Enough has already been said about knowledge in various spheres. But a few words must now be added about the *spirit* of ecumenical efforts. I should like to sum it up in St Paul's phrase: *'Veritatem facientes in caritate'* (Eph 4:15), the truth in a spirit of charity!

(a) In the first place to hold fast to the truth and to bear witness to it: the whole undivided, undiluted Catholic truth, as made known by scripture and tradition and laid down by the teaching authority of the Church. Ambiguities and compromises are never well-advised. No service is rendered to the cause of unity by thus wakening and nourishing hopes which cannot be realized. Even our separated brethren, as their authoritative representatives have declared, wish to hear the whole truth, even when it may at first be distasteful to them. *The whole truth* also in secular sciences. The Church has nothing to fear from the results of modern research when grounded on true science. Genuine scholarship and real scientific investigation must be accounted a service to her.

(b) Any possible resentments must be removed by charity. Charity first in our *speech*. We are not now taking part in the quarrels of the sixteenth and seventeenth centuries, when often enough what was at stake was not the simple truth, but very material and worldly interests as well; and nowadays we do not use the violent language of those agitated times. Our driving force today is *love* for our separated brethren, to whom we may say with St Paul: 'What I claim is yourselves, not anything you can give . . . I will most gladly spend and be spent for your souls' (II Cor 12:14 ff.). With love and because of love we wish to share with those who are joined to us by the grace of baptism, many of whom lead exemplary religious lives, *the whole treasure* of truth and grace, entrusted by Christ to his Church. We will not do this by using hard, contemptuous or offensive words, but through the words of that love which St Paul says is 'patient and kind, which is not arrogant, does not insist on its own way, is not resentful' (cf. I Cor, 13:4-6).

The university teacher can instil this love in the hearts of his students by word and example, in his lectures and academic pursuits. In speaking of the dark and painful events of the past, let us leave judgement of what happened—on both sides—to the Lord God. Let us try today to understand and make amends for the faults and failures of earlier times. The content and method of teaching can be an example of the way in which love of truth and scientific serenity can make the words of St Augustine come alive: 'in necessary things, unity; in doubtful things, freedom: but in all things, charity'.[1] If our university students leave with this attitude they will become authentic apostles of unity; above all, they will have learnt to think in a truly supernatural way and have been led—and this leading falls within the competence of a teacher—to think of themselves as collaborators with God's grace and so to combine with their work, prayer, sacrifice and a truly Christian and holy life.

This century has produced four great religious movements: *Catholic Action*, that is, the apostolate of the laity, the aim of which is to establish a truly Catholic life in every *milieu* of the Christian community; the *liturgical movement*, which invites Christians to be more attentive to interior values within the life of worship; the *missionary movement*, which would lead non-Christians to Christ; and the *ecumenical movement*, which seeks to unite all the baptized in one flock with one shepherd.

At the present time the Holy Spirit appears to be directing the attention not only of Catholics but also of large numbers of separated Christians to the idea of unity. But this idea of unity has unfortunately not yet gone far enough. It has not yet penetrated the consciousness of ordinary Christians. To strengthen and spread this idea is the supreme task of the intellectual leaders of the Catholic people, both of priests and laymen, and it is a most special commission given to those to whom the intellectual formation of future leaders is entrusted at Catholic Universities and Faculties. It was the aim of this survey to give some definite indications as to how this may be done. May the Lord God ensure by his blessing that

[1] '*In necessariis unitas, in dubiis libertas, in omnibus caritas*'.

academic activity may also effectively contribute towards this end:
'*ut fiat unum ovile et unus pastor*' (John 10:16), 'that there may be
one flock and one shepherd'.

8

THE COUNCIL AND CHRISTIAN UNITY[1]

It is a special joy for me to speak to you on the theme 'The Council and Christian Unity', and to treat of this subject before so select an audience, while the day is drawing near for the actual meeting of the Council. Although this Council is, as we know, not to be a 'Council of Union', it will still, as the Pope has said, 'be profitable to those who are separated from the Apostolic See'.[2] The Pope also says how happy he is that many of these separated brethren have also promised the help of their prayers for the success of this important assembly. That is why the Pope expresses the wish: 'That there may come about for the family of Christians of our time what we know existed in Jerusalem after Christ's ascension into heaven, when the newly-born Church, in perfect harmony, gathered about Peter, the shepherd of the lambs and the sheep, and prayed with him.'[3]

It is in this atmosphere of earnest prayer—and our prayer is especially earnest during this Week of Unity—that we wish to study together what the Council can do, in the present situation, to further the unity of all those who, by baptism, are joined to Christ. And for Catholics, this unity is all the more important, nay even necessary, in that they will take part in the Council, being present in the person of their bishop. This has recently been clearly stated by the Assembly of Cardinals and Archbishops of France in a doctrinal

[1] Original text: 'Le Concile et l'unité des chrétiens' (an address delivered in Paris,, at the invitation of the Centre Catholique des Intellectuels Français, 23 January 1962) published in *Informations Catholiques Internationales*, 162 (15 February 1962), pp. 15-25 (without the notes).

[2] Cf. *Humanae salutis*, 25 December 1961, A.A.S. XLIV (1952), 12.

[3] Ibid.

note on the Council: '. . . the bishops are present at the Council . . . not as simple delegates or representatives of the Pope, but as heads of their particular Church . . . So it is that, through us, your bishops, you will all—priests, religious of our dioceses and laity—be present at the Council . . .'[1]

Unity has become the great longing of our days: unity not just national or international, but world-wide, and extending to the religious sphere as well. It is in fact in this sphere that the divisions among men are deeper and more serious in their consequences. Now it is no longer a question of unity merely among Christians in the same country; what is in question is the unity of *all* Christians. At the present time they number some 900 million, of whom 500 million (52 per cent) belong to the Roman Catholic Church, while the other 400 million are divided into hundreds of independent groups, known as 'confessions' or denominations. The fact that the World Council of Churches includes, since the recent assembly at New Delhi, 201 different confessions—and we must also take account of many groups which have remained outside the World Council—illustrates clearly the sad state in which we find the unity of all those who have been baptized in Christ. And yet, is it not the will of the Church's divine Founder that there be '*one* fold and *one* shepherd' (John 10:16)? It is for this unity that he prayed on the night before his Passion: 'I pray . . . for those who are to find faith in me through their (the apostles') word; that they may all be one, as thou, Father, art in me, and I in thee' (John 17:20ff).

The desire for unity among all Christians has never been as strongly expressed as in our days—the ecumenical movement is a very clear manifestation of it—and the Second Vatican Council, which has been announced by Pope John XXIII, comes most opportunely in answer to that longing. A non-Catholic author has said of it: 'This (the Council) is a providential ecumenical incentive. (Its announcement) has awakened great hopes among the Protestant laity throughout the world.'[2] This fact prompts a double question:

---

[1] *La Documentation Catholique* LVIII (1961), p. 132.
[2] F. Roger Schultz, Prior of Taizé, in *La Documentation Catholique*, LVIII (1961), p. 104.

What will be the nature of the forthcoming Council? What will it do to further unity?

The lively *interest* which the mere announcement of the Council has aroused throughout the world is so remarkable that the Holy Father himself has said: 'This respectful interest, even outside the Catholic Church . . . consoles us and gives us a foretaste of the joy of seeing all who believe in Christ fully united.'[1] The extent of that interest is especially striking when we recall the cold, even hostile, reception which non-Catholics gave to the announcement of the First Vatican Council. At that time the thought of taking part in the Council was stiffly dismissed and every invitation was considered an interference by Rome in the internal affairs of the other Churches. This time, on the contrary, the Central Committee of the World Council of Churches made a statement as early as 1959, following the announcement of the Council:[2] 'As leaders of a movement which stands for Church Unity we cannot be indifferent to an event which affects so large a number of Christians and which cannot avoid having a bearing on relations among the several Churches.' At the recent meeting in New Delhi, the General Secretary of the World Council, Dr. Visser't **Hooft**, quoted — and shared the conviction of the author—these words of Professor Schlink of Heidelberg: 'It is unquestionably of great importance for Christianity and for the world that it should be clearly seen from the decisions they will make that these two assemblies (viz. the Vatican Council and the New Delhi Assembly) have not been convened in opposition to each other, and that each will not seek its own advantage, but will seek only to serve the Lord Jesus Christ.'[3]

In the light of these favourable reactions, we can ask ourselves: why has the Council awakened this respectful interest everywhere?

(a) It is clearly not enough simply to answer that at first it was regarded by some as a 'Council of Union'. It is true that its very title of 'Ecumenical Council' could suggest this incorrect interpretation. The word 'ecumenical' in fact means, in our modern

[1] *Address*, 14 November 1960, cf. *A.A.S.* III (1960), p. 1009.
[2] Cf. *The Ecumenical Review* XII (1959 60), p. 68.
[3] Cf. *La Croix*, 15 December 1961, p. 4.

language, 'what is common to all the Christian Churches' and so it
might be inferred from the words of the Pope that he intended to
invite all the Christian denominations to a council in somewhat the
same way as was done during the formation of the World Council
of Churches. But that was not the meaning of the Holy Father's
words. The word 'ecumenical' is a very old term in canon law, and
means only the 'catholicity' or 'universality' of the Church, which
of course implies the communion of the individual Churches with
the See of Peter. So an ecumenical council is a council to which are
invited all the bishops of the world who are in communion with
the pope. No doubt, Pope John could have convened a 'Council of
Union' like those of Lyons (1274) or Florence (1439). But it is the
results of those two councils that now suggest prudence. Both
ended in the restoration of unity with the representatives of the
separated Eastern churches, but this unity was never effective,
because the clergy and faithful had not been spiritually prepared.

(b) The misunderstanding, however, about the nature of the
coming Council was soon cleared up by the Pope himself, although,
at the same time, he let it be known how dear to his heart was this
unity of all Christians and how much he hoped from the Council
in this regard. Scarcely two months after the announcement of the
Council, the Pope declared that the Council itself should be
impressive evidence of the unity and concord which prevail in the
Church, and in that way serve as an invitation to brethren separated
from the Holy See to take their place again in the fold which
Christ entrusted to Peter.[1] He spoke in similar terms in his first
encyclical: this Council must be a friendly invitation 'to seek and
regain that unity for which Jesus Christ so ardently prayed to his
heavenly Father'.[2] John XXIII constantly returns to this idea; he
repeats it on every possible occasion. The fact that he set up a
special Secretariat for Christian Unity, at the same time as the
various Preparatory Commissions for the Council, shows clearly
what a great interest he takes in the question of unity. He says

[1] Address to the Directors and Delegates of the Federation of Catholic Universities,
1 April 1959, cf. *A.A.S.* LI (1959), p. 300ff.
[2] Encyclical *Ad Petri Cathedram*, 29 June 1959, cf. *A.A.S.* LI (1959), p. 511.

plainly that this institution is to 'show our affection and good will towards those who also bear the name of Christian . . . so that they too can follow the work of the Council and more easily find the way to the unity desired by Christ'.[1]

(c) We can easily appreciate the *deep impression* which this attitude of the Holy Father could not fail to produce upon all who long for unity. The new Anglican Archbishop of Canterbury, Dr. Ramsey, speaking at a press conference, previous to his nomination, said: 'The present Pope has, I think, a great amount of Christian goodwill and charity. And where you have charity the results are incalculable.'[2] Dignitaries of the Orthodox Church have also paid tribute to the Holy Father, as for example Monsignor Cassien, the Rector of the Institut Saint-Serge in Paris, who says: 'His Holiness Pope John XXIII has seen what others did not see . . . He has seen Christian unity and the supreme effort which is demanded of our faith in the ways which lead to it.'[3] Many similar statements could be quoted: they all show, as a Protestant writer has said, that the separated Christians 'are expecting something from the Council for all Christianity, for us who are divided into so many communities, towards the united testimony which we must give to the world'.[4] From that arises the next question: what can the Council do to promote unity?

What can the Council do to promote Unity?

I would like to answer this question in the words of Saint Paul: 'We are to follow the truth in a spirit of charity, and so grow up in everything into a due proportion with Christ who is our head' (Eph 4:15). Truth and charity are inseparable in this task. Truth without charity becomes intolerant and repelling; charity without truth is blind and does not endure. So the Council must keep the two most closely bound together, both truth and charity.

[1] Motu Proprio *Superno Dei nutu*, 5 June 1960, cf. *A.A.S.* LII (1960), p. 436.
[2] Quoted by B. Sketchley, 'Le Concile oecumenique et les Anglicans' in *Unitas* (French edition) XIII (1960), p. 298.
[3] Cf. *La Croix*, 10 November 1961, p. 4.
[4] Pastor R. Baumann in *Lebendige Seelsorge* XII (1961), p. 205.

Truth above all! The Lutheran Bishop Lilje of Hanover Province has very rightly observed that it would be 'unthinkable for a council to raise doubts about the basic dogmas of the Catholic Church'.[1]

(a) In this the Lutheran bishop very clearly perceives the limits to the powers of every council, much more clearly than did the Dutch Protestant Union, which recently asked the bishops of Holland to plead with the Vatican to abolish certain tenets of faith, such as the Catholic doctrine on justification, transubstantiation and others, for which Protestant theologians 'cannot find foundation in scripture'.[2] But it is evident that there can be no question of seeking a compromise on dogma, on divinely revealed doctrine. We would be showing a very misguided love for unity and our separated brethren if we allowed them to hope that we will not demand of them anything more than the recognition of 'fundamental articles', that we will no longer ask for the acceptance of the dogmatic decrees of the Council of Trent, or that we are ready to revise the dogma of the primacy or the infallibility of the pope. When the Catholic Church once and for all declares a certain truth to be an article of faith, she does not act on her own unaided and independent discretion, but acts under the guidance of the Holy Spirit, that Spirit whom Jesus promised to send to the Church 'to guide you into all truth' (John 16:13). Our Lord gave this Spirit of truth to his Church in order that the Church might guard and explain revealed truths, and not make even the least of changes in them. The apostles realized the meaning of this charge, for we find St Paul writing to the Galatians with almost brutal frankness: 'though it were we ourselves, though it were angel from heaven that should preach to you a gospel other than the gospel we preached to you, a curse upon him!' (Gal 1:8). The apostles and their successors have no sovereign power over the deposit entrusted to them; they are only 'servants and stewards' (1 Cor 4:1). Their duty is to watch faithfully so that nothing is altered or lost. All the councils have realized this and they have never decreed *new* articles

---

[1] Quoted by H. Schnell, 'Anbruch des johanneischen Zeitalters?' in *Informationsblatt f.d. niederdeutschen luth. Landeskirchen*, 29 February 1959.

[2] Cf. *Informations Catholiques Internationales*, 157, 1 December 1961, p. 6.

of faith or revised old ones; their role has always been to decide, with the help of the Holy Ghost and in accordance with scripture and the tradition of the Church, what is a divinely revealed truth. The second Vatican Council will act likewise. It will not, through some mistaken idea of eirenic aims, dilute or explain away any truths of the faith.

Besides, non-Catholics with clear minds and sound judgement have no such expectations. The General Secretary of the Lutheran World Federation said as much in an interview: 'Efforts at Church Unity have no chance of success unless they take their stand on the firm ground of truth. Any other way of seeking unity which left truth out of account, would only result in a fictitious unity.'[1]

(b) On the other hand, without sacrificing anything of revealed truth, the Council can give effective help in recognizing the whole truth more clearly. Anyone who knows the situation realizes only too well how many wrong notions and misunderstandings of Catholic doctrine are obstacles on the road to unity. These misunderstandings go back in part to the early years of the Reformation, but they are also caused by the differences in theological terminology and by the many philosophical trends which have affected Protestant theology during recent centuries. While it is true that systems of philosophy express the outlook of an age yet they, in turn, have a considerable effect on men's way of thinking. That is why it is inevitable that they also influence the language of theology, all the more so when a theology is less bound to tradition and less controlled by doctrinal authority. So we can easily understand that the different systems of modern philosophy have considerably influenced the religious thought and theological language of our separated brethren, so that non-Catholics often have great difficulty in grasping Catholic doctrine when it is presented to them in the Church's traditional terminology.[2] So we must, as the Holy Father says 'by going back to the pure sources of revelation and tradition,

[1] Quoted in an *Oggi* (Milan) enquiry, December 1961, p. 10. This statement was confirmed for me by the author himself.
[2] H. Asmussen, 'Das Konzil und die evangelischen Christen', offprint from newssheet *Die Sammlung*, p. 2.

give new value and force to the very substance of Christian thought and living, of which the Church has been for centuries the guardian and teacher'.[1]

To the difficulties of theological terminology there is joined another factor, even more important.

Several of our theological assertions, by means of which a definitive and unchangeable doctrine is expressed today, are to be explained by the historical context in which they were formulated, and they sometimes present only a *certain aspect of the doctrine* rather than the truth in all its depth and fullness. Pius XII, dealing with this point in the encyclical *Humani Generis*, observes that 'this twofold spring of doctrine divinely made known to us (scripture and tradition) contains, in any case, treasures so varied and so rich that it must ever prove inexhaustible'.[2] Here is a wide field for theological investigation—in this treasury of revealed truth, to search out and find those elements which, in *our* time, are most important for our separated brethren. Thus in clarifying certain matters that are particularly pertinent to our time, the Council can not only dispel much misunderstanding about Catholic doctrine, but can also draw out from the depth and riches of the truths of faith those truths which are of special concern today.

The present age is *especially favourable* to this type of study. Modern scientific study is characterized by a remarkable renewal of interest in history and sociology. Every effort is made to discover the origin of ideas and their historical evolution, in what environment they were born, how they came down to us, and what influences affected them. The individualism, which had long held sway in the intellectual world, exercising an unhealthy influence on theological studies, is now giving way to this historico-sociological method, and religious thought and theological research are now again allied to tradition.

This modern method is particularly fruitful when applied to the study of sacred scripture. For example, in a review of Kittel's *Theologisches Wörterbuch*, an eminent professor of the Protestant

---

[1] *Allocution*, 15 November 1960, cf. *A.A.S.* 52 (1960), p. 1006.
[2] *A.A.S.* 42 (1950), p. 268; English translation, C.T.S., London, 1961, para. 21.

faculty of theology in Zurich University states: 'Here we have the authentic word of the New Testament and not some classic piece of denominational exegesis. . . . In the light of *Theologisches Wörter-buch* certain traditional theological teaching of our fathers appear biblical only in a very limited sense.' The reviewer quotes the examples of the doctrines of original sin and predestination, observing also that Luther's conception of justification by faith alone cannot, without qualification, be identified with Saint Paul's.[1] We have another example in the *definition of unity*. One group of Reformation theologians had opposed the idea of a visible unity, while now at the New Delhi General Assembly, following on a joint study by the various denominations, the following definition was drawn up:

'We believe that the unity which is both God's will and his gift to his Church is being made visible as all in each place who are baptized into Jesus Christ and confess him as Lord and Saviour are brought by the Holy Spirit into one fully committed fellowship, holding the one apostolic faith, preaching the same Gospel, breaking the one bread, joining in common prayer . . . and are united with the whole Christian fellowship in all places and all ages . . .'[2]

Although this definition of unity may not yet be identical with the view held by Catholics, it nevertheless shows the results of a deeper study of scripture and Christian tradition. Last November at one of the conferences organized by 'Humanités Chrétiénnes' in Strasbourg, the president, Marc Boegner, spoke on the subject of Mary and of Peter and declared that he could never accept the Protestant 'nihilism' on Mary, and that, concerning Peter, they must honestly study the problem and then accept the consequences.[3]

These are only examples to show that a more rigorous and perfect scientific method in theology can greatly lessen the differences

[1] Cf. *Beilage zu 'Theol. Wörterbuch z. Neuen Testament'*, ed. G. Kittel, vol. IV, August 1940.
[2] Cf. *The New Delhi Report*, London, 1962, p. 116, quoted by Cardinal Bea from *La Croix*, 16 December 1961, p. 7. Cf. above, p. 43, n.3.
[3] According to a private source of information, at the conference organized by 'Humanités Chrétiennes' in Strasbourg, 15 November 1961.

which have heretofore existed on the doctrinal plane. In the same way this method can be a means by which the Council—and after the Council the scientific work of theologians—will make several truths of the Catholic faith more accessible to our separated brethren, by showing that they are strictly scriptural. In this way many doubts and difficulties can be resolved. The Archbishop of Canterbury, Dr. Ramsey, observed very pertinently at New Delhi: 'You can see, among Roman Catholics, Lutherans, the Orthodox, Reformed and Anglican Churches, an interest in the Bible, the Fathers, and the liturgy, which is changing the emphasis in thought and teaching and bringing to light new approaches in dialogue and association.'[1]

(c) This last observation can be of particular value regarding *doctrine about the nature of the Church*. This is the deep ravine which divides Catholics and Protestants and, to some extent, divides the Orthodox from both. On the Protestant side, there has been a growing and widening realization of the supreme importance of the true doctrine on the Church of Christ. On this subject, the phrase a 'rediscovery of the Church' has become familiar.[2] 'Indeed,' says a present-day Swiss Protestant theologian, 'the problem of the Church is the one problem to which Protestant research has as yet found no solution.'[3]

It is here that the coming Council can do something to lessen the area of divergence. The question of the nature of the Church had been posed since the time of the Council of Trent. But neither at that Council nor at the First Vatican Council was it possible to deal thoroughly and completely with that fundamental question. It is for the coming Council to complete that task, which indeed will be much more easily accomplished at the present time, thanks to the great work done by qualified theologians and especially thanks to the deep insight into the nature of the Church as the mystical Body of Christ, given us by Pope Pius XII.[4]

[1] Quoted by *La Croix*, 16 December 1961, p. 7.
[2] Cf. K. G. Steck in *Evangelisches Kirchenlexikon*, vol. 2, p. 889, quoted by H. Schutte, *Um die Wiedervereinigung im Glauben*, 4th edn., Essen, 1961, p. 187.
[3] E. Brunner, *Gebot und Ordnungen*, 1939, p. 508.
[4] Cf. *A.A.S.* XXXV (1943), pp. 193-248.

Certain competent Protestant teachers have admitted that Pius XII's encyclical had given them an idea of the Church previously unappreciated by them.

What of the most difficult point for our separated brethren, the *primacy* of the Pope? Here, John XXIII has created a much more favourable climate in showing by his charity, goodwill and humility that 'the Roman Church understands and exercises the primacy—in the words of Monsignor Dumont—not as an ambition to dominate but, as it ought to be, a service, a "diaconia" '.[1] The very act of convoking an ecumenical council shows that the Pope in no way sets aside the collaboration of the bishops in ruling the Church.

The doctrine proclaiming the Church the 'mystical Body of Christ', the cooperation of the pope with the bishops, and this attitude of humble service—all these throw a different light on a whole complex of difficulties which many non-Catholics used to regard as compelling. In that light many of their fears appear, if one may say so, quite without basis.

This is not the place to develop this subject at greater length; besides it has been excellently dealt with in a statement on doctrinal instruction which was recently published by the Assembly of French cardinals and archbishops.[2] I am content to indicate that it is especially about the nature of the Church that the Council may be able to bring us enlightenment.

(d) Another point may be considered here: the nature of the *ecumenical work* of the Church. When we speak so freely these days of 'separated brethren', it is not just a polite way of speaking but the expression of a profound Christian truth. All who have been validly baptized in Christ, even outside the Catholic Church, have through their very baptism been organically united to Christ and to his mystical Body and 'in spite of our ecclesiastical, theological or human differences (they are our) brothers, because we all know that we depend solely on the grace of our same Lord Jesus Christ'. So spoke Philippe Maury, the General Secretary of the World

[1] Cf. *La Documentation Catholique*, LVIII (1961), 1186.
[2] Ibid., 1341-1346.

Federation of Christian Students, at the *Pax Romana* Congress in Fribourg, Switzerland.[1]

We must then hope and pray and labour that all who have been baptized may share in all the gifts of truth and grace which flow from Christ, the Head, and the dispensation of which he has confided to the Church. Unfortunately, only too numerous are those who remain outside the Church and this stream of life-giving grace that flows from it. It is true that, by baptism, they possess a union of grace with Christ, and this union enables them to have the authentic religious life which we admire in many of our separated brethren; it helps them to develop their life of faith and gives them the strength to overcome the difficulties and obstacles to that life of faith. But how great are the graces they forgo! Those, for example, which they could gain from the sacraments of the Church . . . That is why the Church feels itself obliged in charity, apart from Christ's explicit command, to help them to find the way leading to this fullness of grace. This effort of the Church does not spring from any form of 'imperialism', or from 'an impulse to dominate', or from 'totalitarianism', or from 'questions of prestige'. It arises from a sincere and genuine affection, such as a mother has for her children. The Church believes—and must believe—that Christ has entrusted to it the salvation of all who have been validly baptized and who are, by virtue of that baptism, 'children' of the Church, as the Holy Father called them in an important document, the Apostolic Constitution *Humanae Salutis* of 25 December 1961.[2] From that springs the motherly anxiety of the Church for all. It is understandable that our separated brethren do not share our faith. But this cannot be, and must not be, regarded in any way as a reason for doubting the sincerity of the Catholic Church or for attributing its attitude to some hidden and unavowable motives when it shows its interest in 'union' and 'reunion'.

(e) The Church, it is often said, bears *the responsibility for the separation* and for that reason it must, in repentance, admit its fault

[1] Cf. *La Liberté*, 28 July 1961, p. 5.
[2] *A.A.S.* LIV (1962); p.12.

openly. Certainly it is with great sorrow that we recall that the divisions were caused by selfishness and arrogance and refusal to accept our Lord's teaching: 'Learn from me, for I am meek and humble of heart.' Yet we must bear in mind that there is no question here of the whole Church, but of *members* of the Church, men who, in the eleventh or sixteenth centuries, governed the whole Church or particular Sees, or simply lived in the Church. Dogmatic and moral responsibility must not be confused. The reform decrees of the Council of Trent clearly shows that the Church, on the practical level of morals, needed reform; but in the field of dogma and doctrine, it was still guided by the Holy Spirit and had not gone astray; it could not. Besides, have we today the right to judge the men of those distant days? God alone has the right to pass judgement on them. The people who have come after the rupture can never unravel that tangled skein of genuine religious yearning, human passion, and base personal or political interest. It is simply impossible to estimate the degree of blame to be attached to individuals or even to groups. Let us rather leave the past in peace and busy ourselves in winning back what was lost: the unity of all baptized Christians.

(f) However, another *problem* arises here. In the view of a Protestant theologian, 'a holy Church of Christ according to the Gospel' is nothing more than 'the fellowship of Christians desirous of living by faith and grace, that is by Christ, and pursuing their way to their eternal goal'. According to him, this unity is not 'organizational' in character; 'the true Church of Christ already exists in all our churches, despite the differences in doctrine and faith'.[1] We too have clearly and forcibly affirmed this fact of the interior unity of all who have been baptized. But is that all? Was it the will of the divine Founder of the Church to create nothing more than an invisible unity? It is a question which cannot be settled simply by refering to 'the conception which the Roman Church has of itself', the '*Selbstverstandnis*' of the Church, as the Germans say; the question must be decided in the light of the

---

[1] Cf. H. Bornkamm, 'Eine heilige, christliche Kirche, evangelisch gesehen,' in *Sonntagsblatt*, 27 November 1960, p. 19ff.

Gospels and the writings of the apostles, and even of the Old
Testament prophecies referring to the future kingdom of God.
Man is not competent to decide for himself what is the 'unity'
desired by Christ. We must accept humbly and obediently what an
impartial, objective and methodically exact study of the scriptures
shows us to have been the express will of the divine Founder of the
Church. There also, it is for the Council guided by the Holy
Spirit, the Spirit of the mystical Body of Christ, to speak the
decisive word. Then, in sincere endeavour and a spirit of fraternal
charity, theologians will have the task of showing the scriptural
foundations of the Catholic teaching on the real unity of the
Church. I am happy to say that in New Delhi the Faith and Order
committee asked for 'special provision to be made for conversations
with Roman Catholics' and asks 'member Churches and local
councils to take whatever initiative seems possible'.[1] Friendly
discussions between Catholic and non-Catholic theologians will
show how true was the saying, a few days ago, of an eminent
figure in the French Reformed Church: 'However great are the
questions dividing us, what unites us is far greater still.'[2]

(g) I hope that this rough outline may throw into relief the
importance of the Council as regards doctrine about the Church
and about unity. There are, of course, a number of other doctrinal
topics about which the Council could give us light. Merely for
the sake of giving examples, I mention the question of the laity's
role in the Church (a special Preparatory Commission has been set
up for this purpose), the possibility of communion under both
kinds, the incorporation of the ancient hierarchies of the Eastern
churches into the general structure of the Church. On all those
questions, the Council will take into account the 'ecumenical'
situation to take decisions and offer solutions to the different
important problems of separated brethren. The Council will
certainly not suffer from any lack of suggestions and proposals
about inter-church relations. They are simply pouring into our

[1] The *New Delhi Report*, London, 1962, p. 175. Cardinal Bea quoted from *La Croix*,
15 December 1961, p. 4.
[2] *La Croix*, 17 May 1962.

Secretariat. We do our best. We confer about them, turn them over to individual experts for assessment, discuss them in our general sessions and then, if it seems wise, send on a digested version to the appropriate Commission of the Council.

Outside the domain of dogma lie the vast areas of canon law, public worship and religious practices of a more or less private nature. In all these matters, about which there is generally no explicit command by God, Christ has left the Church much more free and, as the history of canon law, liturgy and forms of devotion shows, the Church has always shown great consideration for the needs of the times, the different customs of peoples and pastoral requirements. That the Council will do likewise we already know from the words of Pope John himself. Speaking on 25 January 1959, the Holy Father numbered among the tasks of the Council 'the reform of canon law, which is so much desired and expected'.[1] A short time ago, the Cardinal-Secretary of the Holy Office made clear how this reform, and others in practical matters, must be carried out: 'Once the truth is recognized, that truth on which the Church cannot compromise, then all children who turn to her will find her a mother ready for the fullest liberty possible in the human matters of liturgy, traditions and discipline.'[2]

This brief outline should suffice to show that the preparatory organs of the Council are well informed on the various aspirations and proposals touching unity. Already at the disposal of each member and consultant of the Preparatory Commissions there is an immense amount of material in the fifteen folio volumes containing reports from all the bishops of the world, faculties of theology and universities and other institutions as well. The Commissions and especially the Central Commission are made up of experts from all parts of the world. It seems unnecessary to emphasize how much valuable and detailed information about the state of religion in every part of the globe is forwarded to these Commissions, which are themselves so international in character. All this will greatly assist the Council. Then there is also, apart

[1] Cf. *A.A.S.* LI (1959), p. 68.
[2] Cf. *La Civilta Cattolica*, IV (1961), p. 77.

from the publications in different languages concerning the Council, an immense amount of correspondence from many countries to the heads or members of the Commissions, dealing with every possible subject. So we can be certain that nothing essential is overlooked. We might also remark that many of these letters come from lay people interested in the life of the Church and are of great assistance in preparing for the Council. It can be said without hesitation that, in all the 2,000 years of the history of the Church, no council has been so thoroughly prepared for as the present one.

There is another field in which the Council can do fruitful work: encouraging the ecumenical movement. I have already spoken of the theological basis underlying the Catholic work for unity. It is a very special grace of the Holy Ghost given to our generation that the idea of unity constitutes such a potent force in our time. This grace itself calls on all Catholics to work with all our strength towards the re-establishment of unity among all Christians—to strive to overcome any prejudices that may linger on—and to forget inherited wounds and susceptibilities. Here, also, the Council could make an emphatic declaration about the imperative duty incumbent upon every Catholic to take an interest in the welfare of his separated brethren and therefore to pray, to make sacrifices and work for the unity of all who have been baptized in Christ.

Activities for Christian unity—is it possible that they are still, even today, too individualistic and uncoordinated? Much has, indeed, been done: think of the Week of Prayer for Unity in which we now take part together with our separated brethren. Think of all the theological conversations which are having fruitful results, and of the numerous conferences, articles and publications dedicated to the cause of unity. But the Council, without any attempt at centralization or uniformity, can give general directives and indicate attainable objectives. It can make more precise the part, collective or individual, that all Christians can take in this immense task. Above all, it can point out the means that are open to all 'children' of the Church.

Of these means, prayer is the most important. This the Holy Father has repeatedly said with great conviction. This the World

Council of Churches at New Delhi stressed, 'laying upon the hearts and consciences of all the member Churches the importance of constant prayer for their Christian brethren in every part of the world'.[1] Prayer must be accompanied by *sacrifice*, by the daily offering of our sufferings, difficulties and disappointments, for the great intention of unity. It must be accompanied by that *charity* which St Paul extols in his epistle to the Corinthians, (cf. 1 Cor 13:4-7) and of which the Holy Father gives a wonderful example in preferring, as he says, 'to emphasize what unites men and to go with each as far as possible without prejudice to the demands of justice and truth'.[2]

Then the Council may call attention to the possibilities of close cooperation in areas not affecting the faith, in affirmation of convictions about the moral law or convictions which are the common heritage of all Christians, in concern for the suffering and the oppressed. It can commend and encourage the serious theological discussions which, as I have just said, our separated brethren also desire. Finally it can ensure that future priests, while still in the seminary, are taught the importance, aims and methods of the unity movement, and are won over to it. So, while it is not a 'Council of Union', the Second Vatican Council can make important contributions towards unity, and lay the foundations which will permit—in God's good time when we and our separated brethren have been sufficiently prepared—the holding of a real 'Council of Union', which can carry out the will of the Saviour: that there may be only 'one flock and one shepherd'.

Conclusion

Hope of attaining our goal—is it a mere Utopia, a sheer illusion? You will agree, I think, that I have not been starry-eyed, but blunt and realistic. The obstacles are still enormous. Our separated brethren and ourselves stand far apart on many issues. Illusions here

[1] *The New Delhi Report*, London, 1962, 'Relations with Non-Member Churches', p. 151. Cf. *La Croix*, 15 December 1961, p. 4.

[2] *Allocution*, to the Pax Christi Pilgrimage, 26 July 1961, cf. *La Documentation Catholique*, 43 (1961), vol. 58, p. 1010.

could be most damaging. But it would be more damaging to lose courage and sit torpid with folded arms.

Recall the words of Mgr Cassien: 'It is God who directs history. But the effort which is asked of us—a striving towards understanding and charity—is, even while we are separated, an expression of our unity.'[1] One thing is absolutely certain: the unity of all who have been baptized is the *will of God*. It was for that our Saviour so earnestly prayed his heavenly Father on the eve of his passion: 'Holy Father, keep them true to thy name, thy gift to me, that they may be one, as we are one . . . that they too may be one in us . . . so that the world may come to believe that it is thou who has sent me . . . while thou art in me, I may be in them, and so they may be perfectly made one' (John 17:11, 21, 23). We can and must work with all our strength to fulfil this divine will. Let us not forget, however, what St Paul once said to the Corinthians about his apostolic work: 'It was for me to plant the seed, for Apollo to water it, but it was God who gave the increase . . . we are only his assistants' (1 Cor 3:6-9). The outcome, the increase, is God's business. But God is *all-powerful*. Remember our Lord's reply to his disciples who, in their fear, had raised an objection: To men, says the Saviour, that is impossible, but not to God: for all things are possible to God. That is why we go forth full of confidence and courage, in a spirit of charity, prayer, sacrifice and work, on the way which leads to the unity of all who have been baptized in Christ, mindful of the words of St Paul: 'Both the will to do it and the accomplishment of that will are something which God accomplishes in you, to carry out his loving purpose' (Phil 2:14).

[1] *Allocution*, to the Strasbourg ecumenical discussions, cf. *La Croix*, 10 November, 1961, p. 4.

9

PROTESTANTS AND THE COUNCIL

I. Agreements and Disagreements[1]

On 25 January 1959, the Holy Father, John XXIII, announced 'an Ecumenical Council'.[2] He did so, he tells us, 'trembling with emotion, but also with humble though firm resolution'. The world, both Catholic and non-Catholic, was greatly surprised. Catholics were surprised because they did not know that Pius XI had considered convoking a General Council. Neither he, however, nor his successor, was able to do so because of the great difficulties of the time (Fascism, Nazism and the Second World War).

Non-Catholics were surprised because at first they thought that there was question of a Council which would bring together the representatives of all the Christian communities to discuss the question of unity. This interpretation was founded on the meaning of the word 'ecumenical', used today to signify the coming together of all religious groups which call themselves Christian.

The misunderstanding was quickly cleared up. In fact it was to be an Ecumenical Council in the canonical sense, that is, one in which all the Catholic bishops of the *oikoumene*, the world in communion with the Apostolic See, would take part.[3]

[1] First published: 'Il Concilio sulla via dei protestanti: consensi e difficoltà (I)' and 'Il Concilio sulla via dei protestanti: i suoi possibili contributi (II)', *La Civiltà Cattolica*, 1961, III, pp. 561-572; and IV, pp. 3-13.

[2] *Acta et documenta Concilio Oecumenico Vaticano II apparando*, ser. I, vol. I, Citta del Vaticano 1960, p. 5.

[3] *C.I.C.*, can. 222f.—J. P. Michael, 'Eine schwere Entscheidung', (in *Die Welt*, no. 73, 28 March 1959: heading 'Das Forum derWelt') rightly remarked that this use of the term 'ecumenical' was not an arbitrary creation by the Code of Canon Law without any foundation, but is supported by almost two thousand years of the history and tradition of the Church, which in turn reflected the Catholic dogma on the nature of the universality of the Church. On the other hand the second meaning of the term 'ecumenical', to designate the representatives of all the Christian denominations, grew up more or less together with the 'ecumenical movement', and only in the last century. Cf. also P. Bourguet (art. cit. p. 131 below), pp. 23-28.

But the thought of 'separated brethren' was in the mind of the Holy Father. Little more than two months after the first announcement, he himself declared in an address of 1 April 1959 that the Council, giving striking evidence of the unity and concord reigning in the Church, should be an invitation to separated brethren who bear the name of Christ to return to the universal flock entrusted by Christ to St Peter.[1] The Council was therefore to have, at least indirectly, a unionistic purpose.

Yet the misunderstanding had one considerable advantage, for it revealed the intense and powerful longing for unity which holds sway among our separated brethren. Thus, even with its more limited purpose, the Council continues to arouse a lively interest among them, so lively that the Holy Father was able to say: 'This respectful interest consoles us and gives us a foretaste of the joy of seeing all who believe in Christ fully united.'[2]

This interest is more remarkable when one compares it with the reactions of the Protestant communities to the form of invitation sent them on the occasion of the First Vatican Council and indignantly rejected, because, as they said, it signified an interference by Rome in their internal affairs.[3]

Now, instead, the Central Committee of the World Council of Churches noted in its meeting at Rhodes (August 1959) that 'as leaders of a movement which stands for Church Unity we cannot be indifferent to an event which affects so large a number of Christians and which cannot avoid having a bearing on relations among the several churches. We hope and pray that the bearing will be of a constructive nature, and that it will serve the cause of unity according to the will of Christ.'[4]

---

[1] *Acta et doc*, op. cit., p. 15.

[2] *Allocution* 14 November 1960: *A.A.S.* LII (1960), 1009; cf. also A. Ebneter (art. cit. p. 132 below), p. 229.

[3] Cf. *Stimmen der Zeit* 163 (1958-59), p. 463; A. Fliche-V. Martin, *Histoire de l'Eglise*, Paris 1952, vol. 21, p. 314.

[4] Cf. the official Report in *The Ecumenical Review* 12 (1959-60), p. 68; cf. also H. Schnell, 'Anbruch' (art. cit. p. 132 below), p. iv. Similar declarations have been made by representatives of various Protestant groups: by M. Boegner, former President of the Protestant Federation of France (cf. *La Croix*, 19 January 1960, p. 4); other declarations by Calvinist circles: P. Marcel in the foreword to the article of P. Bourguet, loc. cit., p. 1 and in *Unitas* (French), 1959, pp. 118-121; from circles in the United

The interest in the Council is as great among the Eastern Orthodox churches as it is among the Protestants; but for the present I shall speak only about Protestants because they are numerically much stronger (250 million as against 165 million Orthodox Christians), and because they are more active in furthering the ecumenical movement in the non-Catholic Christian world.

In speaking of 'Protestants' I am aware that the term is disliked by some of our separated brethren and that it is not fully suitable. The term, however, is commonly used to include groups which differ greatly from one another: Lutherans, Calvinists, Anglicans, and some 250 'denominations' or 'sects' in the United States,[1] some of which have very little Christian character. All the same, it is possible to give some picture of the reactions among them, favourable and unfavourable, to the Council, a picture sufficient to illustrate their outlooks and the actual situation that faces us with regard to unity.[2]

Evangel.-Lutheran Church of Germany (VELKD), cf. *Kath. Nachrichten Agentur, Informationsd.*, 21 January 1961, p. 6, based on information from the Evangel. Pressedienst; for Anglican circles see *Unitas* (French), 1959, pp. 65, 117f.; for Swedish Protestantism cf. *Eirenikon* 32 (1959), pp. 489-492; the statements of certain individual authors: of W. Sucker (art. cit. p. 132 below); of P. Votel-Sanger, in A. Ebneter (art. cit. p. 132 below); of P. Meinhold, 'Was erwarten ...' (art. cit. p. 132 below), pp. 30-40; of R. Schutz (art. cit. p. 132 below), p. 103; of M. Thurian (art. cit. p. 132 below), p. 106; of J. R. Nelson, member of the 'Faith and Order' Commission of the World Council of Churches, in *Unitas* (English), 1960, pp. 142-144.

[1] Cf. *Weltkirchenlexikon, Handbuch der Ökumene*, edited by Franklin H. Littel and H. Hermann Walz, Stuttgart 1960, p. 1530.

[2] We offer here a select bibliography fairly representative of the chief currents of thought among the Protestants of different countries. Where one of these publications is cited elsewhere in the course of the article, for the sake of brevity only the beginning of the title will be given.

'Le Concile à la mi-temps de sa préparation: L'état de l'opinion', in *I.C.I.*, 135, 1 January 1961, pp. 28-39.

Asmussen H., 'Das Konzil und die evangelischen Christen', special issue of *Sammlung* 1959; *Das kommende Konzil nach dem Stande vom 10 Nov. 1959*, Meitingen, 1959.

Baumann R., *Der Berg vor dem Konzil*, Tübingen 1960.

Bourguet P., 'Opinions sur le Concile', in *Revue Réformée* 12 (1961), pp. 1-75. (The author is President of the 'Conseil National de l'Eglise réformée de France'; a preface, p. 1f., observes that the article gives the author's personal point of view, but this is certainly one which strongly appeals to many of the Reformed (or Calvinists), not only in France but in the whole world.)

Boyer Ch., 'Le Concile et les chrétiens séparés d'Occident', in *Unitas* (French) 14 (1961), pp. 18-24.

Brandenburg A., 'Evangelische Christenheit in Deutschland am Vorabend des II

Vatikanischen Konzils', in *Katholischer Sicht* (Fromms Taschenbücher 'Zeitnahes Christentum', 11), Osnabruck 1961. (The present article was practically completed when this work reached the author.)

Butler Salv., S.A., *Protestanti ed ecumenismo*, Rome 1961.

Cornelis J., 'Dans la perspective du Concile: précisions nouvelles et réactions des frères séparés,' in *Unitas* 12 (1959), pp. 107-121.

Ebneter A., 'Die Protestanten und das Konzil', in *Orientierung* 24 (1960), pp. 229-233.

Jaeger L., *Das Ökumenische Konzil, die Kirche und die Christenheit. Erbe und Auftrag*, Paderborn 1960. (English translation, *The Ecumenical Council, the Church and Christendom*, London 1961.)

Kleine E., 'Sie wenden sich ans Konzil, Evangelische Stimmen, die Gehör verdienen' in *Echo der Zeit*, 17 January 1960, p. 6.

Küng, H., *Konzil und Wiedervereinigung, Erneuerung als Ruf in die Einheit*, Vienna, Freiburg, Basel 1960. (English translation. *The Council and Reunion*, London 1961.)

Lackmann M., 'Erwägungen zur Vorbereitung des Konzils', in *Sammlung*, 1959, n. 8, pp. 1-8.

(Lehmann W.), 'Bericht zur Lage', in *Evangelisch-Katholisch* (= *Sammlung*), Fastenzeit 1961.

Leuba Jean-Louis, 'Was erwarten evangelische Christen vom Ökumenischen Konzil', in *Ökumenische Rundschau* 9 (1960), pp. 77-90.

Meinhold P., 'Was erwarten evangelische Christen vom angekündigten Ökumenischen Konzil', in *Una Sancta* 15 (1960), pp. 30-40. 'Die christliche Ökumene', in *Wort und Wahrheit* 16 (1961), pp. 101-116; *Der evangelische Christ und das Konzil* (Herder-Bücherei, 98), Freiburg i. Br. 1961.

Richter, W., 'Was hat die Ankündigung des römanischen Konzils der nichtrömischen Christenheit vom evangelisch-ökumenischen Gesichtspunkt aus zu sagen?' in *Una Sancta* 15 (1960), pp. 266-279.

Schnell, H., 'Enttäuschungen sollen erspart bleiben', in *Christ und Welt*, no. 16, 16 April 1959, p. 8; 'Anbruch des johanneischen Zeitalters?' in *Informationsblatt f. d. niederdeutschen luth. Landeskirchen* 1959, (29 February), offprint.

Schoch M., 'Die Annäherung zwischen Rom und den Reformationskirchen. Keine "Wiederherstellung" der Einheit', in *Neue Zürcher Zeitung*, 25 November 1960, p. 3.

Schütte H., *Um die Wiedervereinigung im Glauben*, Essen 1960;' Evangelische Christen und das Konzil', in *Rhein. Post*, 21 January 1961.

Schutz R., 'En vue du Concile', in *La Documentation Catholique* 43 (1961), vol. 58, pp. 103-105.

Sketchley B., 'Le Concile oecuménique et les Anglicans', in *Unitas* (French ed.) 13 (1960), pp. 294-299.

Smulders P., 'Das Konzil und die von uns getrennten Christen', in *Orientierung* 23 (1959), pp. 181-182.

Spiazzi R., *Il Concilio Ecumenico e l'unità della Chiesa*, Rome 1959, pp. 29-35.

Spindeler A., *Das 2. Vatikanische Konzil. Wende oder Enttäuschung?* Köln 1959.

Stakemeier E., 'Das kommende Konzil und die Einheit der Christen', in *Der Dom* (Paderborn), 1959, pp. 388, 412, 436f; 460ff. (The same article is also in *Lebendiges Zeugnis*, 1959, II, pp. 3-24); 'Wird das kommende Konzil uns der Wiedervereinigung der getrennten Christen näher bringen?' in *Gottes Wort im Kirchenjahr* I (1960), pp. 11-17.

Sucker W., 'Das Konzil des Papstes', in *Sonntagsblatt* (ed. H. Lilje), no. 5, 29 anuary 1961, p. 44.

Thurian M., 'Le Concile et l'unité visible', in *La Documentation Cath.* 43 (1961), vol. 58, pp. 105-107.

I

Favourable Reactions

In his address of 14 November 1960 Pope John XXIII spoke of the 'respectful attention on the part of separated brethren',[1] and indeed the announcement of the Council roused lively interest among Christians of all denominations. One Protestant writer thinks that the interest was greater than that preceding the Assemblies of the World Council of Churches.[2]

Since it is clearly impossible here to give many quotations, I shall try to indicate the broad lines and the main problems raised by the different and differing statements made.

1. The person and the personal qualities of the Pope manifestly carry great weight and account for a more general eirenic and optimistic attitude. One or two statements may be taken as indicative of a general feeling. The Anglican Archbishop of York, Dr Ramsey, recent successor to the Archbishop of Canterbury, said in a press conference: 'It seems to me that the present Pope has great Christian goodwill and charity. Where there is charity the results are incalculable.'[3] A Protestant bishop of Pittsburgh dedicated an entire pastoral letter to Pope John XXIII and unity, declaring in it that he expected much from the Council.[4]

Even when expectations are not high, there are hopes neverthe-

Volpi J., *Il dramma dei fratelli separati dinanzi al Concilio Vaticano II*, Assisi 1960 (see especially pp. 5-49).

Zahrnt H., 'Wenn jeder wirklich ein Christ wäre . . . Die Protestanten, die Orthodoxen und das Konzil', in *Die Welt*, no. 73, 28 March 1959 ('Das Forum der Welt'); but compare with this: 'Die Konzilsankündigung—ein grosser Bluff?' in *Deutsche Tagespost*, 14 July 1959, p. 8.

[1] Cf. *Allocut.*, 14 November 1960: *A.A.S.* LII (1960), p. 1009.

[2] So H. Asmussen, 'Ein höher Preis ist zu zahlen,' in *Christ und Welt*, 16 April 1959.

[3] B. Sketchley (art. cit. p. 132 above), p. 298; for other declarations from Anglicans see Ch. Boyer (art. cit. p. 131 above), p. 19f.; J. R. Nelson, in *Unitas* (English), 1960, p. 143.

[4] *I.C.I.* (op. cit. p. 131 above), p. 34; M. Schoch (art. cit. p. 132) sees an indication of very great humility in the fact that the Pope foresees that union will be attained only gradually, in a series of preparatory steps, first an approach and then a drawing-together.

less for some good results. Hans Lilje, Lutheran Bishop of Hanover and President of the Federation of the Evangelical-Lutheran Churches of Germany, while granting that it is 'unthinkable that the Council could call into question the dogmatic foundations of the Roman Church', believes that 'it could prove in many ways that there is a desire for different and more active relations with the other Christian churches', and this could be 'very useful, at least in other fields, such as religious freedom or the problems arising from atheism, for example'.[1]

2. More important than verbal statements are facts which demonstrate the interest of non-Catholics in the Council. In the Benedictine Abbey of Maria-Laach in Germany a meeting of Catholic and non-Catholic journalists was held from 19 to 22 June 1959, to discuss the theme: 'The Council and the Unity of Christians'.

In this meeting there was unanimous agreement that the announcement of the Council had been received with great enthusiasm even among non-Catholic Christians, and that the hopes and desires expressed by non-Catholics of weight and standing showed the interest they had in the Council and the importance they attached to it.[2] Similar conferences on the Council were held elsewhere, for example at Frankfurt-on-Main and in the Benedictine Abbey of Niederalteich in Bavaria, and the outlook was the same.

Another very significant fact was the welcome given by non-Catholics to the Secretariat for Christian Unity, set up by the Holy Father on 5 June 1960, together with the other Preparatory Commissions of the Council.[3] The motion proposed by the Executive Committee of the World Council of Churches, and approved by its Central Committee at the meeting at Saint Andrews, Scotland, in August, 1960, stated, after referring to the institution of the Secretariat:

[1] H. Schnell, 'Anbruch . . .' (art. cit. p. 132), pp. ii, v.

[2] Cf. O. Roegele, 'Im Blick auf das Konzil', in *Rhein-Merkur*, 3 July 1959, p. 4; E. Stakemeier, 'Bericht über das 4. ev.-kath. Publizistentreffen in Maria Laach 19, 22 June 1959' (*Theol. Berichte über Protestantismus und ökumen. Bewegung*: J. A. Möhler-Institut, Paderborn, 1959); Okr. E. Wilkens, 'Mehr Klarheit über das Konzil', in *Sonntagsblatt*, 5 July 1959, p. 31; *Unitas* (French) 1959, pp. 100-106 (A. Wenger).

[3] Motu proprio *Superno Dei nutu*, n. 9; *A.A.S.* LII (1960), pp. 433-437.

'The fact that a dialogue with the Roman Catholic Church now becomes possible is to be welcomed . . . The opportunity of a dialogue is welcome, but it means that the real difficulties are bound to come to the fore.

'The World Council will profit by the opportunities which present themselves to make known to the new Secretariat the basic convictions and concerns of the World Council of Churches (for example, on religious liberty and on Christian social action, etc.).'[1]

Dr Fisher, then Archbishop of Canterbury, who availed himself of the good offices of the Secretariat to make known to the Holy Father his desire for a 'courtesy visit'—having been informed more accurately on the purpose and activity of the Secretariat itself—held that his visit to the Pope had been important but fleeting, while the Secretariat was a permanent institution whose work will continue to exercise its influence.[2]

The interest of the general public in the Secretariat is also shown in the many requests for interviews from representatives of the Press, radio and television. These are so frequent that it is not possible to satisfy them all, even in the distant future.

Immediately after the publication of the papal declaration *Superno Dei nutu* (5 June 1960), in which the setting up of the Secretariat was announced,[3] the present writer was interviewed at New York by five correspondents of important newspapers. These were then followed by another five interviews in Rome, and four others in Germany.

One of these interviews was on the Italian radio-television network, one on German television, and one on French television, not to mention many private conversations on the same matter held by both the President and the Secretary of the Secretariat.

[1] *The Ecumenical Review* 13 (1960), p. 46.

[2] A similar declaration on the importance of the Secretariat was made by K. Slack, General Secretary of the British Council of Churches at the Congress of that Council in Dublin, 24-25 April 1961 (cf. *The Irish Times*, 26 April 1961, p. 9). Cf. also C. J. Dumont, 'Le Secrétariat pour l'unité' in *Vers l'unité Chrétienne* 13 (1960), pp. 65-69, 88; O. Roegele, 'Um die Einheit der Christen', in *Rhein. Merkur*, 9 September 1960, p. 3; M. Thurian (art. cit. p. 132 above), p. 106; W. Lehmann (art. cit. p. 132 above), p. 6; *Verbum Caro* 14 (1960), p. 298; also in favour, though more critical, is the judgement of P. Bourguet (art. cit. p. 131 above), pp. 46-49.

[3] *Acta et doc*, pp. 93-99; see p. 95, n. 9.

All this shows that the Council has given rise to considerable favourable reaction, or at least to very great interest, in the Protestant world, and one certainly understands how the Holy Father, having noted the 'respectful attention of separated brethren' for the Council, found in it a cause for consolation that gave him 'a foretaste of the joy of seeing all who believe in Christ fully united'.[1]

But at the same time he asked that trustful prayers 'should rise up from every place on earth' so that he could 'feel himself supported by his venerable brothers and beloved children in all parts of the world'.[2]

The Holy Father is fully aware that as well as agreements there are also discordant voices and grave obstacles which must be faced and overcome.

II.

Difficulties and Obstacles

To gain a true idea of the situation existing in the Protestant world regarding the Council, one must avoid exaggerated optimism as much as excessive pessimism, and must look courageously and accurately at the elements unfavourable to union in order to find a way of overcoming them. They warn us not to build our work on the sands of poor human foundations, but on the bedrock which is Christ, the divine Founder and Head of the Church. Having built upon such an unshakable foundation, we will face the task with

[1] Allocutio 14 November 1960: A.A.S. LII (1960), p. 1009.
[2] Ibid., p. 1013; the Holy Father has not hesitated to ask for prayers for the Council also from brethren who are separated from the Holy See (cf. encyclical Ad Petri Cathedram; translation, C.T.S., London). Characteristic of the atmosphere in the denominations today, and a very promising sign, is the fact that various representatives have recommended their faithful (or all Christians) to pray for the Council. Thus, first of all, the Central Committee of the World Council of Churches, cf. The Ecumenical Review 12 (1959-60), p. 68; and also W. Sucker (art. cit. p. 132 above); the Hauptpastor in Hamburg, H. H. Harms (Eirenikon, 33, 1960, p. 366f.); P. Meinhold, 'Was erwarten . . .' (art. cit. p. 132 above), p. 40; M. Thurian (art. cit. p. 132 above) and most recently His Grace Doctor G. Fisher, former Anglican Primate of all England, at the Convocation of Canterbury on 1 May, who explicitly associated himself with the Pope's appeal to pray for the Council in the week between the Ascension and Pentecost (cf. The Church Times, Friday, 5 May 1961, p. 1); cf. also H. Schnell, 'Anbruch . . .' (art. cit. p. 132 above), p. iv.

courage, seeking to do whatever can be done to clarify misunderstandings, dispel and overcome prejudices, answer objections and prevail against obstacles and opposition.

1. We shall not delay over the difficulties of a general order which one encounters even today in certain Protestant circles, which speak of 'Romanism', 'papism', 'thirst for power', 'exclusivism' and the like. These are propaganda terms, answered and refuted a thousand times by wise and responsible men.

Someone has even asked if the World Council of Churches does not perhaps consider the announcement of the Ecumenical Council as an attempt in grand style to disturb, neutralize or bring under its own control the ever-increasing co-operation of the member churches of the World Council itself.[1]

The General Secretary of the World Council, apropos of the announcement of the Ecumenical Council, released the following declaration which was later adopted by the Executive Committee of the World Council:

'All Christians, to whatever denomination they belong, hope and pray that this historic event may be useful to the cause of the Christian unity for which our Lord prayed.'[2] This truly seems to be the only attitude worthy of a generous love for Christ, the only attitude responsive to Christ's will for the unity of all those who believe in him.

2. More serious are the objections springing from a different concept of dogma properly so-called, and from its immutability. He who 'encloses himself in a dogmatic prison', says one influential member of the German Evangelical Church,[3] 'will be of no service to unity'. The Secretary of the Church Union, the Anglo-Catholic Coleman, doubts that the Council is disposed to effect changes in the doctrinal situation which exists between Rome and the Anglican

[1] Cf. H. Schnell, 'Anbruch . . .' (art. cit. p. 132 above), p. iv.
[2] Ibid.
[3] H. Schnell, 'Enttäuschungen . . .' (art. cit. p. 132 above); cf. also P. Bourguet (art. cit. p. 131 above), p. 59f.; M. Schoch (art. cit. p. 132 above), p. 2; H. Zahrnt, 'Wenn jeder. . .' (art. cit. p. 133 above; but the thought of the author is not quite clear).

Church. Indeed, he does not even expect that 'the Roman theologians of a more liberal spirit met with in certain circles' will be
able to make themselves heard efficaciously in the Council.[1]

This objection is certainly serious and touches the very essence of
the Catholic Church. No well instructed Catholic will believe that
the Council could or would change even a single dogma. The full
and integral preservation of the doctrine transmitted by tradition
is a duty from which the ecclesiastical authority, the Pope and the
Council, cannot depart, and no love for our separated brethren can
move us to touch even in the slightest the sacred deposit of the faith.

Any 'conciliatory' attempt to water down or explain away
dogmas would be an infidelity to the command received from
the Lord and, moreover, would destroy its own purpose. The most
responsible among separated brethren themselves repudiate any
idea of unity at the expense of truth.

'The great possibility that Rome and Wittenberg may meet
peacefully on the occasion of the Council must not be destroyed by
unlawful compromise', said Asmussen,[2] and the President of the
German Evangelical Federation, Professor Bornkamm, stated that
'the way to unity must require from no one the sacrifice of convictions imposed by conscience', and that doctrinal differences must
not be set aside at the expense of truth.[3]

The General Secretary of the World Council of Churches expressed himself in the same sense at the Saint Andrews meeting.[4]
A communiqué of the German Evangelical Lutheran Federation
(VELKD) said: 'Only where the situation is seen clearly and soberly
can genuine progress be achieved in relations between the denominations. This awareness requires on the part of all renouncement of an
ingenuous silence about differences, renouncement of superficial
outlooks which give rise to emotional expectations, and renounce-

[1] B. Sketchley (art. cit. p. 132 above), p. 298; cf. also *I.C.I.*, loc. cit., p. 34f.

[2] In 'Ein höher Preis . . .' (cf. note, p. 131 above); charity, truth and unity *make one
single entity*, as J. R. Nelson very justly observes, loc. cit., p. 143.

[3] Cf. *Kath. Nachr. Agentur, Informat.-Dienst*, 1 October 1960, n. 39, p. 11; the same
idea is found in W. Lehmann (art. cit. p. 132 above), p. 9; Meinhold, loc. cit., pp. 101.
116.

[4] *The Ecumenical Review*, 13 (1960), p. 56; cf. ibid., also p. 46.

ment of the tendency to find the whole solution in the words "charity" and "union".[1]

This however does not preclude tactful and patient efforts to show our separated brethren the solid foundations of Catholic doctrine, its inherent consistency, its religious and moral loftiness. The meaning and import of individual dogmas can be made clear so as to remove the wrong interpretations which are only too common[2] as, for example, the confusion between infallibility in solemn definitions and impeccability, between infallibility in *ex cathedra* definitions and other papal declarations or teachings. We shall speak of the correction of such misunderstandings in another article.[3]

3. Equally grave is the difficulty about the authority of the Church and in particular of the pope. A Protestant author notes that Catholics, because of their conception of the Church, can never consider Protestants as equal to them, the Catholic Church being for them not just one 'denomination' among many, but the only true Church of Christ, to which the others must return.[4]

Sometimes, instead of attempts being made to understand this attitude of the Church and to give weight to the doctrine involved, it is forthwith stigmatized as 'centralism', 'curialism',[5] thirst for power. There is a peremptory antecedent demand that the Catholic Church begin by placing itself on the same level as the other denominations and dealing with them on a brotherly basis of equality.

[1] *Cf. Kath. Nachr. Agentur., Informat.-Dienst.* 21 January 1961, p. 6. None who knows the diversity in the characters of men will be surprised at finding this sort of eirenic excess on the Catholic side, also, but it is really difficult to understand how one could affirm that this false eirenicism meets with 'l'approbation chaleureuse . . . du catholicisme le plus hautement hiérarchique' (so P. Bourguet [art. cit. p. 131 above], p. 68; cf. also p. 48).

[2] Cf. J. L. Leuba (art. cit. p. 132 above), pp. 88f.

[3] See below, p. 143ff.

[4] So H. Zahrnt, 'Wenn jeder . . .' (art. cit. p. 133); W. Sucker (art. cit. p. 132) and also at a congress held at Loccum, cf. *Der christl. Sonntag* (Freiburg) 11 (1959), p. 43; cf. also P. Bourguet (art. cit. p. 131 above), pp. 31-33, 62.

[5] Cf. *I.C.I.* (loc. cit. p. 131), p. 35; cf. P. Bourguet, (art. cit.), p. 63; basically the Church is acting for reasons of prestige! To be fair, however, one must add that there are much more moderate people who take full account of the problem and can face it serenely: see e.g. J. L. Leuba (art. cit. p. 132 above), pp. 78-81; R. Baumann, *Der Fels der Welt*, Tübingen 1959, pp. 62ff. and the various statements collected by H. Schütte *Um die Wiedereinigung* . . . (op. cit. p. 132 above), pp. 110-136.

It should associate itself, like the other Christian denominations, with the ecumenical community of the World Council of Churches.[1]

Here also Catholics can only respond with a '*non possumus*' (we cannot). The very nature of the Church, willed and sanctioned by Christ, is contrary to any compromise in matters of doctrine. Any weakening in this respect would compromise faith itself.

This is no obstacle, however, to treating our separated brethren with true charity and with the 'fullness of courtesy' which, as the Pope said, marked his conversation with Archbishop Fisher.[2] Nor is it true that responsible and frank exchanges, even on doctrinal matters, cannot take place between Catholics and Protestants. The experience of recent decades proves exactly the contrary.

4. Akin to doctrine about the nature of the Church is the conception of the unity of the Church. According to certain authors it is useless to search for unity because it already exists, consisting in 'the community of Christians who wish to live the life of faith and grace, that is of Christ, and follow the path which leads to their eternal goal'.[3]

The unity of the Church, according to them, is not a unity of organization or of an ecclesiastical and political nature. For them, an organizational structure is not essential for the Church. To ask of non-Catholic Christians a 'return' to Mother Church is then an arbitrary demand, contrary to the Bible and therefore not Christian.

Thus argue Dr Schnell[4] and others. Another author writes: 'The road to unity, if unity is taken to mean an organization, is and remains a utopia.' Not even the primitive Church, he says, had an organized unity: Paul and Peter, James and John, notwithstanding

---

[1] These are ideas which keep turning up in different articles; see e.g. H. Schnell, 'Enttäuschungen . . .' (art. cit. p. 132); H. Zahrnt, 'Wenn jeder . . .' (art. cit. p. 133); B. Sketchley, (art. cit. p. 132), p. 298; cf. also *Unitas* (French), 1959, p. 121; P. Bourguet (art. cit. p. 131), p. 62.

[2] Discourse of 3 December 1960, at the close of the spiritual exercises; cf. *Osservatore Romana*, 4 December 1960.

[3] H. Bornkamm, ' "Eine heilige christliche Kirche", evanglisch gesehen' in *Sonntagsblatt*, Hamburg, 27 November 1960, p. 19; the exclusion of the 'organizing' element there is also found in a statement the well-known Protestant theologian R. Bultmann made to the review *La Rocca* 20 (1961), no. 7, p. 37; cf. also *Oikoumenikon* 1, 1 (1961), p. 79.

[4] H. Schnell, 'Enttäuschungen . . .' loc. cit.

all differences and conflicts of opinion, recognized themselves as united in Christ.[1] The ideal for these controversialists is not the 'one, holy and catholic', but the World Council of Geneva, which unites all Christians without wishing to be a 'super-Church'.[2]

This position would make all efforts at unity 'stale, flat and unprofitable'. Work for unity would be futile. But the position cannot be sustained. It is certainly true that all validly baptized Christians are united in Christ by a union which not even heresy or schism can completely destroy. Because of this union, all baptized persons are 'brothers' among themselves and 'sons' of the same Mother, the Church.

But this union is certainly not that complete union willed by our Lord, as is attested by the Gospel itself and by the letters of Peter and Paul. One who reads with critical objectivity the relevant biblical texts inspired by the Holy Spirit could never acquiesce in a purely spiritual unity created by common faith in Christ, nor in that fundamental unity which comes from baptism. It is impossible to escape from the Scriptural teaching that Christ meant his Church to be embodied in a concrete organization, and that the Church from its earliest days was inexorable in maintaining its concrete organization against those who would cut themselves off either from the doctrine it openly professed or from the government it imposed.[3]

In saying this, I make no charges against those who in recent times turned away from the Church. No man can judge their responsibility. Such things must be left to God. And yet the objective truth must be understood and underscored: there is an authentic and correct conception of the unity of the Church; and there is a heavy responsibility resting upon those who bring separation from her teaching, her means of holiness (sacraments) and her guidance.

5. The final serious difficulty in the search for unity is the lack of authority with which one can deal in non-Catholic circles. A Pro-

[1] G. Hummel, 'Was ist eine heilige Kirche?' in *Christ und Welt*, 6 October 1960, p. 6.

[2] So Dr Bornkamm in the 'Assemblea della Federazione Evangelica' of 23-27 September 1960, cf. *Kath. Nachr. Agentur, Informat.-Dienst.*, n. 39, 1 October 1960, p. 10f.

[3] Cf. *La Civiltà Cattolica*, 1961, I, pp. 115f.

testant author remarks correctly that 'the Evangelicals do have no common evangelical church government . . . each evangelical denomination always remains autonomous in its decisions'.[1]

Even the World Council does not consider itself competent to discuss doctrinal questions in the name of its members. The General Secretary, Dr W. A. Visser 't Hooft, gave an explicit warning at Saint Andrews that to enter into doctrinal negotiations with the Church of Rome would be 'a dangerous deviation from the true task of the World Council'.[2] The report of the Executive Committee, then, established in precise terms that, in questions regarding the union of churches, 'the World Council, according to its constitution, is not authorized to act for the churches in such matters'.[3]

This difficulty of the lack of any unifying authority among our separated brethren seems, as things show at present, insuperable. Long and patient work will be required, work on a long-term basis, perhaps beginning in relations with some particular groups of separated brethren who have more cohesion among themselves. Dialogue between theologians offers the best prospects, for theologians have considerable influence, if not authority, with other members of their group or denomination.

In the face of all these difficulties, some among us may feel discouraged and be tempted to abandon all efforts. Nothing could be worse. It would be a false conclusion to draw, even granted the natural hopelessness of the present situation. To conclude so would be a proof of trust in mere human resources. It would be to forget the omnipotence of God, to forget the irresistible efficacy of prayer and of the activity of Christ, to forget the power of Christ's divine Spirit. Of course human co-operation is wanted, perhaps especially the co-operation of the church's diverse organs, and so of the Council (of this more in the next chapter), yet in the beginning and the end our trust must rest upon no action of men, but upon the all-powerful grace of God.

[1] H. Asmussen, in *Christ und Welt*, 16 April 1960; cf. also P. Meinhold, 'Was erwarten . . .' (art. cit. p. 132 above), p. 37.
[2] Cf. *The Ecumenical Review*, 13 (1960), p. 46.
[3] Ibid.

10

PROTESTANTS AND THE COUNCIL

II. Possible Contributions to Church Unity[1]

As WE have already indicated, the immediate aim of the forthcoming second Vatican Council is not the union of the Christian world, or even reunion with particular religious groups. But there can be no doubt that from a long-term point of view the Council may serve to prepare the way for Church Unity by smoothing out many of the existing difficulties.[2]

1. With regard to doctrine generally: the preservation of dogmatic integrity does not require that nothing should be done, merely because there are difficulties in the field of doctrine. All too often difficulties arise because the true meaning of a dogma is ill-understood or even distorted. We have to remember that man's way of looking at things and his ways of expressing his thought have changed greatly with the passage of time. Our separated brethren, cut off from the Church for several centuries past, have experienced the influence of many philosophical systems (rationalism, empiricism, hegelianism, kantianism, phenomenalism, existentialism) and these have shaped their outlook and their terminology in such a way that they often have difficulty in understanding adequately the dogmatic teachings expressed in the traditional language of the Church. Here the Council will be able, on several heads, to carry out a useful work of explanation and so remove many misunderstandings. The present moment is particularly favourable for such a work.

[1] Original Text: see note 1 to Chapter 9.
[2] Cf. especially, A. Brandenburg, 'Evangelische Christenheit in Deutschland am Vorabend des II Vatik. Konzils', in *Kath. Sicht* (Fromms Taschenbücher 'Zeitnahes Christentum', 11), Osnabruck, 1961, pp. 63-73; H. Küng, *Konzil und Wiedervereinigung. Erneuerung als Ruf in die Einheit*, Vienna, Freiburg, Basel, 1960, pp. 127-152; English translation by Cecily Hastings, *The Council and Reunion*, London, 1961.

In days gone by, Protestantism, especially in its Lutheran form, had a distinctly individualistic character. It separated man from society, from history and from tradition: the rule of a man's life was his personal faith; he was to live in God's sight quite simply, reading and interpreting the Bible under the guidance of the Holy Spirit, who enlightened him and directed his life. For this reason he never looked back to the past, to tradition, and felt no need of a visible Church through which the deposit of faith would be handed down to him. But today contemporary thought is marked by a re-awakening of the sense of history and of the social structure of life. We examine the origin and history of ideas; we examine the intellectual climates in which they were born and propagated; we look into the different influences which they have undergone. This modern method, based as it is on social history, draws doctrines out of their isolation and places them in the great current of tradition. Fundamentally it is the method of the Catholic Church, which is anti-individualist. Today, therefore, the wide-awake theologian will find it easier to demonstrate the historical and objective source of doctrines, and their development down the centuries. It is true that this does not take us to tradition in the dogmatic sense of the word, i.e. a divinely guaranteed means of the accurate transmission of truths revealed by God. But that purely historical tradition which we do reach is in itself very precious as a point of departure for future progress.[1]

This modern method is particularly fruitful when it is applied to the study of holy scripture. It will be enough to quote here the words of a Protestant Professor of Theology at the University of Zurich, who, speaking of the famous *Theologisches Wörterbuch* of the New Testament published by Professor Kittel, writes: 'Here it is the New Testament itself that speaks, not some classical exegesis of confessional tradition. Faced with the results of the *Theologisches Wörterbuch* certain classical theological doctrines of our forefathers reveal them-

---

[1] Cf. E. Kleine, 'Sie wenden sich aus Konzil. Evangelische Stimmen, die Gehör verdienen', in *Echo der Zeit*, 17 January 1960, p. 6; A. Ebneter, 'Die Protestanten und das Konzil', in *Orientierung* (1960), p. 232 (A. Schlatter); P. Meinhold, 'Was erwarten evangelische Christen vom angekündigten Ökumenischen Konzil', in *Una Sancta*, XV (1960), p. 36.

selves as biblical only in a very limited sense.' He then mentions as an example the doctrine of original sin and predestination, noting that Luther's conception of justification by faith alone cannot, without qualification, be identified with that put forward by St Paul.[1]

With these recent studies as a basis, the Council will be able not only to support the doctrine of the Church with an interpretation that conforms to modern methods but, more generally, to show that the right understanding of the teaching of holy scripture, and even the assessment of what constitutes the canon of scripture, is not possible without recourse to tradition, at least in its human and historical aspects. It is true that if we use this method of historical research the deficiencies of men in the past and their errors will come to light; but more strikingly, there will also be revealed the miracle of the continuous preservation and constancy of the Catholic Church, which has triumphantly weathered so many crises and has constantly re-affirmed herself before the world.

2. Which points particularly need explanation today? Primarily the Church, her doctrine, her conception of dogma and its unchanging character, her authority and especially the authority of the Pope.[2] These in fact are the fundamental problems, and *not*, for example, the question of justification or of the Mass as a sacrifice. Protestants themselves are becoming more and more aware of this, so much so that nowadays they speak of a 'rediscovery' of the Church.[3] In this field the Council may very well produce many beneficial results. The problem of the Church was posed as far back as the Council of Trent, but was not adequately dealt with either then, or at the first Vatican Council, which was prematurely interrupted by the Franco-Prussian war. The most authoritative modern historian

[1] E. Brunner, 'Die Bedeutung des theol. Wörterbuches zum N.T. für die Theologie', in a supplement to Vol. IV of the same Dictionary, 1940. Cf. a similar statement by Rudolph Hermann of Berlin at the 2nd Congress of Lutheran Studies (August 1960). Cf. A. Ebneter, op. cit., p. 232.

[2] Requests for such explanations have already been made by more than one non-Catholic: cf. P. Meinhold, loc. cit., pp. 35, 37ff; Cf. J-L. Leuba, 'Was erwarten evangelische Christen vom Ökumenischen Konzil', in *Ökum. Rundschau* IX 1960, p. 82ff; cf. R. Schutz, 'En vue du Concile', in *Documentation Catholique* XLIII, (1961), 58, col. 103; cf. W. Sucker, 'Das Konzil des Papstes', in *Sonntagsblatt* (ed. H. Lilje), n. 5, 29 January 1961, p. 44.

[3] K. G. Steck, in *Evang. Kirchenlexikon* II, p. 889.

of the Council of Trent aptly remarks that its teaching does not require reformation but completion.[1] Today the path towards the completion of both these Councils has been paved by theological study and research, as well as by the directive compiled and authoritatively set out in the encyclical *Mystici Corporis Christi* of Pius XII, on the Church as the mystical Body of Christ.[2] Even Protestant writers have admitted that this encyclical presented an aspect of the Church which they had hitherto scarcely taken into consideration. The infallibility of the Church and of her head, the successor of St Peter, the hierarchical structure of the Church, the relation between the power of the pope and that of the bishops, the important position and function of the laity within the Church, the efficacy of the sacraments—these, all difficult questions for Protestants, are explained and clarified by the doctrine of the mystical Body in such a way as to make plain that the Church is not that merely juridical body rejected by Protestants as contrary to Christ's ideal. At the same time, however, it becomes more obvious that the Church must be a well-ordered and regulated organism. When all this has been set out and explained, the Church will appear to our separated brethren in a much clearer light, and many prejudices and misunderstandings may well disappear.

Pius XII's encyclicals *Mystici Corporis* and *Mediator Dei* throw light on the position of baptized Christians who are separated from the Church: they do in fact belong in some way to the Church, albeit not in the full sense and not sharing in all the graces derived from Christ, the head: graces which give members fully joined to the head so much light and strength.

It would be an important step forward if the Council, with its supreme authority, could explain these doctrines and their implications and thus, as the Pope puts it, 'give splendour to the visage of Christ's Church, restoring the simpler and purer beauty of the time of her birth', re-discovering anew 'the traces of her more fervent youth, in such a way as to show forth her triumphant power over those modern spirits that have been tempted and compromised by

[1] Thus Prof. H. Jedin, in a conference given at Rome in November 1960.
[2] *A.A.S.* XXXV (1943), pp. 193-248.

the false theories of the Prince of this World'.[1] Such an achievement, besides helping the Church herself on her difficult journey, would also meet the needs and aspirations of our separated brethren and would indeed be a 'gentle invitation' to them to seek and obtain the unity for which Jesus Christ prayed so ardently to his Father.[2]

3. The restoration of its native splendour to the visage of the Church, of which the Pope speaks, can be brought about also in what concerns Canon Law. There are laws given by God himself, which therefore cannot be changed: for example, the existence of the Episcopacy and Primacy in the Church, or the indissolubility of marriage. But there are others which have a human origin also, one which results from the conditions and requirements of earlier times and are incomprehensible to modern man. The Pope himself seems to indicate the possibility of a reform which would take into account the needs of the present day when he speaks, in his *Allocution* of 25 January 1959, of 'a timely and welcome modernization of the Code of Canon Law' as a result of the Diocesan Synod of the city of Rome, and of the Council. He speaks more specifically of this revision in his first encyclical, *Ad Petri Cathedram*. In this Council, writes the Pope, bishops from every part of the world will come together to discuss important religious issues, and particularly the problem of how ecclesiastical discipline might be better adapted to the needs and the mentality of our times. Such adaptations have already been put into effect during the pontificates of Pius X, Benedict XV, and Pius XII: for example, the laws dealing with frequent Communion, with the required age for first Communion, with the Eucharistic fast: the change in the Latin translation of the Psalter, the reform of the Roman Curia under Pius X, the increase in the number of Cardinals under John XXIII. Pius XII, referring to a reform which he had both instigated and brought about, once remarked that 'it took a lot of courage'. It will also take a great deal of courage to reform certain other laws. But the Council, like the divine Founder of the Church, will have the gifts of the Holy

---

[1] *Allocution* of 13 November 1960, *A.A.S.* LXX (1960), p. 960.
[2] Cf. the encyclical *Ad Petri Cathedram*, in *A.A.S.* LII (1959), p. 511; English translation, C.T.S., London, 1959, para. 44.

Spirit, and among these gifts are fortitude and counsel. It will know how to take into account the needs of the present day, thus making the way towards union clearer and easier.[1]

4. Finally, there is one other way in which the Council may do much to help the ecumenical movement: namely by giving its approval, and by arousing and fostering in the whole Catholic Church both interest and action for union. It is true to say that this is already happening to a great extent. We need only call to mind the immense interest and response which the Pope's various pronouncements on this subject have produced, a response reminiscent of the enthusiasm that met the appeals of St Pius x and Pius xi for Catholic Action and the lay apostolate, or the missionary zeal aroused by Pius xi. This does not mean that interest and initiative in the ecumenical movement has been shown only in recent times; it is enough to bear in mind the immense popularity of the Church Unity Octave. At the moment, however, it is our duty to strive to make these efforts less sporadic and isolated, to direct and co-ordinate them with an eye to differences of situation and circumstance, and above all to make the whole Church progressively more aware, in her every department, of the essential duty in charity of collaborating in the great cause of the union of all baptized Christians.

We must therefore hope and trust that the Council will greatly increase the enthusiasm of all for the work of unity. There is no doubt that, if the opportunities which the Council affords and which we have outlined here are seized, we shall have both a useful foundation and an effective stimulus for the movement as a whole.

To this we ought to add more explicit advice, special directives and suggestions for the possible formation of study-groups, or for the foundation of permanent institutions at the diocesan, national, and international levels. Without wishing to interfere in the slightest with the ultimate decisions of the Council or even to make suggestions, we shall try now in the light of directives already given by the Church to trace out the main lines along which the ecumenical

---

[1] Requests and suggestions have been made along precisely these lines by authoritative Protestant scholars, e.g. Prof. J-L. Leuba (Switzerland) loc. cit., pp. 81-9.

activity of groups and individual members of the Church might be expected to proceed.

(a) The first and most effective contribution, one that has innumerable applications, would appear to be this: each of us who meets non-Catholics in his everyday life can do much to prepare them mentally for union by a wholehearted attitude of *charity*. Just as the Pope's deep charity in speaking and dealing with our separated brethren has contributed greatly to an improvement in the 'atmosphere', so also the approach of each one of the faithful has its importance. Charity will preserve the Catholic from impatience and discourtesy in his relations with non-Catholics, from resentment and prejudices caused by unpleasant events in the past for which they are in no way responsible, from the uncalled-for judgement and the rash generalization. In short, it will bring him to use, in his relations with them, the great rule of charity set forth by the Apostle of the Gentiles: 'Charity is patient, is kind, feels no envy . . . hopes, endures to the last' (1 Cor 13:4, 7). This sort of a united effort by Catholics from all walks of life would reflect their fidelity to the precept of the first pope, St Peter, which has been practised in so exemplary a way by his successor John XXIII: 'Carry out your charge as God would have it done, cordially, not like drudges . . . not tyrannizing, but setting an example to the flock' (1 Peter 5:2). An effort of this kind would be a practical way of showing our separated brethren that, though the Catholic Church carefully guards the integrity of the dogma and faith of her own children, she is a loving mother for them also, and now anxiously wonders whether this terrible quarrel of the past may be made up today, through greater sanctity, prayer and sacrifice.

(b) *The example of a way of life that is eminently religious and moral* will also have much importance in preparing the minds of non-Catholics for union. Each individual Catholic must apply to himself what the first Vatican Council says of the Church in general; each must be 'a signal beckoning to the peoples' to lighten, as it were, by his exemplary conduct, the way towards the union of all separated Christians.[1]

[1] Cf. Is 11:12; Vatican Council 1 Sess. III, cap 3; Denz. 1794.

(c) *Fraternal collaboration with our separated brethren*, in any work
that does not directly involve Catholic doctrine, would be a
partial, advance realization of the union that we all hope for. Such
collaboration is today both esteemed and desired by non-Catholics.
Dr H. Schnell writes on this point: 'The formula, "practical
collaboration as a means for drawing the churches closer to one
another", might form the basis of an agreement between the ideas
expressed by the Pope in his radio broadcast (1958) and the suggestions of the World Council of Churches of 12 February 1959.'[1]
Only recently the General Secretary of the World Council stated
in his report to the Meeting at St Andrews: 'We have made it
abundantly clear that full unity is and must be the goal of the World
Council of Churches, but we believe at the same time that there are
urgent common tasks to be performed even now, and that the
performance of these tasks will help us to advance towards unity.'[2]
These urgent common tasks concern social problems and the pro-
mulgation of Christian principles in civic, social and cultural life,
as also in the life of charity and particularly in the relations between
nations.[3] It has been observed, and rightly so, that the idea of such
collaboration is not a new one. This was a constant theme in the
teaching of Pius XII, reflected in the Instruction of the Holy Office,
De motione oecumenica (20 December 1949). This instruction approves
of 'congresses of the various denominations to discuss the ways in
which we may work in common to defend the fundamental
principles of the natural law and the Christian religion'.[4] This
teaching has been repeated and insisted upon by the present Holy
Father, John XXIII, who makes a solemn appeal for 'good will to
be at the service of order, justice and brotherhood among all
Christians, that they might work together in a common effort of

[1] H. Schnell, 'Anbruch des johanneischen Zeitalters', in *Informationsblatt f.d. niederdeutschen luth. Landerskirchen*, 29 February 1959; and cf., also, H. Zahrnt, 'Wenn jeder
wirklich ein Christ wäre . . . Die Protestanten, die Orthodoxen und das Konzil,' in
Die Welt, n. 73, 28 March 1959 (Das Forum der Welt).
[2] Cf. *The Ecumenical Review*, XIII (1960), p. 56.
[3] Cf. the Report of the Central Committee for the World Council of Churches on
the Congress of Rhodes, August 1959, in *The Ecumenical Review* XII (1959-60), p. 67ff
Cf. 'Konzil und Gespräch', in *Wort und Wahrheit* XIV (1949), p. 243.
[4] *A.A.S.* XLII (1950), p. 145.

understanding and a spirit of mutual respect in religious, civil and social life'.[1]

(d) A special form of collaboration with our separated brethren is *theological discussion between specialists*; that is between the theologians of either side. This work is especially to be recommended, because it will tend gradually to affect the deepest roots of division, which are found in attitudes and mentality; it will also serve to clarify the misunderstandings and wrong interpretations which may exist on points of doctrine.[2] Moreover these specialists, who are usually university professors, enjoy great prestige in the Protestant world and it is they who educate the future ministers of religion. Many non-Catholics are anxious for such discussions, and set great store by them. It is significant that the Central Committee for the World Council of Churches, in a resolution of August 1960, welcomed joyfully the creation of the Secretariat for Christian Unity, and expressed the desire and the hope that informal discussions between theologians would continue, seeing that these contributed greatly to the cause of union.[3]

(e) It is clear that not everyone will be engaged upon active collaboration, which depends upon the varying circumstances of public and social life. But there is a type of collaboration that is open to all, one which is essential for the success of the Council and of the efforts of the Council directed towards church unity, namely *prayer*. We must not forget that the gift of true faith is above all the work of grace, which gives us the light to see and to recognize truth and to accept its practical consequences, as well as the strength to overcome obstacles. This is true for each individual, and even more so for entire religious communities, handicapped perhaps by age-old prejudices, misunderstandings, social and family considerations. We shall quote a single but very significant example. In 1958-9 a congress on Catholicism was held at the Ecumenical Institute of Bossey (Switzerland). Its purpose was the study of the

---

[1] Christmas Broadcast, 23 December 1958. In *A.A.S.* LI (1959), p. 10ff.

[2] On the method, efficacy and results of these discussions, cf. E. Stakmeier, 'Wird das Kommende Konzil uns der Weidervereinigung der getrennten Christen näher bringen?', in *Gottes Wort im Kirchenjahr* I (1960), pp. 13ff, 16ff.

[3] Cf. *The Ecumenical Review*, XIII (1960), p. 46.

structure of the Church, the missions, ecumenical history; three Catholic professors were invited to attend. Also taking part were some fifty theologians of twenty-two nationalities who belonged to eleven different religious denominations. At the end of the congress the 'Octave of Prayer' was held with great fervour. All who had taken part signed a round-robin addressed to the General Secretary of the World Council of Churches. This letter was read aloud and discussed at the meeting of the Central Committee of the World Council at Rhodes in August 1959. Here is a brief extract from it: 'We believe that we must frankly confess our inability to break down the barriers that divide us, without the unifying strength of the Holy Spirit working within us . . . we feel obliged to communicate to you our great concern, namely that it should be recognized that we live today at a moment of critical importance for the renewal of prayer for church unity.' Finally there is this practical and most edifying conclusion: 'We pray that the forthcoming Ecumenical Council may encourage such discussions (between theologians of different denominations) in an atmosphere of charity.'[1]

In the same way, all the recent popes have constantly exhorted the faithful to prayer, to prayer in common, and especially to the 'Octave of Prayer', either in preparation for the feast of Pentecost (Leo XIII), or (since St Pius X) from 18 to 25 January. John XXIII also expresses 'the pious desire that this practice may be propagated everywhere in the world, as widely as possible, especially in view of the coming Ecumenical Council, during which time it is to be hoped that our separated brethren may be abundantly enlightened and strengthened by the Holy Paraclete'.[2] The Church herself prays daily, through the priest in the Holy Mass, asking God to deign to 'lead the Church into unity'. This is above all the prayer of our Lord himself, on the night before he died: 'I pray for those who are to find faith in me through their word; that they may all be one; that they too may be one in us, as thou, Father, art in me, and I in

[1] Cf. M. Villain, *La prière de Jésus pour l'unité chretienne*, Tournai, 1960, pp. 17-22.
[2] Letter to the Superior General of the Franciscans of the Atonement (28 October 1959), *Acta et Documenta*, I-I, p. 54.

thee' (John 17:21). We trust entirely in this prayer of the divine
Founder of the Church, not letting ourselves be discouraged by the
difficulties which still lie between us and the attainment of the
precious gift of the unity of all who carry the image of our Lord in
their hearts and, through baptism, a seal upon their souls that
cannot be effaced.

In conclusion, we must point out that what we have said is
necessarily incomplete; the discussion is, and will continue to be,
unfinished, because the literature on the subject is so vast, and needs
such continuous revision. Besides, there are matters which can be
spoken of only in private, which affect the secrets of the conscience
and cannot be made the subject of public discussion. However what
has been set down here, based as it is upon public statements and
reports, will be enough to show how important is the movement for
Church Unity today, and in what ways the Council may help to
advance its cause. 'This heart-breaking problem of the disunity of
Christ's heritage,' says the Pope, 'remains, to the prejudice and
hindrance of our best efforts, and the way ahead is paved with
difficulties and doubts.' But the Pope knows that the peace of the
world depends upon this unity, and therefore upon how we work
and how we pray to bring it about. He therefore insists that we
should not lose courage, but 'continue to extend a loving invitation
to our dear separated brothers, who like us bear the name of Christ
and read his holy Gospel, who listen also to the promptings of
religious piety and of a charity that blesses and benefits'.[1]

Let us, like the Pope, not be discouraged, for we know 'what is
impossible for men is possible for God'.

[1] Christmas broadcast, 23 December, 1958.

PART TWO

THE SECRETARIAT FOR THE PROMOTION
OF THE UNITY OF CHRISTIANS

II

ORGANIZATION AND METHOD OF WORK[1]

Q. YOUR EMINENCE, what is the exact competency of the Secretariat for the promotion of Christian Unity?

A. The immediate reason for the setting up of the Secretariat is the forthcoming Council. For several reasons, the field of work assigned to it includes relations with all non-Catholic Christians, except the Eastern Orthodox.[2] It is to supply separated brethren with authoritative information on the work of the Council, and to receive and assess their wishes and suggestions relative to the Council and, where feasible, to apply them.

Q. Have any such wishes or suggestions been communicated to your Eminence?

A. Indeed they have. Our files include a fair amount of correspondence on the subject from different nations and denominations, and I must say that the suggestions, in general, are valuable and weighty.

Q. Why was a Secretariat, and not a Commission, set up in this important field? Does the fact that it is a Secretariat imply that it is of lesser importance?

A. It is not a question of degree of importance, but merely one of organization. Contact with non-Catholic Christians is of many different kinds and introduces an element which has nothing in common with the other preparatory commissions of the Council;

---

[1] Original text: 'Fernseh-Interview am Norddt Rundfunk', published in *K.N.A.* (22 January 1961).

[2] Subsequently, the formal document which convened the Council, *Humanae Salutis*, entrusted to the Secretariat arrangements about the presence at the Council of delegated 'observers' from all other Christian Communities, including the Eastern Orthodox.

this necessitates different procedures in our Secretariat. For this reason we prefer the more general term 'Secretariat'.

Q. Will the Secretariat continue to exist after the Council?

A. In establishing the Secretariat, the Council and its needs were the primary considerations. The outcome of the discussions in the Council and their bearing on the question of reunion will show whether the work of the Secretariat should continue, and what form it should take.

Q. Is it at all possible that through the work of the Secretariat, Catholics may arrive at some form of association with the World Council of Churches?

A. There is no objection to this in principle. Since, in fact, the World Council of Churches does not hold doctrines irreconcilable with Catholic dogma, association or co-operation would, in principle, be possible. First of all, there spring to mind non-doctrinal fields: social work, charitable activity, work for peace and the like. The whole of humanity, for instance, would be influenced by the fact that all Christians acted in agreement about such problems of decisive importance as atomic war, disarmament, the means to preserve and promote world peace! Obviously, I do not mean to make any official pronouncement on these difficult problems—that is outside my competence; I merely wish to draw attention to the contemporary situation.

Q. And now, concerning the Council: does it aim at an immediate reunion of Christians?

A. No. The Holy Father has expressly excluded this. He is not thinking in terms of a council of reunion, such as those of Lyons in the thirteenth and Florence in the fifteenth century. These councils discussed and attained a union with the Oriental Christians, but unfortunately the union was not a lasting one. The Holy Father hopes that the forthcoming Council may be a kind of invitation to our separated brethren, by letting them see in its day-by-day proceedings the sincerity, concord and love which prevail in the Catholic Church. So we may say, rather, that the Council should make an indirect contribution to union, breaking the ground in a long-term policy of preparation for union.

Q. What can we expect from the Council with regard to the union of Christians?

A. It can help to improve the atmosphere between Catholics and non-Catholics by removing at least some misunderstandings. Then again, it can prepare the ground for union by solving problems which have a bearing on efforts towards unity either in general, or in particular groups of non-Catholic Christians. Think for example of the persistent question of the allowances which may be made regarding institutions and customs which exist among evangelical Christians in areas which are not directly connected with the faith: for example, the use of the vernacular in the liturgy, the hymns and anthems which they use, Communion under two kinds and so on. These are only a few of the thorny questions which might be submitted to the Council for consideration and decision, with a view to taking a first step on the long road to union.

Q. At present what, in your Eminence's judgement, are the principle obstacles standing in the way of the union of Christians?

A. In answering this question let us leave aside the separated Oriental churches and restrict ourselves to the field with which the Secretariat is directly concerned. And here, for the sake of brevity, I shall mention only one of the chief difficulties, which involves different concepts of the Church and of its unity.

The Catholic conception of the Church involves the following: it is essential to the Church that the bishops derive their powers in uninterrupted succession from the Apostles, that they possess an authority in teaching which must be final for the faithful, and that, where faith and morals are concerned, they can oblige in conscience both in acceptance of doctrine and in its application to Christian conduct. The Evangelical side rejects all these tenets. At this point, quite apart from the doctrinal difference, there arises a huge practical difficulty in efforts towards unity: the Catholic Church is not faced with a partner who speaks with equal title and authority in the conversations and negotiations. For example, an Evangelical theologian proposed to me that our Secretariat should discuss specific problems with theologians nominated by the Evangelicals. I replied that this could be done, if he could indicate to me who, on his side, had the authority to nominate such theologians and to ensure that the eventual results of the negotiations would find acceptance among the Evangelicals.

The situation is such that at present unofficial conversations between theologians of different denominations affords one of the principle means of clarifying doctrinal differences and thus in the long term, promoting unity.

12

THE SECRETARIAT AND THE COUNCIL[1]

Q. REGARDING THE Council and Christian unity: what part is the Council likely to play in the efforts towards unity?

A. To put it very briefly, the Council cannot and will not be, properly speaking, a council of reunion. The time is not ripe for this, either among Catholics or non-Catholics. The Council, however, both can and will make long-term plans for unity, first by clearing the air and improving the atmosphere between denominations, by removing misunderstandings and misinterpretations of Catholic doctrine, adapting canon law to present-day outlooks and to the needs of our separated brethren and, finally, by giving new impetus and better co-ordination to the ecumenical work of the Catholic Church.

Q. Could you, in a few words, outline the difficulties that the Orthodox, the Anglicans and the Protestants find in this matter of reunion?

A. First of all, with regard to the Orthodox, misunderstandings and traditional resentments apart, the main difficulty is the primacy of the pope, and particularly his infallibility. Regarding Protestants and Anglicans, reference should indeed be made to the doctrine of justification, the sacraments, and devotion to Mary, but the principal difficulty on which everything ultimately depends and by which everything will be decided, is the concept of the Church, of its teaching office and its authority. When we come to Lutherans and Calvinists there is the added difficulty of the lack of any hierarchy which they admittedly reject on principle. This lack of any authority

[1] Original text: Interview with the Catholic International Press Agency, 15 November 1961. First published in *K.N.A.*, 22 November, 1961.

binding the faithful in conscience is, moreover, the main practical difficulty when it comes to meetings and negotiations. The question is always with whom to hold discussions, and who has the authority to implement what is eventually decided?

Q. Have you, in fact, received any proposals or requests from non-Catholics concerning the Council?

A. I have received either personally or through the Secretariat many such proposals and requests. All these were thoroughly sifted and considered, sometimes against the background of relevant publications. This work was done in some cases by sub-committees and in others by the Secretariat as a whole in the four plenary sessions, some of which lasted several days. Such progress has been made that some proposals have been accepted, drafted in definitive form and given to the Central Commission of the Council.

Q. How is the Secretariat made up?

A. It consists of members entitled to vote, and consultant members. Both categories have fully international representation. There are eleven members entitled to vote: two each from Germany, England and France, one each from Belgium, Italy, Holland, Switzerland and the United States. Of the fifteen consultant members, three are from the United States, two from Germany, England and France, one from Belgium, Canada, Holland, Scotland, Switzerland and Slovenia. As you can see, the countries which are most strongly represented are those in which the non-Catholic Christians are most numerous.

Q. Is any difference of status or importance implied by the terms 'Commission' and 'Secretariat'? Will your Secretariat go on functioning even after the Council?

A. No difference of status is implied, but merely a difference of organization. Our many and varied contacts with non-Catholic Christians introduce an element not found in the other preparatory Commissions. To some extent this brings about a difference in the procedure of our Secretariat. This is the reason why the more general term 'Secretariat' has been preferred.

As to the Secretariat's continued existence after the Council, it can be said that the primary purpose in instituting the Secretariat was the Council and its requirements. The outcome of the Council's deliberations and their significance for the question of union will show whether the Secretariat is to continue and, if so, in what form.

Q. Is there any possibility of closer co-operation with the World Council of Churches? It is notable that the Swiss bishops have asked the faithful to pray for the success of the Assembly of the World Council of Churches at New Delhi.

A. There is no direct connection between this request of the Swiss bishops and Catholic co-operation with the World Council of Churches. Prayer for the success of the World Council Assembly at New Delhi is to be welcomed and extended; but it does not imply any direct co-operation, and is based primarily on the significance such as assembly has for Christianity as a whole. About co-operation by the Secretariat with the World Council of Churches, there is no difficulty in principle. In so far as the World Council of Churches does not stand for any doctrine irreconcilable with Catholic dogma, co-operation would in principle be perfectly possible. What come to mind are those fields which do not directly touch on matters of belief, such as social work, *Caritas*, work for peace, assistance to under-developed countries.

For instance, what would it mean for humanity if all Christians could act together in such important matters as nuclear war, general disarmament and the means for preserving and advancing world peace?

It is needless to say that I am not voicing any sort of official attitude on these difficult questions—I have no authority to do so—but I should like simply to call attention to the existing situation.

It may also be added that private and unofficial contacts already exist with the World Council of Churches. And that is not all. This year, for the first time, five official Catholic observers are taking part in the General Assembly of the World Council of Churches in New Delhi: a Frenchman, a Dutchman, an American and two from India, since the General Assembly is being held in New Delhi. This sending of observers has been cordially welcomed by the officials of the World Council of Churches.

Q. It has already been stressed more than once that the forth-coming Council is not one of reunion. Should we then say that the paths to future reunion must be made smooth, and this applies even apart from the Council, both by experts and by 'ordinary Christians'?

A. To say that the Council cannot be one of reunion but is only to make long-term preparations for unity, as I emphasized at the beginning, is also to say that the real work for unity will not be begun until after the Council. After the Council has improved the atmosphere and created a certain amount of common ground by clarifying difficult points of doctrine, by adapting certain of the Church's rulings to the mentality of our separated brethren, by giving Catholic ecumenical work a new impulse and mandate, then can ecumenical activity be intensified and grow stronger and better. When I say this, I am thinking in general terms of co-ordinat-ing (without unduly centralizing) the various Catholic ecumenical activities which already exist, and of theological discussions between experts, and co-operation in various fields, for example charitable and social activities, as has already been mentioned.

But I am convinced above all that, among large sections of the faithful, there is need to arouse and reinforce an awareness of the serious duty to work for the unity of Christians. The efforts of recent popes have brought home to the laity the urgent obligation of their co-operation with the apostolate of the hierarchy, and of prayer and sacrifices for the missions. In exactly the same way, and in a certain sense even more urgently, every Catholic should be made aware of the serious duty obligatory on him to work for the union of Christians. I say even more urgently, because our separated brethren, baptized in Christ, are infinitely nearer to us than the non-Christian peoples in missionary countries. This duty of which I speak, each of us will fulfil according to his position and profession but all are, and must be, united in the love we bear towards our separated brethren, in the example we give of genuine religious life, and in our prayer and sacrifice for unity. No one who is conscious of the supernatural character of ecumenical work could under-estimate the importance of these means.

Q. Do you think that in the present threatening state of the world a common Christian peace front could be set up?

A. The term 'peace front' is ambiguous and might have political implications. But that Christians should form a single 'front' is, in the present world situation, greatly to be desired. In saying this, I am making no official démarche, but am voicing what is in many minds. We ought to do all we can to create such a 'front' for peace; we should pray that Christians take a united stand for peace. Whether such a 'front' could be set up and what success it would have—this is a secret of divine providence. Nevertheless, today all of us are involved, and all of us should exert ourselves in this cause, by prayer and by sacrifice and, where possible, by determined action.

13

A REVIEW OF THE WORK OF THE FIRST
TWO YEARS[1]

WHEN, ON Christmas Day, 1961, in the Apostolic Constitution *Humanae Salutis*, Pope John XXIII officially announced the second Ecumenical Council of the Vatican, he spoke of the various Christian bodies which are separated from the Church of Rome, and expressed the hope that they would be able to send to the Council representatives who could observe its actual proceedings. He had previously created a special office, a 'Secretariat', to facilitate relations with these bodies. In the Motu Proprio *Superno Dei Nutu* of 5 June 1960, with which he set up the Secretariat for the Promotion of Christian Unity, he wrote: 'In order to show in a special manner our love and good will towards those who bear the name of Christ, but are separated from this Apostolic See, and in order that they may be able to follow the work of the Council and find more readily the way to attain that unity for which Jesus Christ besought his heavenly Father, we have established a special Office or Secretariat.'

This Secretariat which Pope John instituted has now been in existence for a year and a half: on the occasion of this Octave of Prayer for Unity it may be interesting to make a brief survey of its reception, its development and its work. The purpose of this account is not to highlight the merits and achievements of the Secretariat and its members—that would be completely out of place; nor do these pages aim at any commendation of the Catholic Church or the Holy See. The intention is rather to show how the Spirit of God

[1] Original text: 'Das Konzil-Sekretariat zur Förderung der Einheit der Christen: Organisation-Entwicklung-Tätigkeit'. An interview on Radio Bavaria, 21 January 1962, published in *K.N.A.*, 21 January 1962.

which today, both within and outside the Catholic Church is working so powerfully in the cause of the union of Christians, has made use of this instrument to bring a gradual remedy to the 'scandal of division', that calamity of Christianity which is so frequently and so deeply lamented by our separated brethren as well as by Catholics. One is tempted here to say with the Apostle Paul: 'As our fault (which is division) was amplified, grace has been more amply bestowed than ever' (Rom 5:20). If in the exposition which follows we are compelled to speak of ourselves, we shall do so in the spirit of these words of St Paul: 'After all, it is not ourselves we proclaim; we proclaim Jesus Christ as Lord, and ourselves as your servants for Jesus' sake' (2 Cor 4:5).

Catholics were not alone in greeting the establishment of the new Secretariat with lively satisfaction; in non-Catholic quarters also the move was hailed as a valuable service to the furthering of Christian unity. Shortly after the Secretariat was set up, the Executive Committee of the World Council of Churches, at the meeting of the Central Committee in St Andrews, Scotland, in August 1960, made the following comment: 'The fact that a dialogue with the Catholic Church has now become possible is to be welcomed. We must make use of this opportunity for discussions: as the dialogue proceeds the real difficulties are bound to come to the fore.' The World Council of Churches might use available opportunities to make known to the new Secretariat in Rome the basic convictions and concerns of the World Council of Churches (e.g. on religious liberty and on Christian social action, etc.). In the General Assembly of the World Council of Churches held at New Delhi, the General Secretary, Dr Visser 't Hooft, once again cordially welcomed the establishment of the Secretariat and saw in it a new and promising development in work for Christian unity.

In accordance with the Pope's wishes, the organization of the Secretariat had to be identical to that of the eleven Commissions which were established at the same time in preparation for the Council. Hence the Presidency of the Secretariat was entrusted to a Cardinal; he has a secretary and several assistants. Mgr Willebrands was appointed Secretary; for almost ten years he had been President of 'The International Catholic Conference for Ecumenical Questions', founded in Holland. This post had brought him a very full awareness of the problems involved, and many valuable contacts and friendships. The Secretariat has sixteen *Members* who have the right to vote, and twenty *Experts*—consultants without the right to vote: members and consultants were chosen in such a manner that almost all nations with a notable number of non-Catholic Christian communities are represented in the Secretariat. The distribution is as follows: France seven, Germany six, England five, the United States five, Belgium, Holland, Italy and Switzerland two each, and Canada, Jugoslavia, Scotland, South Africa and Israel one each.

The activity of the Secretariat is directed first of all towards arousing the greatest and deepest possible interest in all problems concerning unity, and towards indicating ways by which it may be possible to help the cause of unity. There is a keen public desire for information and explanation, as was immediately apparent. The very day after the creation of the Secretariat, the President, who was at that time in New York for a short visit, was asked for an interview by correspondents of five of the most important newspapers and agencies in North America. Similar interviews followed in quick succession: five at Rome, five for the German information services, one for each of the following countries: France, Spain, Norway, Brazil, North America and Switzerland; three of these—France, Italy and German—were television interviews. For the same purpose, public lectures were given in Italy (Ferrara, Rome, Genoa, Milan, Turin), Switzerland (Lugano, Berne, Basel, Fribourg, Zurich), and in France (Strasbourg). Most of these, especially in Switzerland and North Italy, were attended by numerous non-Catholics and, as far as can be judged, contributed to a fostering of mutual understanding, a dissipation of misunderstanding and misinterpretations and the creation of an atmosphere more favourable to religion.

Soon the Secretariat began to receive many letters from Catholics and non-Catholics, especially from lay-people interested in religious questions. In these letters, and also in conversation, members of different faiths belonging to many different nations voiced wishes and suggestions for a better understanding between different Christian communities and Rome, and pointed out difficulties and obstacles which stand in the way of union, both in doctrinal and in practical matters. Particularly numerous were the suggestions concerning the Council and the decisions that it ought to take: very many of these proposals are valuable and deserve the greatest consideration, and they proved extraordinarily useful in the preparation of the Council.

Naturally preparation for the Council has been one of the Secretariat's most important tasks. Even if the Council is not to be a council of reunion, as were those of Lyons and Florence—the time is not yet ripe for this—nevertheless, it is the Pope's intention that it should offer non-Catholics ever-widening opportunities to come to know, understand and appreciate the Catholic Church, and thus make smooth the paths which lead to union. Material related to these topics which had accumulated in the course of the months at the Secretariat—both official comments from numerous bishops, who are particularly interested in the problem of the union of Christians, and letters and opinions of every sort—was systematically classified and appropriate sections given to each of the fourteen sub-committees, made up of members and consultants of specialized competence. The reports and recommendations of these sub-committees were then commended by the appropriate spokesmen to the plenary sessions of the Secretariat, and discussed fully by the members and consultants present. To date there have been five of these plenary sessions of the Secretariat generally lasting a week: in November 1960, and in February, April, August and November 1961: another, and probably the last one before the opening of the Council, as all the material will have been worked through, will be held at the beginning of March 1962. Once the reports and proposals have been discussed and drafted, they will be submitted to the vote of the members of the Secretariat and then, in final form, sent to the competent Commission of the Council. As regards the ground we have covered, it may truly be said that everything that may be of importance to the Council has been taken into account. Indeed, for some months past practically no proposal has been submitted to us that had not already been discussed in the preparatory sittings of the Secretariat. It may be said without hesitation that the material passed on to the Council is sufficiently extensive and valuable for the problem of unity to be given full consideration; this material comes from people who have specialized knowledge, and from countries and nations where interest in unity is lively and active.[1]

There have been activities of the Secretariat which for the time being cannot be made public, but these apart, the Secretariat has had some small success which is fairly widely known. First, there was the official sending of Catholic observers to the third General Assembly of the World Council of Churches, held at New Delhi from the 18 November to the 5 December. At the two previous Assemblies, Amsterdam (1948) and Evanston (1954), official Catho-

---

[1] Here we may print extracts from two interviews—not reproduced in full in this book—concerning delicate problems handled by the Secretariat, in view of the Council.

'The problem of mixed marriages is certainly a difficulty which must not be underrated. It has a great bearing on the relationship between the different denominations and is a matter of capital importance in connection with liberty of conscience. It requires attentive study. At different times the Catholic Church has regulated this matter in different ways. Our Secretariat has gone very deeply into the question and has forwarded proposals to the Central Commission. Suffice it to say that the Secretariat is seeking the best possible solution to this difficulty, and is taking into consideration all legitimate desires.' From an interview granted to Herr Werner Stratenschulte and published in Welt am Sonntag, 25 March 1962, II, pp. 179-180, and in La Civiltà Cattolica, 1962, II pp. 179-180.

'No doubt you know, from a recent bulletin released by the Press Office of the Council concerning the last session of the Central Commission held in June, that a scheme concerning the relationship between Church and State was examined there. On this occasion our Secretariat had drafted proposals concerning religious liberty.

'Notice that I do not say "tolerance", which is a somewhat negative thing, but "religious liberty", which consists in the positive recognition of the right of a man to follow the dictates of his conscience in matters of religion. It is therefore the duty of civil society (the State) to respect and protect in practice the inalienable right of the citizen to religious liberty.

'In our proposal we have grappled with the problem which Pius XII treated in his well-known address to Catholic jurists in 1953. The theme is of great importance in the pluralistic society of today: a fact fully recognized in the proposals drawn up by the Secretariat. I should like also to add that we conceive religious liberty as having an absolute value whose application must be universal and not restricted to any particular countries. Naturally great prudence is required in applying general principles to particular situations and in particular circumstances.' From an interview granted by Cardinal Bea to Fr. Eugene C. Bianchi, S.J., published in America, 11 August, 1962, p. 587.

lic observers were not present. In the meantime, the relations of the World Council of Churches with the Catholic Church had changed to such an extent and mutual interest in each other's work had so developed that one could say that by 1961 they had entered upon a new phase. Thus it was possible for five official Catholic observers to take part in the third General Assembly of the World Council of Churches. These observers were chosen by the Secretariat so as to include one expert in each of the principal problems before the Assembly. They were Professor Grout of Holland, whom the Dutch Bishops put in charge of ecumenical work in that country; Père le Guillou, a Dominican, Professor of Theology at Le Saulchoir, member of the French Ecumenical Centre 'Istina'; Fr Edward Duff, a Jesuit, Director of the Institute for Sociological Research and editor of the review *Social Order* (St Louis, U.S.A.), who has also published a special study on the social thought of the World Council of Churches; the other two observers were chosen by agreement with the Indian Episcopate: they were Fr Joseph Edamaran S.J., Superior of the new Jesuit province of Kerala, knowledgeable about ecumenical questions in India, and the Rev. Ivan Extross, much interested in relationships between Christianity and Hinduism. These Catholic observers were received with great kindness in New Delhi, and besides taking part in the Plenary Sessions and at the sittings of the special Commissions and Group Meetings, they were able to establish personal contacts and relations of considerable importance. The sending of official Catholic observers has surely made a useful contribution towards fostering relations between the Catholic Church and other Christian communities and making possible future dialogue and discussions.

Other more or less widely know events to whose preparation and successful outcome the Secretariat made an essential contribution are the various visits of prominent non-Catholic personages to Pope John XXIII. First and foremost we should recall the earliest and most important of these: the visit of Dr G. F. Fisher, Archbishop of Canterbury, Primate of the Church of England, in December 1960. One of the fruits of this visit, besides the notable improvement of relations between the Anglican Church and the Catholic Church, was the appointment of Canon B. Pawley to act as a link between the Anglican Primate and the Roman Secretariat. In November 1961 another important visit took place; that of Dr A. Lichtenberger, presiding Bishop of the Episcopal Church of North America. In December came Dr J. H. Jackson, President of the National Baptist Convention of the United States, whose membership includes five million negro members. The statements made by these prominent churchmen concerning their conversations with Pope John XXIII show that through these visits an entirely new understanding has been attained between the organizations they represent and the Catholic Church. In this regard the declaration made by Dr Fisher in the House of Lords shortly before resigning the Primacy is worthy of particular prominence: he said that the movement towards Christian unity was gathering momentum; his visit to John XXIII had led to a 'new friendship' and had shown that many causes of strain could be mitigated and many obstacles removed.

Dr Fisher's successor as Archbishop of Canterbury, Dr. Michael Ramsey, spoke in similar vein at New Delhi. When asked how the visit of Dr Fisher to Pope John XXIII had been received in England, he replied: 'We in the Church of England are most thankful that this visit took place; it is the symbol of a new spirit.' He was of the opinion that this visit had opened the way to personal relationships.

All this goes to show that God has blessed John XXIII's decision to establish a Secretariat for Christian Unity. We repeat that our intention in giving this account is not to enhance the importance of the Secretariat but simply to show, in the light of definite facts, what has followed Pope John XXIII's initiative. Any good results must be attributed to a situation which has been created not by men but by the Spirit of God himself. As early as 1949, the Congregation of the Holy Office, in an Instruction on the Ecumenical Movement, took note of the great changes evident in many parts of Christendom, both in the general situation and in outlook and feeling, and attributes this to the united prayer of the faithful and to the very breath of the Holy Spirit, the source of abundant grace. In the hearts of many who are separated from the Catholic Church, this document says, there grows day by day hope and yearning for the restoration of the unity of all who believe in Christ our Lord. The grace of God is at work, and gives us an unwavering confidence that step by step this high goal of unity will at last be reached.

At the end of one of my lectures I was asked an unexpected question: was I an 'optimist' or a 'pessimist' about the restoration of unity? I answered that I was neither an 'optimist' nor a 'pessimist', but a 'realist'. Anyone who is in touch with the situation is only too well aware that the difficulties in the way of union are still weighty; but he is aware, also, that with the grace of God much has already been done to lessen them; and that constant prayer, generous sacrifice and tireless work for the cause of unity must in the end, with the grace of God, lead to the achievement of this aim. A non-Catholic correspondent, speaking after a talk I gave at Zurich, expressed his agreement with what I had been saying, in these words: 'Divine grace is visibly at work in the longing for unity. We ought not to draw back from it. We do not yet see the ways and means to achieve it, but let us trust firmly in God to find them and lead us to them.'[1] That sums it up. But this confidence in the grace of God is also a summons for us to co-operate with it, according to our ability, by prayer, sacrifice and action. First place must always be given to prayer, because the problem is one which simply cannot be solved by mere human resources: the obstacles are so great that only the grace of God can overcome them. We must ask for grace: Pope John XXIII, in the Apostolic Constitution summoning the Council, laid the greatest stress on his renewed appeal for prayer. He extended this appeal to 'all Christians of the Christian churches not in communion with Rome'. 'We know', he says, 'that many of our children are rightly desirous of achieving unity and peace, according to the teaching of Christ and his prayer to the Father.' He went on to express his joy that they too should have promised to pray for the success of the Council, and hence that it might bear fruit in the service of Christian unity.

The Octave of Prayer in which we, in union with so many of our separated brethren, are now joined, gives us a welcome opportunity

[1] *Neue Zürcher Zeitung*, 29 November 1961, p. 17.

of praying for the great grace of the unity of all those who have been baptized in the name of Christ, so that what Christ, on the night before his Passion, begged of the Father from the loving heart of God made man, may soon be realized: 'That they should all be one, as we are one ... so let the world know that it is thou who has sent me, and that thou has bestowed thy love upon them, as thou hast bestowed it upon me' (John 17:11, 23).

I4

POSSIBILITIES OF CO-OPERATION[1]

Q. YOUR EMINENCE, during this Church Unity Octave all Christians are praying for unity in the one Church of Christ. What part could the coming Council play in this matter?

A. Perhaps it would not be out of place to begin by underlining the fact that, contrary to what many people thought when it was first announced, there is no question of its being a 'Unionist' Council, that is to say that the immediate object of the Council is not to discuss and achieve union with any particular Christian community. It is rather that the Council may promote union among Christians by showing, as the Holy Father himself has said, in its very methods and procedures the sincerity, concord, and charity that exist and are paramount in the Catholic Church. In this way, His Holiness hopes it may be a gentle invitation to our separate brethren to accept their share of the great benefits which the Church gives her children. The Council may also improve the atmosphere between Catholics and non-Catholics and thus create conditions more favourable to union and solve some of the problems connected with union in general or with particular communities of our separated brethren.

Q. Separated brethren are those who belong to the Orthodox Churches and to those stemming from the time of the Reformation. What are the main obstacles to unity from the point of view of the Orthodox Churches?

A. For the Orthodox Churches the main obstacles of a doctrinal

[1] Original text: Interview on Radiotélévision française, 22 January, 1962. First published as 'Dans une interview télévisée accordée au R. P. Wenger le card. A. Bea explore les chemins de l'unité', in La Croix, 24 January, 1961.

character are the primacy and infallibility of the pope, and in fact anything defined since the definite separation of the Eastern Church from Rome in 1054. Connected with the question of primacy is the whole matter of the position and function of bishops. Just as the office of bishop undoubtedly devolves from the divine Founder of the Church, so do a bishop's specific functions and responsibilities. However, these episcopal functions have been differently interpreted and differently put into practice at various times in the two thousand years of the Church's history, both in the East and in the West. In the East, bishops and regional councils of bishops, called synods, had and still have very wide powers. One can well understand that the East is anxious to retain what we may call 'local autonomy'. There are, too, other obstacles of a historical and practical nature: the difference of mentality between East and West, and resentment about certain deplorable historical incidents, such as the so-called Fourth Crusade and the creation of the Latin Empire in Constantinople in the thirteenth century.

Q. These are pre-Reformation questions. The problem of unity in connection with the post-Reformation Christians is therefore somewhat different?

A. The problem here has two principal aspects. The first concerns doctrinal differences in general. Even at the actual time of the Reformation there were doctrinal disagreements which had various and striking ramifications: certain doctrinal convictions were indeed held in common by groups numerically large; but even within these groups there were considerable disagreements which proliferated in the course of the centuries. On the continent of Europe the number of groups divided from one another is large enough, but is comparatively limited. In the English-speaking world, however, there are more than two hundred of what are called 'denominations', often in radical disagreement with one another. The question inevitably rises: how is it possible to discuss union with so many groups, all so different from one another?

There is another fact which throws a still darker shadow over our present situation. The whole Reformation world rejected in principle any authority in the Church which could oblige the consciences of the faithful to follow it. From this stems a very practical obstacle to all efforts at unity. The Catholic Church must ask herself, in the case of each community of Christians, this question: 'Who is authorized to demand that members of his denomination should recognize any agreement which may finally be reached?'

Q. Granted this situation, Your Eminence, what can be done to help further some *rapprochement* between separated Christians?

A. Leaving aside what the Council itself may eventually do, let me say one word about the means that may be used apart from the Council. A first and most important step would seem to be theological discussions between experts, that is between theologians, on each side. Such discussions are invaluable, for they go to the roots of divisions and gradually bring changes in conviction and habits of thought; they can clear up misunderstandings and set straight false interpretations. Moreover, such specialists are generally university professors, and are influential because of their prestige in the Protestant world. It is they, too, who educate and train future Protestant ministers. To this must be added the effect of more intimate personal acquaintance and the mutual friendship and understanding which this fosters. So the way is being paved to practical co-operation in non-doctrinal fields, such as social better-ment, general Christian service, and the defence of human values, of religious liberty, of human life and of peace.

Q. Your Eminence mentioned the defence of peace. Do you think that a common stand by all Christians would make any notable contribution towards preserving world peace?

A. Yes, I think so. In saying this I am obviously not issuing an invitation—I cannot do that—but merely drawing attention to simple facts. The Catholic Church numbers about 500 million members, the Eastern Churches about 165 million and the Pro-testants about 240 million. All told, then, Christians amount to about 1,000,000,000 spread all over the face of the earth. I leave it to you to work out what it would mean for mankind if these Christians and their representatives in public life were in complete agreement about such matters as, for example, nuclear weapons, disarmament and peace, and applied their Christian principles and the practical consequences thereof to international negotiations.

Q. That would assuredly be a great step towards peace. Your Eminence spoke just now about meetings of specialists, of Catholic and non-Catholic theologians, but it seems to me there should be more than that alone. In the mind of the Holy Father the Secretariat for Unity should also serve to bring about a *rapprochement*. Your Eminence has been given charge of this Secretariat. In what way and to what extent does this Secretariat work for *rapprochement*?

A. A first practical step would be to make it possible for our separated brethren to follow the work of the Council. This we can do by supplying them with accurate information on how things are going or by accepting and studying their wishes and suggestions and passing them on to the appropriate Council authorities. In this type of work occasions turn up to correct misunderstandings and to suggest solutions of problems about union in general or as regards some particular community. Take one example: the question is not seldom raised about meeting the wishes of our separated brethren in matters of discipline or worship where no matter of faith is involved, and about respecting their institutions and customs, for example the use of the vernacular, popular hymns, Communion under both kinds. These are problems which have frequently been raised and discussed in print. The Secretariat will be able in due course to collect all such material, subject it to careful study by competent persons and prepare from it matter for later discussion by the Council.

Q. May we suppose that the Secretariat will be the means of contact with the World Council of Churches?

A. There is no difficulty of principle about this, I think, since the Council of Churches does not support any doctrine contrary to Catholic dogma. A certain amount of co-operation is therefore possible, although in saying this I am, once more, not taking any official step. Co-operation could be very fruitful in matters not directly concerning doctrine—that is, as we have already said, in defence of human values and such matters.

Q. In this connection, surely the visit of Dr Fisher to the Holy

Father and to Your Eminence must have done much to smooth relations between Rome and the Church of England?

A. To that, the answer is an unhesitating Yes, as indeed I had occasion to write in a recent article. Obviously we cannot expect any immediate, spectacular results from it, but it was an event of undoubted significance, as proof of a notably improved atmosphere and as promise of further improvement. As such, it marks a definite stage, almost a landmark, in the noble work of uniting all the baptized, a work whose consummation the Holy Ghost has manifestly, during these last few decades, been preparing, slowly, indeed, but irresistibly. It is the task of all baptized persons to co-operate by prayer, by a holy life and by sacrifice so that Jesus Christ, the Divine Founder and Head of the Church may bring this work to a happy conclusion.

15

THE WORK OF PIUS XII AND THE COUNCIL[1]

SIG GIORGIO BERLUTTI: An Ecumenical Council at the dawn of the new atomic age is certainly an event of outstanding historical and supernatural importance; the divine inspiration is clear. The Ecumenical Council affects, directly or indirectly, every individual, every race and nation.

Modern men, even unbelievers, atheists and Marxists, cannot fail to realize, still less can they ignore, the moral and spiritual scope of an Ecumenical Council and the decisive influence which it will have on the destiny of the world, of a world which used to seem so vast and has now become so small.

To seek clarification of certain important aspects of the Second Vatican Council, I approached His Eminence Cardinal Augustin Bea, former confessor of Pius XII and now President of the Secretariat for Christian Unity, one of the Preparatory Commissions of the Council. He gave me a paternal welcome and kindly answered the following questions.

Q. Pope John XXIII, in speaking of the purpose and scope of the Ecumenical Council, often stresses Church unity, moral reform and a revivifying of faith. But this would be nothing short of miraculous. While a sense of well-being and a hedonistic concept of life prevails everywhere, euphoric moral and spiritual decadence has become so advanced, so animal and satanic, that it seems impossible to call a halt. What means can the Ecumenical Council use, Your Eminence,

[1] Original text: Interview with Giorgio Berlutti, published in *La Casa sollievo della sofferenza* (San Giovanni Rotondo, Foggia), 12, no. 5 (1-15 March, 1961), p. 2, and reprinted in *Il Quotidiano*, 16 February, 1961, p. 7.

to change the present dangerous and frightening world situation, or at least to stem the break-down of moral, ideal, traditional and religious values?

A. In answering your question it is not simply my own personal ideas that I shall be putting forward. Pope John himself, when inaugurating the preparatory work of the Commissions for the Council, told us what should be done. He made it clear, in fact, that it was not a case of expounding any particular point of the Church's doctrine or discipline—as was the aim of more than one of the Councils in the Church's history, but of 'restoring to its true value and splendour the substantial concept of human and Christian living of which the Church has been guardian and teacher throughout the centuries. It is a question also of seeking out the characteristics of the Church's more fervent youth, and restoring them in order to bring their all-conquering power to bear on jaded modern minds beguiled by the almost exclusive pursuit of material goods, and either forgetful of spiritual and supernatural principles or indifferent to them.'

Q. Don't you think, Your Eminence, that humanity is becoming more and more alienated from God, and approaching a new form of barbaric decadence?

A. Certainly there are moments when evil seems so paramount as to make us think that this is so. And there is clearly a grave danger that things will come to such a pass, but we must not lose sight of the brighter and more consoling aspects of our time.

Besides, in her almost two thousand years the Church has known situations of equal or even greater peril, but she has always survived them. She relies on the words of her divine Founder: 'The gates of hell shall not prevail against thee.'

Q. The Council proposes to re-establish the unity of all baptized persons. But how is this to be done?

A. Certainly the Council proposes to do this; or, rather, the Pope has in a certain sense given it the aim of promoting the unity of Christians. This, however, does not mean that the Council will enter into direct dealings with the representatives of the non-Catholic Christian communities on the problem of unity. By the very manner in which it functions the Ecumenical Council should give striking evidence of the truth, sincerity, concord and charity which prevail in the Catholic Church, and in *this* way furnish a gentle invitation to non-Catholic Christians to seek that unity which Christ willed, and for which he prayed so earnestly a few hours before sacrificing himself for mankind. Furthermore, the Council should stimulate a profound renewal within the Catholic Church herself.

Q. Could Your Eminence tell me what Pius XII thought about the problem of the unity of Christian communities separated from Rome?

A. It is not always realized what encouragement is to be found in Pius XII's writings on this point. For instance, in his encyclical on the Church as the mystical Body of Christ, Pius XII expressed such tender love for our separated brethren as may surprise us, coming from such a jurist. In addition, it is well known how often he expressed a desire for closer co-operation of all Christians in fields not directly concerned with faith, as for example in social and relief activities, in working for peace, and so on. One remembers too the fatherly kindness which he showed in receiving all well-intentioned non-Catholics who came to him for stimulus and encouragement.

Q. Does Your Eminence think that the speeches and messages of Pius XII can be regarded as a valid contribution to the solution of the problems to be examined by the Ecumenical Council?

A. Undoubtedly. But I do not mean that the Council ought to or will follow mechanically the whole programme set out by Pius XII. Every pontificate has its own character which corresponds to the personality of the Pope, to the needs of the time and, above all, to the mysterious intentions and plans of the Holy Spirit, who always animates and guides the Church. The last, most eminent Pope left twenty volumes containing a wealth of valuable doctrinal material. Among these writings will be found, in general terms at least, solutions to many modern problems which no one concerned with renewal in the Church can possibly ignore.

Q. I think that the spiritual unity of the world, although delayed and hindered by man, will inevitably come about, because that is part of God's plan. But do you believe, Your Eminence, that scientific and technical progress can help us reach this final goal?

A. You are certainly right in saying that the spiritual unity of the world is bound to be achieved. But as far as scientific and technical progress go, it must be borne in mind that although this is a powerful means of speeding up and furthering the unification of mankind, it is essentially a human activity and can, therefore, like man himself, lead equally to mankind's destruction. Everything depends upon the use we make of it.

Your question seems to suggest that the spiritual unification of mankind depends solely and entirely on man. This is not so. There is, in fact, the infinitely more essential and finally decisive factor of God's providence and the redemptive work of Christ, the Saviour of mankind. So although the present state of mankind sometimes make us tremble for its future, we must not lose sight of God nor of Christ's work, which can make straight man's tortuous ways.

16

VISIBLE AND INVISIBLE UNION[1]

Q. WHAT IS the Pope John XXIII's impression of present efforts around the world to promote Christian unity?

A. The Holy Father is pleased at the generous and increasing efforts being made in all parts of the world.

Q. What is the Holy Father's precise purpose in calling for Christian unity?

A. Along with every Catholic, he wants to restore the unity—including the *visible* unity—of all Christians. This visible unity is—in the Holy Father's words—'the communion of all believers in a *single* profession of faith, in the *same* practice of worship, in obedience to the *same* supreme authority'. This unity corresponds to the intentions, commands and prayers of the divine Saviour.

Q. Does this include another unity—an invisible unity?

A. Yes, it presupposes it; invisible unity means unity in grace, in sharing God's own life. Such unity comes about through baptism. This means that each true baptism produces a *oneness* between Christ and the baptized person. Not only that, but also a *unity* among the baptized themselves. Added to this internal unity from baptism is the unity that comes from charity and from professing, at least partially, the same faith.

We do not, then, reduce the Catholic Church to a mere external, juridical organization. Yet the Church affirms—even if everyone is not pleased with it—that one cannot be content with *only* interior unity. There must be also a *visible* unity. In the words of Christ, 'one flock and one Shepherd'.

[1] Original text: Television interview, given in English to the American Broadcasting Company on 6 January, 1961. English version first published in this book.

Q. What, then, does this two-fold unity mean in the Christian's daily life?

A. It means an *internal* union of all the baptized in the same charity and the same faith. And an *external* unity in professing this same faith, using the same sacraments, recognizing one authority.

Q. What authority?

A. The authority which Christ gives to his shepherds or bishops —united among themselves—and united with the successor of St Peter, the pope.

Q. Are Christians ever going to be able to attain such unity on this earth?

A. Some theologians say: Christ has reserved this perfect unity— visible and invisible—of all Christians in one Church, until the Church reaches her final glory at the end of time. There is no objection to this, if we mean that the Church on earth is on the *way* to this perfect unity, that the unity which Christ has already given to the Church, is in the process of perfection.

Q. Well, then, what are your objections?

A. The Roman Catholic Church objects to taking this as a motive of resignation, that is, to do *nothing* about healing the scandalous divisions now existing among the children of God and brothers of Christ. We cannot be content to remain *separated* brothers. Doing nothing would be fatal.

The will of Christ is clear and demanding. On the eve of his death, Christ fervently begged of his heavenly Father for the unity of all those whom the Father had given to him, his Son. That ardent prayer did not envisage a unity which should be attained only at the end of the world.

Q. Then, you believe this unity may come about before the end of time?

A. God will give his gift when he *wills*. Who are *we* to put limits on the action and power of Christ and the Holy Spirit? Christ told us: 'Such things are impossible to man's powers but not to God's. To God, all things are possible.' Therefore, we Christians must co-operate with the action of Christ and the Holy Spirit to further perfect Christian unity. The words of St Augustine apply: 'God does not command impossible things. But, in commanding, he asks us to do what we can—and to ask for what we cannot.'

Q. From your experience, is there a real desire for Christian unity in the world today?

A. Yes, and this desire is growing. There is a craving for Christian unity today among the baptized in Christ. And, more and more they are praying for unity. These desires and prayers are bringing consolation to a world torn by anxiety. Full and perfect unity has not yet been reached, But there is great consolation in the fact that it is growing—according to the command and prayer of Christ: 'that all may be one'.

17

PREPARATIONS FOR THE COUNCIL[1]

Q. WHAT REAL, practical contribution does Your Eminence think the Council has made up till now towards the cause of Christian unity?

A. It has been recognized even by non-Catholic writers that the announcement of the Council and the preparatory work for it have already proved to be a providential stimulus for the movement towards the union of all Christians. Thus, for example, representatives of various non-Catholic communities have asked their followers to pray for the Council, and the Holy Father has more than once been rejoiced by the interest taken in the Council and by the prayers offered for it. During their last Assembly in New Delhi the General Secretary of the World Council of Churches, referring to the Assembly, to the Pan-Orthodox Conference at Rhodes, and to the convocation of the Vatican Council and its preparatory work, said that all these things gave one the impression of being in the presence of a 'general ecumenical mobilization'.

Getting down to details, one can say that another more concrete result has been the creation of the Secretariat for Christian Unity which has been so well received by almost everyone, including non-Catholics. It is enough to mention the welcome given it by the Central Committee of the World Council of Churches scarcely two months after the Secretariat was set up in August, 1960, and more recently by the General Assembly in New Delhi.

In this improved atmosphere contacts have begun to be made. Here I want to mention only the most outstanding of those we

[1] Original text: Radio interview with Michele Sima, 7 April, 1962; first published in *De Linie* 7 April, 1962, pp. 2ff.

know about, for it is obvious that there are many others which for the present must remain hidden under a veil of discretion. Among those we know about, the first—and not only chronologically the first—is the visit of the then Archbishop of Canterbury, Dr Fisher, to the Holy Father in December, 1960, a most courageous and Christian act: after that, came the visit of the presiding Bishop of the American Episcopalians, Dr Lichtenberger, then that of Dr Jackson, President of the National Baptist Convention of the United States, which embraces five million coloured Baptists, and finally the visit of Dr Craig, Moderator of the Church of Scotland. In the same context we must consider the presence of official Catholic observers at the General Assembly of the World Council of Churches at New Delhi. This last was a milestone, for it was the first time in the history of the ecumenical movement that the Catholic Church has been officially represented at an Assembly. All these, the contacts and, above all, the better atmosphere, are real, practical results, and in fact the only possible results at this stage in inter-denominational relations.

Q. Could Your Eminence now explain to us the work which your Secretariat has done so far in preparation for the Second Vatican Council and also in the wider context of hopes for the union of the entire Christian world?

A. The Secretariat supplies those of our separated brethren who request it with authentic information about the preparations for the Council, and receives from them information about their wishes, their corresponding suggestions and, should they desire it, their criticisms as well. Besides this, we deal with the question of the representatives of communities of separated brethren who will attend the Council—'observers' as they are called. Once the Holy Father had settled the matter in principle and made his decision known in the Bull *Humanae Salutis* summoning the Council, and had confided to our Secretariat the responsibility for putting this into practice, it remained to see which of these communities would like to be invited, and the form the invitation should take. It is not hard to see that this charge is delicate and involves a making of contacts and an exchange of views. It is also plain that this charge involves no small responsibility, since we must make sure that the presence of these representatives of our separated brethren results in no worsening of our relations with them but in an improvement and a real advance in *rapprochement*.

Another aspect of the Secretariat's work is similar to the work of the other preparatory commissions: that is, the Secretariat examines and studies carefully the wishes, interests and problems of our separated brethren in matters which will be discussed by the Council. Many such wishes and suggestions have been expounded in various periodicals, and many come to us among the masses of personal letters from heads of communities, and from their theologians and others. To give one example at random, there is the problem of the exact position of non-Catholic Christians, who are validly baptized, in the mystical Body of Christ, and of their relation to the one true Church of Christ. Beyond that rises the question of religious liberty, a matter of crucial importance in so many ways if the denominations are to live together. Mixed marriages are but another instance, and there are other questions besides.[1]

Such problems, or groups of related problems, are examined and studied by subcommittees of the Secretariat consisting of a small number of members (with a vote) and consultants (experts). The work of studying questions is thus shared between about fifteen subcommittees whose conclusions are then examined at a plenary session of the Secretariat where all members and all consultants are present. When the conclusions have been discussed and, if necessary, amended, and a definite text has been obtained, this is sent either to the appropriate preparatory Commission of the Council, or if there is no Commission dealing with such matters, directly to the Central Commission of the Council. In fact the Secretariat cannot and does not want to act independently of the other preparatory bodies. Its task is to furnish them with ecumenical aspects of questions within the competence of each Commission so that these aspects will be given due consideration in its deliberations.

To sum up: the specific function of the Secretariat in the general

[1] Cf. above, Chapter 13, p. 170, note.

field of Christian unity has become clearer from what we have said. It is a matter of gradual improvement in the inter-denominational atmosphere, of giving help to the slow but definite progress of *rapprochement* between Christians and of making proposals, doctrinal or practical, which could foster this *rapprochement*. In other words, we are involved in long-term preparatory work for unity.

Q. What could be the contribution to unity of Your Eminence's Secretariat during the Council and during the post-conciliar period?

A. No official decision has yet been published about the permanence, during the Council, of the various preparatory bodies

In any case it is obvious that *during* the Council the representatives from different non-Catholic Christian communities will have to be looked after. Information must be given them to enable them to prepare themselves to follow the proceedings of the sessions at which they are present; and information, also, about the proceedings in sessions, or in Commissions, which they do not attend. Every assistance must be given them to help them to fulfil their function and mission as 'observers'.

As regards the permanence of the Secretariat *after* the Council, and the form it should take, this is a matter which really depends upon the decisions and the general results of the Council itself. Supposing a continuance of the Secretariat, several tasks await it, and delicate ones, e.g. the maintaining and extension of contacts with non-Catholic Christians, the general guidance and co-ordination —without any undue centralization—of different Catholic organizations and efforts in the field of unity and similar matters.

Q. Do you think, Your Eminence, that anything useful arose from the Third General Assembly of the World Council of Churches in New Delhi in relation to the problem of unity and the forthcoming Second Vatican Council?

A. At present, I cannot judge that since I was not present and the Report has not yet been published. I shall therefore confine myself to mentioning three things that seem to me to be of considerable importance for the ecumenical movement. The first concerns doctrine and is the definition of the goal of the movement submitted to the General Assembly by the Commission on Faith and Order. Although this definition does not yet fully coincide with the Catholic concept, it does make an important step forward in that it rejects the idea of a purely invisible Church and is a notable advance towards the Catholic position. The second matter of importance at the New Delhi Assembly was a statement by Dr W. A. Visser 't Hooft, General Secretary of the World Council. He referred to the Pan-Orthodox Conference at Rhodes, to the New Delhi Assembly and to the Vatican Council, and then recalled the following words of Professor Schlinck: 'It is unquestionably of great importance for Christianity and for the world that it would clearly be seen . . . that these two assemblies have not been convened in opposition to each other, and that each will not seek its own advantage, but will seek only to serve the Lord Jesus Christ.' This is striking evidence of the sincere yearning for unity among Christians.

The third point was this: the New Delhi Assembly invited all the Christian communities within the World Council to urge their members to take a serious interest in all baptized people outside their own denomination and to pray for them.

These are things which are, I am convinced, of great importance for the spirit of mutual understanding, or *rapprochement*, of charity and of a genuine submission by everyone to the one Lord Jesus Christ and of dedication to the service of his Church.

Q. Do you think it desirable, Your Eminence, that committees for Christian unity should be set up in all countries as has been done in England? What would be the practical usefulness of a systematic establishment of such committees in all countries?

A. I am, of course, convinced of the usefulness of such committees, although this does not mean that they should be set up suddenly and almost mechanically, by a stroke of the pen. We should let things take their course. Example and evidence of a real need will produce organizations worth far more than those set up by order. I know, in fact, that committees of this kind are planned in other areas.

As for their practical usefulness, the answer is very simple. The Church has a strict and grave obligation to concern itself with all who have been baptized in Christ; this is an obligation even more serious than that, (which is already serious enough), of bringing the Gospel to those who are not yet Christians, since these baptized persons are already united to Christ, are thereby 'sons' of the Church, (as they were again named by the Holy Father himself in the Bull convoking the Council), and our brothers. Now on whom does this obligation lie if not in the first place on the individual parishes, dioceses and local Church authorities who live in the midst of their separated brethren? There should therefore be bodies capable of co-ordinating and stimulating all initiatives in the field of Catholic relations with non-Catholics. It is not hard to see the vast possibilities of action which offer, and how such action is not only useful but absolutely indispensable.

Q. In view of the particular religious situation of their country and the great number of Protestants in it, does Your Eminence believe that the bishops, clergy and laity of Holland have a particular role to play in the course of union in the Christian world as a whole?

A. Of course, yes. And I know that they themselves are well aware of this. They have in fact been for some time in the vanguard of Catholic ecumenical activity. They are responsible for the creation of the International Catholic Conference for Ecumenical Questions, not to mention other activities. This Conference was later honoured by the nomination of its Secretary by the Holy Father as Secretary of our Secretariat for Christian Unity. In addition, the Dutch hierarchy has on more than one occasion given valuable directives to its faithful on ecumenical work. It has also undertaken the charge of promoting prayers for separated brethren on special occasions such as, for example, the recent General Assembly of the World Council of Churches in New Delhi. I therefore hope with all my heart that Holland will be able to carry on with this pioneer work so as to serve, in close union with the whole Church, as a model, example and encouragement to many other countries, particularly where conditions are similar to those in Holland.

18

A DELICATE BUT URGENT TASK[1]

Q. ESPECIALLY IN the last two years, Your Eminence has had a great deal of contact, both publicly and in private, with personalities from many communities of separated Christians. What are the general impressions you have gained from this?

A. I have received extremely favourable impressions. There is a great improvement in atmosphere. There is immense goodwill. There is willingness to forget the past. There is an awareness and acceptance of our most grave obligation to be concerned with all the baptized and with their unity. There is resolve to labour for the fulfilment of the will of the divine Redeemer and Founder of the Church that all may be one. Not that these men cherish any illusions. They are fully aware of the multitude and intractability of the difficulties. But they face them with their eyes on Christ and on the omnipotence of his grace, which can achieve what is impossible to men.

Q. Your Eminence, is that atmosphere to be felt mainly in a small, select group or equally among the people at large?

A. Principally in a select group of men belonging to different communities; but at the same time this atmosphere is rapidly spreading among the people as a whole. To keep to my own experience, I can say that wherever I have given lectures—six in Switzerland, one in Paris and two in Germany—the interest and attendance of non-Catholics has exceeded the most flattering forecast. The many requests made to me for press, radio and television interviews, which I can only partly satisfy, are further

[1] Original text: Interview with L. Furno, published in *Vita*, 19 April 1962, and reprinted in *La Civiltà Cattolica*, 1962, II, p. 181.

evidence of this atmosphere. I am to give seven more lectures this month and next: four in Germany, two in Austria and one in Italy. We may truly speak—as, in fact, an official document of the Holy See, the well known Instruction of the Holy Office on the ecumenical movement did some time ago—of a strong breath of the Holy Spirit which is pervading Christianity. This is a great gift of God to our time, but one which imposes on us a large task and a heavy responsibility.

Q. Would Your Eminence therefore be rather optimistic about the attainment of union?

A. A few months ago, someone at Strasbourg put the question to me point-blank: 'Your Eminence, are you an optimist or a pessimist in regard to union?' I replied: 'I am a realist.' Let me explain. There is certainly no reason to delude oneself. The difficulties on all sides are vast. But we have to see things with the eye of faith, that is, animated by the faith which can move mountains. We must remember the solemn assurance of our Lord in this respect: 'I promise you, if you have faith, though it be but like a grain of mustard-seed, you have only to say to this mountain, Remove from this place to that, and it will remove; nothing will be impossible to you' (Mt 17:19).

Q. Is this same attitude relevant also to what is hoped for from the Council?

A. Certainly it applies also to this most important field. On the one hand, do not consider the Council, naïvely, as an automatic cure for all ills and misfortunes. As long as she is on this earth, the Church is constantly travelling on the road to perfection. She is always in a state of development, a state where the law of the hidden leaven, the law of the grain of mustard seed and of the little flock applies; in other words, the law of humiliation and the cross. On the other hand, there is no call for discouragement or pessimism. In the forceful words of Pope John XXIII: 'Christ has not abandoned mankind whom he redeemed.' Still less has he abandoned his own followers. In fact, never has a Council been prepared with such care and solicitude as this one. If and when we notice things less perfect and satisfactory, it should stimulate us to insist the more strongly on that spiritual help to which the Council has a claim, on prayer, sacrifice, and personal sanctification. And prayer is really being offered, even by many non-Catholics, for the Council's success. Besides, it must not be forgotten that the Council is guided and enlightened by the Holy Ghost. What St Peter said after the first Council of the Apostles at Jerusalem: 'It is the Holy Spirit's pleasure and ours' (Acts 15:28) applies also to the twenty-first Council, the forthcoming Second Vatican Council. Pessimism, therefore, would be a sign of want of faith.

Q. Your Eminence, allow me to put a somewhat delicate question. At times one hears it said that work for union—and one thinks principally of contacts with non-Catholics—is dangerous; for example, for the purity of faith, involving the risk of indifferentism, and that therefore it would be better perhaps to keep one's distance. What should we think of this attitude?

A. Dangers there certainly are. It has more than once been observed that both Catholics and non-Catholics tend to a rather sentimental use of the word 'charity', which is liable to obscure doctrinal clarity and blur the truth. Consequently I, for my own part, never tire of repeating in lectures and articles the utmost necessity of adhering firmly to the whole of what Christ teaches us through the Church.

Not everyone can do everything. A Catholic who has no theological training cannot risk engaging in a conversation, a 'dialogue', with a learned non-Catholic theologian. One must, therefore, be cautious and not overestimate one's own powers; the same prudence is needed in all matters, even secular ones. Yet the possible risks are not, and cannot be, a reason for evading the sacred duty of prudently and carefully showing concern, for all those who are baptized in Christ and are thus our brothers. Apostolic work in a dechristianized environment has considerable dangers. Nonetheless, the Church has not hesitated to urge all her sons to take part in Catholic Action. In this apostolate of unity then, let us do what we always do in case of danger: take the necessary precautions and then go forward with unwavering faith in God and with true Christian courage.

Q. Your Eminence, one last question. In speaking of the need of working for the union of all Christians, it is usual to emphasize the will of God and of the Founder of the Church. But to me it seems that the dechristianization of society today is a further reason that makes Christian unity absolutely essential. I am not thinking only of professed atheism but rather of that unconscious atheism which is more insidious because it is more agreeable, of the 'practical' materialism which, without any theorizing or expressed intention, tends inevitably to steep men in comfort and pleasure, resulting, in practice, in their ignoring spiritual values such as God, Christ, the Church and the soul. What have you to say about this?

A. I completely agree that the progressive dechristianization of society today makes union a matter of urgency. This idea is in perfect accord with the mind of Christ in his priestly prayer at the Last Supper. He prayed to the Father: 'That they too may be one in us, so that the world may come to believe that it is thou who hast sent me' (John 17:21). The union of Christians, therefore, besides being the will of the Founder of the Church, is also of capital importance for the whole of mankind. The union of all who believe in Christ does in fact constitute the evidence that should lead the world to believe in Christ, and thus to find its salvation in him. So work for union is made imperative by the responsibility of Christians—of all Christians—for the good of mankind. They all have been called to the great honour of co-operating with the divine Redeemer in the salvation of the whole of mankind. What a task and what a responsibility! It is a great joy to see how Christians all over the world are becoming more and more conscious of this immense task and responsibility. I am thinking, for example, of the theme of the last general assembly of the World Council of Churches at New Delhi, held under the motto 'Christ the light of the world'. My wish is that this consciousness and general awareness may grow more and more widespread. That is what mankind, what Jesus Christ and God, expect of Christians.

19

A COUNCIL FOR THE WHOLE OF MANKIND[1]

Statement by Cardinal Bea.

THE COMING Ecumenical Council is, I hope, of considerable interest
to journalists such as yourselves. In the course of nineteen centuries,
there have been only twenty Ecumenical Councils and there has
not been one now for ninety years. Quite apart from the special
importance which the Council has for the Catholic Church, it is
important for all the world's 900 million Christians in general and
for humanity as a whole. No doubt you may have heard the
significant phrase used by a non-Catholic, the General Secretary of
the World Council of Churches at the General Assembly at New
Delhi last November. Referring to the Pan-Orthodox Conference at
Rhodes of the preceding September, to the third General Assembly
of the World Council of Churches and to the Second Vatican
Council, he said that these three events really gave the impression
that there is a 'general mobilization' for the union of Christians.

But I said just now that the Council is of extraordinary importance for the whole of mankind. To understand why, it is enough to
take a quick look at mankind today. As a result of the staggeringly
rapid progress in means of transportation and of communication
media—the Press, radio, television etc.—humanity today seems
to have become more keenly aware of the inevitable interdepend-
ence of all countries and continents and of the overriding necessity
to deal with all our problems in a global context. On the other

[1] Original text: Address and interview given to the Foreign Press Association of
Rome at the invitation of Barrett McGurn, published in *La Civiltà Cattolica*, 1962,
II, p. 491; III, p. 177.

hand, this same humanity is fearful and almost panic-stricken in the face of its own discoveries and advances which threaten unprecedented catastrophes amounting almost to self-destruction. And so it has come to realize, sometimes more instinctively than consciously, that only the strengthening of spiritual values and principles of law, of moral and religious values, can avert this terrible threat and ensure genuine progress, first, towards peaceful coexistence, and then, gradually, towards a real unity of the whole of humanity. Now any realist must recognize the undeniable importance in this situation of the teaching and the moral authority of the Catholic Church. Her faithful number some 500 million and unquestionably exert an influence not to be overlooked, even though it is not always visibly commensurate with their numbers. A realist, then, will likewise admit that the Catholic Church can be a worth-while ally in the struggle for a securely peaceful coexistence of all races, peoples and nations.

The importance of the Council for humanity becomes still clearer if we consider that the Council intends to do more than cope with the Church's internal affairs. It aims also to prepare for the future union of all the baptized, that is, of all Christians. At the present moment, the total number of Christians in the world is about 900 millions. In addition to their numerical importance one must also consider their distribution throughout the whole world, the leading position of many of their representatives and therefore the importance and the value of their influence in all countries and in all social classes. Let me give you a concrete example of the influence that Christians, if they were united, could exercise on world events, an example that I have already quoted in another interview: I am thinking of the problem of peace. Try to estimate what the effect would be on mankind if all Christians were in perfect agreement on the question of nuclear weapons, disarmament and peace. In saying this, obviously I do not mean to issue an invitation—it is not my business to do so—but merely to mention a fact and a possibility of great importance for the Council in so far as it intends, as a long-term policy, to prepare for the union of all Christians.

Mention may perhaps be made of another possible step forward. Pius XII and the present Pope have appealed (on more than one occasion) to all men of good will for the good of mankind and particularly for peace. The problems confronting humanity at the present time are indeed so great and so urgent that it is absolutely indispensable to mobilize all those forces which are in agreement at least in their general ideas about religion and God and the existence of a moral order. In these spheres they can and ought to try to make headway, wherever they can and as far as possible, by working together for the good of mankind. Perhaps also, in the same order of ideas the Council will be able, by giving a more concrete form to the repeated invitations of recent popes, to contribute effectively to the good of mankind.

All that I have said seems to me to show clearly enough that the Council can and must be of interest even to those among you who do not unreservedly accept the Catholic point of view, and to the newspapers you represent, simply on account of the contribution that this Council can make to the good of humanity. And there, I think, lies the principal reason for the great interest in the Council shown by the Press of the world, an interest which should greatly encourage us. I should like to take advantage of this opportunity to ask all of you—and I repeat, on the purely human plane—to be good enough to do your best to explain this aspect of the Council to all levels of world opinion which by virtue of your position you are able to influence and to form.

Answers to questions

I shall now answer some of the very many questions that could be asked about this subject and which have actually been put to me. You will of course understand that I cannot answer all of them for various reasons, principally lack of time. We must confine ourselves to the most fundamental questions or to those of more general interest. In the main I shall answer only those which concern me particularly, those affecting the Secretariat for Christian Unity; only incidentally and indirectly, in dealing with the work of the Secretariat, shall I touch on the question of the Council.

In the first place it should be remembered—and this has already been emphasized on several occasions—that the Council never intended, and indeed is unable, to effect union immediately with any particular group of Christians and that it is not a 'council of union' in this sense but it *is* meant to prepare for unity as a long-term policy.

Q. Since what is at stake is a union of parties to some extent in opposition on doctrinal matters and questions of religious practice the first question that is usually put is this: what concessions can the Council make and what are the limits that cannot be exceeded?

A. This question is sometimes answered by distinguishing between what is 'essential' and what is merely 'accidental'. The distinction is, to say the least, not very clear and does not tell us very much. Rather should we distinguish between those things which belong to the realm of practice and those which are doctrinal. Practice concerns discipline, Canon Law, liturgical rules, forms of piety, traditions. In this sphere, as we know, the Church teaches that her Founder has left her a much wider margin and far greater freedom. And we know, too, that in different periods of history and different parts of the Church there have been differences of practice in these matters. Thus, to give a well-known example, the liturgical rites in East and West are not the same, and in the East there are various rites using languages other than Latin—Greek, Arabic, Syriac, Armenian, Ethiopian, Slavonic etc. Another example is that in the East the law and obligation of the celibacy of the clergy are not so rigorous as in the Latin rite. The differences are such that side by side with the code of canon law for the Latin rite there is another for the various Oriental rites which is in course of being drawn up and has already been partially promulgated.

On the doctrinal level it is quite different. Both in the East and the West it is an absolute rule that all that the Church teaches as a doctrine received from Christ must be admitted and believed. In this sphere, then, there is no room for concessions. The reason for this is very simple. The Church is not the mistress of the doctrine received from Christ. She has received it as a deposit and she is bound to teach it and hand it on intact. In addition, truth is one.

What the Church has once taught as a truth of faith received from Christ she has taught with the help of the Holy Spirit who always assists her in this teaching. She cannot, therefore, declare that it is false and that one is no longer obliged to believe it.

Q. You will ask me then: Is there nothing more to be done in the doctrinal sphere?

A. No. There is something and, indeed, very much to be done. Truth can be better explained by taking account of the mentality and language of modern man or of this or that group of our separated brethren in order to enable them to understand it better. In addition, we can explain more carefully those points of doctrine relating to the particular problems which concern or harass modern man or this or that group. For example, many groups of our separated brethren are particularly concerned about the problem of the Church, her authority, the relationship between the episcopate and primacy, and other similar questions.

Q. Before going on now to examine each group of our separated brethren and the differences between them and the Catholic Church, we can consider a more general question. What does the Catholic Church teach about the relationship with the Catholic Church of those who have been validly baptized, but belong, for example, to an evangelical denomination or an Orthodox Church?

A. Here we are faced with a point which today is of great importance and which might usefully be clarified by the Council. Without wishing to anticipate this clarification I can point out what is so far established. The first point is the general teaching of the New Testament stating that by a valid baptism—even conferred outside the Roman Catholic Church—the baptized person is organically united to Christ and his mystical Body, that he becomes by virtue of grace the adopted son of God and that in consequence all those who are validly baptized are brothers. Now, just as the Catholic Church teaches that she is the true Church of Christ, so she considers all those who have been baptized but live outside her communion as brothers—or, to use the expression that we hear so frequently from the Pope, as our separated brethren. These separated brethren the Church also calls her sons, an expression

8

that she does not use and never would use of the non-baptized, the non-Christian. With these last, there is certainly a general brotherhood on the purely human level but not the specifically Christian brotherhood founded on union with Christ, and the Church does not call them her sons. On the other hand, since our 'separated brethren' do not acknowledge or consider the Catholic Church as their Church, it is clear that in some sort they are separated from her; therefore they are not her sons and her members in the same full sense of the term as Catholics are. What separates them from Catholics are the divergencies in matters of faith and in the use of those vital means of grace formed by the sacraments, and also the fact that they do not recognize the authority of the Church and the pope. These divergencies are certainly very serious. Nevertheless, they do not destroy nor abolish this fundamental and very certain fact of their belonging to Christ, to his mystical Body and to the Church, of which we have spoken above.

Q. Here a new question arises. How are we to understand that well-known doctrine and saying: outside the Church there is no salvation? Is it really true that none of those who are separated from the Church can be saved?

A. Let us confine the answer to Christians, that is, to those who are validly baptized. The expression obviously does not mean that none of those who are separated from the Catholic Church can be saved. Its explanation is to be found in what we have said above about their relationship with the Catholic Church. As they have been baptized and in good faith accept and live the faith in which they were born and brought up, they receive, by virtue of their belonging to Christ, the necessary help for an authentic religious life, for the observance of the law of God and thus, also, for their salvation. Consequently, they are on the way of salvation and that by virtue of this fundamental belonging to the Church of which we have spoken.

Q. It is well known that the divergencies between various groups of Churches and the Catholic Church are neither few nor of little importance. What is the principal one and the most important of all?

A. I believe that the principal one is that which concerns the doctrine of the Church: namely, who holds authority in the Church? What is the extent of this authority? Can it oblige the faithful in conscience to believe certain things and to obey certain laws? Is this authority, in certain cases and within certain limits, really infallible, that is, by virtue of the very special help of the Holy Spirit is it preserved from error?

Q. If it is true that these divergencies have been in existence for several centuries past, what hope is there of our overcoming them?

A. One might be tempted to apply here our Lord's well-known saying recorded in the Gospel of St Mark: 'Such things are impossible to man's powers but not to God's; to God, all things are possible' (Mark 10:27). In fact, we are convinced that God wills union, that Christ wills it, that his Holy Spirit is at work to bring it about. And indeed some progress can be noticed. For example, it has been held for centuries in various evangelical denominations that the Church is and remains invisible; that is, that God alone knows who belongs to it and that thus unity remains invisible. Last year 'Faith and Order', one of the Commissions of the World Council of Churches, proposed at New Delhi a definition enumerating certain signs by which the unity of the Church becomes visible. For example, profession of the same faith, use of the same means of the life of grace, that is, of the same sacraments.

Q. To the extent that men are able to accomplish anything, what are the means to foster this union and bring it nearer at least in some degree?

A. Just now in the example quoted I mentioned an important means. This is a calm and objective study by individuals and theological conversations between specialists belonging to different denominations. Conversations of this sort have already been taking place for a long time past in Belgium, Germany, Switzerland and elsewhere, and they produce excellent results. In these conversations biblical studies occupy a special place. Holy scripture forms, indeed, the basis common to the different denominations. An example of how it is really possible to make progress by means of objective study is the introduction that a Swiss Protestant theologian of great

authority contributed to one of the parts (volume IV, fasc. 13) of the
Theological Dictionary of the New Testament, edited by Kittel,
one of the most important and reliable works of Protestant biblical
research of recent decades. In this introduction the author says that
in the light of the important results of this dictionary several of the
classical doctrines of 'our fathers in the faith' (Protestant), for
example, the doctrine of predestination, that of original sin and
others of the same kind, appear as being only relatively biblical.
Other theologians will certainly differ from this author; nevertheless the declaration in question is a characteristic instance of rethinking old positions as a consequence of a deeper examination
of holy scripture.

Q. The conversations mentioned above concern a relatively
small number of specialists. What can others do?

A. It is true that such conversations concern a very small number
of persons and I would not generally advise them to be undertaken
by non-specialists. They would too easily become fruitless and even
dangerous. But there is one principle which could be applied on a
larger scale: namely, to seek to co-operate with those belonging to
different denominations in spheres which do not directly concern
the faith; in social or charitable activities, for example, the affirmation of the natural moral law in the sphere of family and public
life, of public morality etc. Co-operation is also possible in the
statement of those Christian ideas common to the various denominations. Thus, for example, in India different denominations have
joined together in defence of the schools set up by the missionaries.
In Africa, various Anglican bishops have approved pastoral letters
by Catholic bishops against racial discrimination and have recommended the study of them. This co-operation, in addition to certain
immediate and by no means negligible results, possesses above all
the great advantage of creating between those who take part in it
the spirit of fellowship and of a gradual coming together even on
the doctrinal level.

Q. On this count I have also been asked what are the results and
the purpose of the well-known courtesy visits of the former
Anglican Archbishop of Canterbury, Dr Fisher, of the presiding

Bishop of the Episcopalian Church, Dr Lichtenberger, of the Baptist Convention in the United States, Dr Jackson, and of the Moderator of the Assembly of the Church of Scotland, Dr Craig.

A. Here it is easy to make a mistake either in overestimating or underestimating the results of these visits. We overestimate if we forget the great differences which exist and continue to exist in spite of these visits or if we believe that these differences are easily overcome. We underestimate if we say that they serve no useful purpose because the differences remain the same. It is enough to remember the important role played by the prevailing state of mind both in achieving mutual understanding and, on the other hand, in persistent prejudices, misunderstandings and resentment. Now, Catholics and Orthodox have lived for nine centuries not only without contact but for ever repeating the same old prejudiced opinions, not to say calumnies, on both sides. With the denominations issuing from the Reformation there have been nearly four centuries of struggle, with faults on both sides, struggles in which politics have on occasion intervened with most unhappy results. From this point of view it is already much that nowadays we are beginning to meet each other in charity and that we seek to establish more peaceful and calmer relationships. Of course, the way is long but at any rate we have set out upon it.

Q. Is it from this point of view that we should regard the fact that on the one hand official Catholic observers have taken part in the third General Assembly of the World Council of Churches at New Delhi and that, on the other hand, the presence of non-Catholic observers at the second Vatican Council is being prepared for?

A. Yes indeed, these are most consoling facts.

Q. What can be said of the status of these non-Catholic observers at the second Vatican Council?

A. They will have extensive opportunities of studying and following the work of the Council. Obviously these opportunities will not be confined to presence at the solemn sessions presided over by the Pope at which there is no discussion, but where texts already discussed and approved by a preliminary vote are read and put to formal vote. They will also be able to take part in the plenary sessions called the General Congregations of the Conciliar Fathers—that is, cardinals and bishops—at which further discussion takes place on texts already examined by the different Commissions of the Council (not the Preparatory Commissions which are already in existence). As a general rule, save for exceptional cases, they will not be present at the sessions of the Commissions themselves, though they will be kept informed about them by the Secretariat for the Unity of Christians, which for this purpose will be able to call upon the Fathers of the Council themselves.

Q. I have been asked if the activity of the Secretariat will continue or even perhaps expand after the Council.

A. That obviously depends on the results of the Council itself. If we are to judge by the development occurring in the movement in the first two years of the Secretariat's existence, it may be expected that the work will increase considerably, but its concrete form will depend entirely on the results of the Council.

Q. We can conclude with a question on an entirely different subject. I have been asked as Pius XII's confessor to say something of the personality of this famous, but probably little-known man.

A. As his confessor I can of course say nothing, but fortunately my relations with Pius XII began more than twenty years before I became his confessor, that is, they go back to the time when he was Nuncio in Munich in 1921. In addition, even when I was his confessor I was also in touch with him on matters which had nothing to do with confession. So I can speak of him with an easy mind. In the first place, we can start with the fact that my questioner considers Pius XII as probably little-known. If we look at the private life of Pius XII that is certainly true. We already have at the present time an excellent life of the present Pope written by Professor Algisi of Bergamo, which enables us to get a fair idea even of his spiritual life. We have not had and still have not anything similar about Pius XII. He was too reserved. That Pius XII was little-known is thrown into relief by the fact that the present Pope, by his simplicity and uncalculating spontaneity, straightway won the sympathies and hearts of all men. This fact is the more surprising if we think of the immense stature that is generally recognized Pius XII possessed and, I might add, of the great esteem that John XXIII has for his predecessor.

Pius XII was clearly a man of an entirely different stamp and perhaps fundamentally a lonely man in his greatness and in his keen sense of responsibility, and in this way, too, he was lonely in his personal austerity and life. It should perhaps be added that it will be many years, if not centuries, before the immense work of this Pope and his enduring influence on the Church and even on the history of humanity can be properly evaluated. In the midst of a terrible and catastrophic war and during the period of reconstruction which followed it, his help was solicited from all sides as was no other man's. All classes and professions asked him for guidance or words of encouragement. And it was during all this that uninterruptedly he sowed the seed, almost unbelievably abundant, that is to be found in the twenty-two volumes of his speeches and radio messages. When John XXIII said that he desired nothing better than to follow in the steps of his great predecessor you can be quite sure that these were no empty words or mere compliments. He follows in those footsteps in his own way, of course, but he does follow in them. It can even be said, in a certain sense, that the teaching spread by Pius XII has become the spiritual air that we constantly breathe without even being aware of it. In this sense Pius XII and his work remain fundamental also for the Council; especially on account of its breadth which takes into account every single one of the problems of humanity today and seeks to solve them in the light of the Gospel as it is preserved and taught by the Church, and thereby to reconquer modern man to the faith, to the Church, to Christ and to God.

The following postscript to this interview, provided by the Cardinal's private Secretary, may be of interest regarding Christian and Jewish relations. At the end of the interview the Cardinal was questioned about these relations and some misunderstanding arose. Accurate records were not kept, but the following summary is approved by the Cardinal's private Secretary.

Q. (By Signor Berg): Your Eminence has referred to the fact

that Anglican bishops in Africa approved and commended study of the pastoral letters of Catholic bishops against racial discrimination. May we hope that the Council will study the religious sources of anti-semitism, with special attention to the accusation of deicide made against the Jews, and try to throw light on the whole question?

A. We have had contact with several interested organizations. We looked into the question in several sessions of the Secretariat and formulated proposals about it for the Council.

Q. Is there any prospect that non-Christian observers may be present at the Council?

A. The pertinent fact is that non-Christians, as regards the Council, are in an essentially different condition than Christians, either Catholic or non-Catholic. We paid considerable attention to the matter and concluded that it would not be easy for non-Christians to have any real interest in the Council. But, in general, if a Community felt its interests were involved, we could explore what possibilities lie open.

PART THREE

CONCLUSION

20

ST PAUL'S VISION OF THE CHURCH IN HUMAN HISTORY[1]

THE CHURCH'S passage through the world's history has not been a triumphal march. In the long course of nineteen centuries the religion of Christ has won only about a third part of the human race, and of the 900 million baptized only 500 million are Roman Catholics. And this has been achieved with great sacrifice and labour, with sweat and tears. Entire regions which once were Catholic are today inhabited by populations which are for the most part non-Christian: think of Asia Minor, or of the countries of North Africa. Elsewhere millions of Catholics are undergoing a persistent and an eroding persecution under a militant atheism which endangers the faith and the Christian future of entire nations. For two thousand years countless martyrs have poured out their blood and sacrificed their lives. And within the Church herself, in the course of the centuries, there have been so many dissensions, quarrels, schisms, heresies. There have been the scandals caused so often by those whose lives should have been models of holiness and integrity. And still today there are all those children of the Church who have been baptized and yet remain oblivious of their Christian duties and live in apathetic indifference or complete worldliness, as if supernatural realities simply did not exist.

I have no wish to be a pessimist, like those who see in the Church only the darknesses and the shadows. There has been, and there is, in the Church so much that calls for admiration and even for sincere veneration: so much goodness and progress, such holiness and heroism, such light of knowledge and such energy of action!

[1] Original text: 'Il cammino della Chiesa nel mondo secondo san Paulo', in *La Civiltà Cattolica*, 1961, II, pp. 337-350.

But the strident contrast between the light and the dark, between, loftiness and baseness—it is this that creates a painful problem, evokes objections from outsiders and makes agonizing difficulties for the Catholic faithful themselves.

This is a disquieting and a vexing problem; but it is not a new one. It obtruded itself very forcibly in the life and work of St Paul. He was a new convert, full to overflowing with joy and gratitude to the Lord; he had a passionate love for Christ and the Church, and he blazed with apostolic zeal; no one felt more than he that flagrant contrast between the ideal and the reality, which is the focus of the difficulty. In his letters he gives a solution, brilliant, complete and profound.

I

St Paul's experience

The experiences of St Paul were often painful. Let us examine some of them:

(1) *To the community of Corinth*, more than to any other church, St Paul had devoted his time and his energy: during the period of his first visit, a year and a half of hard toil; then, while he was away, messengers to carry peace and instructions; then two other visits, and at least two great epistles. This community, dear as it was to him, caused him worries, sorrows and tears. In A.D. 56, scarcely five years after its foundation, there are already in Corinth dangerous factions and divisions, parties some of which described themselves of Christ, others of Apollo, of Cephas, of Paul (1 Cor 1:10ff.), threatening unity of doctrine and of charity. With sorrow the apostle has come to know of immorality such as is not admitted even among the pagans, as he himself says (ibid. 5:1), and he feels obliged to forewarn the Christians at Corinth against those who abuse the liberty given them by Christ, making of it a pretext to follow corrupt nature (cf. Gal 5:13) and to revert to the worst vices of paganism (cf. 1 Cor 6:9). Further, in religious meetings the apostle has to deal with the serious abuse of people coming to the agape in a state of drunkenness while others are suffering from hunger (ibid. 11:27). Paul, feeling all this and shaken 'by sorrow upon sorrow', declares

himself to be 'in great anguish and distress of mind, with many tears' (2 Cor 2:3f.); he feels obliged to admonish the guilty energetically, he threatens to come to them 'rod in hand' (1 Cor 4:21), and declares that he is 'prepared to punish rebellion from any quarter' (2 Cor 10:6). He excommunicates the most scandalous of them, handing him over 'to Satan, for the overthrow of his corrupt nature so that his spirit may find salvation' (1 Cor 5:5).

(2) Another hard trial for Paul is *the relative lack of success of his apostolic work* in so many places where he had preached. After the magnificent discourse at the Areopagus of Athens, 'some mocked, while others said, We must hear more from thee about this . . . But there were some men who attached themselves to him and learned to believe' (Acts 17:32-34). The proud and sceptical spirit of the philosophers and intellectuals of arrogant Athens disdained the message of the Gospel. At Corinth there were not, among the converts, 'many wise, in the world's fashion', not many 'powerful', not many of the sort 'who are something'; in the main it was simple people who were converted, people of modest station, contemptible in the eyes of the world (1 Cor 1:26-28). But, saddest of all, the chosen people of God did not accept the Gospel, his own people of Israel. To them St Paul repeats like a sad refrain: 'Now that you do not wish to believe, we shall turn to the gentiles' (Acts 13:47; 18:6; 28:28). Despite all his generous hopes (Acts 22:18ff.), he had always to keep yielding to the sorrowful evidence: only a remnant, a small part of his beloved people, had believed, while the mass of them had remained unbelieving (cf. Rom 11:6), a fact that caused him 'great sorrow . . . continual anguish' (ibid. 9:2). Where indeed was the irresistible power of the Gospel, of the grace of God, of the redemption of Christ?

(3) Grievous as were these disappointments and sorrows, they were perhaps less damaging and wounding than others caused him by some of his own people who were his brethren in Christ and in a sense his colleagues in the apostolate. These were Jews converted to the faith of Christ, who appealed to the authority of an apostle, St

James, and went about maintaining and insisting that circumcision, and therefore the observance of the Mosaic Law, were necessary to all for salvation, even to converts from paganism. The Council of the apostles, held at Jerusalem, had clearly established the contrary, and St James had himself officially declared 'that no burden should be laid upon those of the gentiles who had found their way to God' (Acts 15:13-29, cf. v. 19); nevertheless, these people did not surrender, but went on spreading their pernicious errors with subtleties and subterfuges. These false brethren (2 Cor 11:26) troubled and damaged St Paul's apostolic work and the communities founded by him. In Galicia, they confused the minds of the new converts, and tried to change the Gospel of Christ (Gal 1:5-6ff.). In his own specially loved community of Corinth they were a real threat to the authority of Paul, for they accused him of opportunism, of cowardice, of ambition, of intrigue, of foolishness (cf. 2 Cor 7:2; 10:2; 9:11; 11:7, 16; 12:16-18). These 'false apostles, dishonest workmen, that pass for apostles of Christ' threw suspicion on his preaching and charged that he had not been, like the other apostles, in the company of the Lord, but that he had only come in later, and now pretended to know better than any of those who had been trained by Christ himself (cf. 2 Cor 11:13-15; Gal chaps. 1-2). In fact, it was not merely a personal campaign but one which struck at the very universalism of Christianity: it was in effect a denial of the grace and liberality of Christ which opened the treasures of the Redeemer to all men and peoples without distinction of tongue or race, without reference to the narrow limits of the customs and traditions of the Jewish people. Yet those who preached this narrow-minded particularism maintained that they were the true apostles and preachers of Christ. It is no wonder that the letters of St Paul burn with indignation and that he is so vigorous in unmasking the underhanded intrigues of these pseudo-apostles who threatened to poison the nascent Church in its very constitution and in its sublime mission. These 'false brethren' caused the apostle much more suffering than the disappointments or failures about which we have spoken previously, and more suffering than the persecutions and external dangers which were so frequent and so great: scourgings, stonings, shipwrecks and the like, related in the Second Epistle to the Corinthians (ch. 11): these underhand subterfuges of the pseudo-apostles struck to the very heart of what he held most dear and sacred. And yet St Paul was not discouraged; he did not surrender. Why?

II

The Reasons for the Difficulties

The writings of the apostle show us that he takes full account of the intimate connection between these difficulties and the very nature of the Church. He understands that the prophecy of our Lord 'I shall tell him how much suffering he will have to undergo for my name's sake' (Acts 9:16), does not merely express a transitory phase of God's providence but states an essential law of the Church's work and development. Basing himself on a Messianic prophecy (Ps 109:1), he says of Christ, directly and vigorously: '*His* reign must continue until he has put all his enemies under his feet' (1 Cor 15:25). Since the Church is the kingdom of Christ on earth it is necessary that she should maintain her existence and that in her Christ should gradually triumph victoriously over his enemies. The Church is therefore necessarily indestructible and invincible. On the other hand Paul also knows that this indestructible life is subject to certain laws and conditions which derive from Christ himself. The difficulties which imperfections, weaknesses and sin create for the faith of some members of the Church are due to the fact that they do not know or do not take sufficient account of such laws. What are these laws?

First of all there is the fact that the Church is *a living organism* and hence is subject to the laws of all created life. An organism does not have its perfection right from the beginning; it obtains it only gradually by growth and development. Now it is exactly this that St Paul affirms of the Church. The body of Christ has to be 'built up until . . . we all attain . . . to perfect manhood, that maturity which is proportioned to the complete growth of Christ' (Eph 4:12ff.). Though the organism possesses everything that is intrinsically essential to it from the very moment at which life commences—otherwise it would not be an individual in itself distinct from others—it nevertheless needs a longer or shorter time for development; there is a long road for the baby to travel before he arrives at maturity. Similarly the Church right from her birth out of the pierced heart of the divine Redeemer, possesses her nature, her essential marks of holiness, oneness, catholicity. But these properties must be understood not in a static but in a dynamic sense: while always remaining the same in substance, they must increase, develop, attain their perfection.

And Paul is not unaware that Christians, while by the power of grace they are free from the tyranny of sin, are not for all that immune from relapsing into sin if they relax their effort in the ceaseless struggle against the passions and the desires of the flesh (Rom 8:9; 6:14; cf. Gal 5:13; Rom 6:12; cf. Rom 8:13; Gal 5:24). It is no wonder, then, that throughout the whole time of her development here on earth the Church has so often found herself sullied by the weaknesses, imperfections and sins of her members.

A second law derives from the fact that the development of an organism is in large measure determined or at least influenced *by the milieu in which it lives*. This influence may be favourable, but very often it is harmful, and thus the organism is left exposed to attacks, infections, plagues, wounds. So also the Church. The milieu in which she develops was described by our Lord himself as 'the world', which, as St John says, lies in the power of evil (1 John 5:19). St Paul knows this: he admonishes the Corinthians to protect themselves against the evil influences which come from without, since they cannot immediately 'cut themselves off from the world', that is from the evil influences exerted by the milieu (1 Cor 5:10). He knows that this world is dominated by the spirits of darkness and by their prince, the devil, 'the god this world worships' who blinds minds 'so that the glorious gospel of Christ . . . cannot reach them with the rays of its illumination' (2 Cor 4:4).

The difficulties and dangers raised against the life of Christ in man are notably aggravated by the pernicious influence of the world and its crafty prince, who seek to overthrow man with their attacks, or at least to damage him by flattery, by intimidation, by attrition. It is true that Christ has triumphed over all the enemy powers (Col 2:15), he has freed man from the powers of darkness (ibid. 1:13) and has taken him out of the wicked world (Gal 1:4), but he has not taken away, nor wished to take away, from him and from his Church the law of struggle against the powers of darkness (Eph 6:12).

For this reason the children of the Church must carry 'all the weapons in God's armoury, if they would find strength to resist the cunning of the devil': they must struggle, make headway against the enemy, put out their best effort 'to be found still on their feet, when all the task is over' (cf. Eph 6:11ff.). St Paul is never weary of giving warnings. 'You must not fall in with the manners of this world', he says to the Romans (Rom 12:2)· Christ has schooled us 'to forgo irreverent thoughts and worldly appetites, and to live, in this present world, a life of order, justice and holiness', he writes to Titus (Tit 2:12). As to Paul himself, so also to the Christians, the world must be crucified—and they to the world (Gal 6:14).

It is not surprising that not all Christians prove sufficiently strong to resist successfully the continuous offensive of the world, at times blatant, at times insidious, and to resist its promptings, seductions, menaces, persecutions. In the Church, sins, scandals, falls, defections, can never be lacking, as they were not lacking in the time of St Paul. He foresees that 'the time will surely come when men will grow tired of sound doctrine, ... and so they will provide themselves with a continuous succession of new teachers, as the whim takes them, turning a deaf ear to the truth, bestowing their attention on fables instead' (2 Tim 4:5). He foretells that there will be a rabble of people 'treacherous, reckless, full of vain conceit, thinking rather of their pleasures than of God' (ibid. 3:1, 4, 5).

The third law is that of the Cross, of the mystery of the Cross. The fact that the Church is the mystical Body of Christ and that it lives by his life and by that of his divine Spirit assures not only that it is indestructible and invincible, but also that it must participate in the Cross of her divine Head. The Church is indeed not the glorified body of Christ but, as it were, a prolongation of the earthly life of

Christ the Redeemer. The life of the Church, then, must necessarily be sealed, like the life of Jesus, with the Cross.

The Crucified, 'to the Jews a discouragement, to the Gentiles, mere folly', is held up before the Church as expressing in himself the plan for the Church's life and action (1 Cor 1:23ff.). Through baptism, which makes us members of the mystical Body, every Christian is, as it were, dead with Christ, and with him fixed to the Cross (ibid. 12:13; Rom 6:3, 8; Gal 2:19; cf. Luke 9:23; Mt 16:24), so that pain and humiliation must be the fundamental characteristic of the life of all members of the Church. This law is specially true for the apostle and for his work (2 Cor 4:11ff.), and it is in this perspective that the tribulations undergone by Paul (2 Cor 11:23-31) find their deepest explanation. Paul takes this view of his tribulations: 'I am glad of my sufferings on your behalf, as, in this mortal frame of mine, I help to pay off the debt which the afflictions of Christ still leave to be paid, for the sake of his body, the Church' (Col 1:24). The Church therefore, in order to live, needs ministers and apostles who can, through her, confront the Cross as her head and founder dared to do, with joy and certainty that they are thereby labouring together for the 'life of the world' (cf. 2 Cor 7:4; John 6:51).

Going yet deeper, the apostle explains to us the ultimate reason for this law of the Cross. The life and work of the Church is sealed with the Cross so that the work of redemption may appear not a human work, but as a work of the mercy of God: 'If anyone boasts, let him make his boast in the Lord' (1 Cor 1:31). The apostle is actually nothing other than an instrument and, like the candle, must be consumed in order to give light to others. Why then be upset, when across the way of the Church rise mountainous difficulties and obstacles and when the cross seems to grow ever larger and more weighty?

III
Present-day difficulties

When we contemplate the Church's painful course across the centuries, it is obvious that the imperfections, the weaknesses, the evil and the sin found in her are many and grievous—there is no point in trying to hide them or to put a fair face on them. The sorrowful experience of St Paul constantly repeats itself: it is the more sharply felt the more Christ, his Church and the souls to be saved are loved. And today, with the growth of the Church, concern is not confined to a limited field, to small communities of one or two cities or one or two nations. Today everything has acquired world-wide dimensions. As the good has repercussions on the whole Church, so also has the evil. Then, with the deepening of the doctrine of the mystical Body of Christ, the members of the Church are coming more and more to understand how much the sin of individuals, whatever their social station, damages the whole organism of the Church, and how much it impedes the flow of grace. For this reason, sin found in the members of the Church is no longer regarded merely as a dishonour to the loftiness of the Christian calling, but it is considered as a bacillus, an infection threatening the whole supernatural organism, and consequently sorrow for the sin which is found in the Church grows far more piercing and penetrating. Sin has assumed such proportions today that we almost have that vast chilling of charity foretold by Christ (cf. Mt 24:12). So many Catholics practise their religion only on Sunday, or only at Easter, or even less frequently. This ought to be, for all who love Christ and the Church, a 'continual anguish', comparable to that of St Paul for the unbelief of his own people (cf. Rom 9:2).

No less vast are the proportions of the evil which affects *the unity of the Church*. Here also the pain and anxiety today take on world-wide dimensions. Concern is no longer about this or that local disunity, however sad it may be. Today we face the 'distressing problem of the shattered unity of the heritage of Christ' as the Holy Father puts it.[1] There are 400 million baptized who are separated from the visible organism of the Church and are therefore deprived of the enjoyment of so many privileges, so many graces which Christ grants to those who are fully and therefore visibly united with his Church. This is the other great scandal which today is before us in the Church and which—let us say so frankly—becomes

[1] Christmas Broadcast 1958, in *A.A.S.* LI (1959), p. 9; in *Civiltà Cattolica* 1959, I, p. 7.

a temptation to many, and leads them to doubt the authenticity of the mission of the Church, her truth and her holiness.

These are some aspects of the problem of evil in the Church which have made an impact upon the modern mind. It is upon them that we must turn the searchlight of the principles given us by St Paul to explain the imperfections, the weaknesses, the evil and the sin which exist in the Church.

Indestructibility and invincibility. The deep shadows we have seen in the Church should not make us doubt her divine mission and her divine greatness, just as St Paul did not doubt them, in spite of his most painful experiences.

Look, for instance, at the holiness of the Church. It must be admitted that there is much in the Church that contrasts with holiness. St Paul, too, was by sad experience aware of this. Nevertheless, he held firm to the fact that the Church *is and remains holy* in her principles, in the revealed doctrine which she preaches to men and which is a source of light to the Christian intellect and power to the Christian will, in her sacraments which are the channels by which she communicates to souls the root of all personal holiness, sanctifying grace, and which supply special graces for every condition of life and vocation. The fruits, and likewise the evidence of this holiness, are the countless Christians who live faithfully according to the precepts of the Gospel and, above all, there are those truly great human beings who have attained heroic virtue, the topmost heights of sanctity. What St Paul writes, then, is true, and remains always true, 'Christ shewed love to the Church when he gave himself up on its behalf. He would hallow it . . . he would summon it into his own presence, the Church in all its beauty, no stain, no wrinkle, no such disfigurement' (Eph 5:25ff.). He who has fully understood this essential, fundamental holiness of the Church will never be disturbed in his faith, even when he sees the great scandals in the Church and the great sins committed by the children of the Church in the course of the centuries.

The same must be said of the *essential unity* of the Church. The Church of Christ cannot be other than one: she is, as has been seen, the mystical Body of Christ and, as such, is one as Christ is one.

Christ himself speaks of the Church as of one edifice built upon one fundamental 'rock', which is the apostle Peter and his successor (Mt 16:18); he speaks of the one flock and the one fold to which he must lead all the sheep (John 10:14-16). This essential unity consists in the fact that the members of the Church profess the same faiths that in the whole Church the same means of salvation—that is, the sacraments—are administered and received, and that the body of the Church loyally follows its shepherds, united among themselves and with the Chief Shepherd, the Roman Pontiff, successor of St Peter. In its essentials this unity, which Christ wants in his Church and through his Church, is guaranteed by the divine promises: 'I am with you all until the consummation of the world . . . the gates of hell shall not prevail against it' (Mt 28:20; 16:18). To be sure, not merely some individual members, but also entire regions and nations have unfortunately become separated from her in the course of history, whether by heresy—that is, by denying this or that truth of faith—or by schism—that is, by refusing to accept her rule. History recounts so many of these divisions and St Paul himself foresaw them. In his farewell discourse at Miletus he had spoken of 'ravening wolves', of men who 'will come forward with a false message, and find disciples to follow them' (Acts 20:29ff.), and he is grieved because some 'have made shipwreck of the faith', straying from the truth, and others are working 'the overthrow of the faith in some minds' (1 Tim 1:19; 2 Tim 2:18). But despite such divisions and schisms the Church of Christ has always preserved, though often in the midst of most grievous distress and suffering, her essential unity, her full unity in government and in the faith.

The mystery of the Cross. Keeping firmly in view the invincibility of the Church, one must however not lose sight of these special laws which are characteristic of the life, progress and victories of the Church. They are summed up in a certain fashion in the mystery of the Cross, insofar as this means humiliation and suffering. Taken in this wide sense, it explains first of all that adaptation made by God and by Christ of their designs for the Church to the human laws of organic growth. Certainly in human fashion we might have preferred unbroken and resounding triumphs, a triumphal march through history, just as even the apostles looked forward to and ardently desired—before Pentecost—a sudden glorious coming of the Kingdom of God. Christ on the contrary had preferred to pass through all the stages of human life, birth, infancy, youth . . . maturity, and then the stage of laborious preaching with all its vicissitudes. And in the same way he has also wanted a Church which should be born, should live, as it were, in swaddling bands and through the tears of childhood, and that her growth and maturation should follow step by step that of humanity itself and of its history.

There is yet more. Christ did not choose for himself an ordinary and peaceful human existence but a life liable to all sorts of adversity: opposition, persecutions, painful defeats and humiliations from the world and its Prince, as long as 'the hour of the powers of darkness' should last, according to the plans of God (Luke 22:53). In the same way he has also placed his Church in the midst of the world and wills that it should live in obscurity, that it should conquer through defeats, that it should become great through deep humiliations.

But here one must at once remark a most important difference between Christ and the members of his Church: of him it is written that he was tried in every way and yet was 'sinless' (Heb 4:15), remaining 'holy and guiltless and undefiled, not reckoned among us sinners, lifted high above all the heavens' (ibid. 7:26). In contrast to him, his members stain themselves time and time again with sins, as we have seen, and often with most serious sins. Here is the crucial point of our problem: how is it and why is it that God permits sin even in his Church, redeemed by the blood of his Son, given life by his own Spirit? When we say 'permits', our meaning is clearly not that he approves it, but only that he tolerates it, in other words, that he respects the free will given to men and does not prevent sin by making use of all the means open to his omnipotence, by which he would certainly be able to prevent it.

And let it be kept in mind that the distressing problem of the lack of unity among Christians eventually comes back to the same question of the how and why of sin in the Church. By this we clearly do not mean to say that all those who are today unhappily separated from the visible organism of the Church are separated because of their own personal guilt: God forbid! But we do mean to say that such separation in itself—whether it has come about through heresy or schism—is a sin and a very grave sin. In this sense then the problem of the lack of unity coincides with the general question: 'How and why is there sin in the Church of Christ?'

In general terms the reply to our question is here supplied by the classic answer of St Augustine that God has judged it better to draw good out of evil, rather than to permit no evil.[1] In the omnipotent hand of God's all-wise Providence, weaknesses and even sins are transformed so that they can serve and benefit the Church. Let us try to explain some aspects of how they may so serve.

The first and principal aspect we have already indicated in speaking of the mystery of the Cross. God's will is that no one should glory in himself, but that he who glories should glory in the Lord (1 Cor 1:29, 31; cf. 2 Cor 10:17). He wishes, then, to teach men not to trust in themselves, nor to attribute to themselves the good that they possess or that they have done, but to put their trust in God alone and to attribute success to him alone. Now for this purpose there is no means more efficacious than the thing which most humiliates man, detaches him from himself and casts him into the arms of the merciful heavenly Father: sin admitted, repented, pardoned and atoned.

A great good which he can draw from sin is to restore to modern man *trust in the mercy of God our Lord*. Too often the man of today thinks that after his worst falls and most grievous offences against God nothing remains but to flee like Cain before the wrath of an outraged God. The man who can preach the mercy of God because he has experienced it himself, and who, like the Church, tries to be merciful according to the example of our Lord, is a benefactor to humanity. The Encyclical *Mystici Corporis* sees a particular sign of the infinite mercy of the Lord in that he does not immediately exclude from the Church those who commit grave sin, and Pius XII

[1] *Ench. de fide, spe et caritate*, cap. 37. P.L. 40, 245.

goes on to point out that Jesus during his earthly life did not deny a place at the banquet to sinners.[2] It is not possible here to speak at length about the merciful love Jesus showed towards sinners; he said that he was not come to call the just, but sinners (Mt 9:13; Luke 5:32); yet one cannot fail to point out how much good and how many consolations the Church brings to the whole world and to individual men through her mission of mercy to the weak and the sinful. It can almost be said that without the confessional the Church would lack a precious element of her nature as mother of men. It is certainly true that sins and scandals make a cross which is sometimes heavy and hard; but it is equally true that this school of Christian patience is a source of great graces for all of us. Seeing with the eye of faith the sins and weaknesses which are present among the children of the Church, we may indeed be saddened at the sight: it may make us suffer, as it made St Paul suffer, but it will not trouble our faith and our love of the Church, nor will it disconcert us. It will rather be an effective stimulus to widen our charity still more, that charity of which the apostle said: 'Charity is patient, is kind . . . sustains, believes, hopes, endures to the last' (1 Cor 13:4, 7).

Another blessing that God allows to spring from the distressing experience of lack of unity is this, that Christian people may go on discovering anew the value of this priceless gift of God, go on asking for it with humble perseverance, and that they may recognize the true Church precisely because of the attitude she takes toward the tragic fact of division. To her untellable grief, she is in fact involved in the frightful breaking of bonds that are sacrosanct, and she is conscious, especially today, of her own duty to do everything possible to bring into the one fold all who are without. This heartfelt motherly love and anxious concern is the true answer to the tormenting problem of the separation of so many children whom she holds as her own. It is a problem which is not solved by despairing doubt about the oneness of the Church founded by Christ; it can be solved only by prayer, sacrifice and work, that the will of our Lord may draw closer to realization, 'that they all may be one'

[2] *A.A.S.* xxxv (1943), p. 203.

(John 17:21)—a holy yearning in the heart of Paul, touchingly expressed at the end of his letter to the Romans: 'May God, the author of all endurance and all encouragement, enable you to be all of one mind according to the mind of Christ Jesus, so that you may all have but one heart and one mouth, to glorify God, the Father of Our Lord Jesus Christ' (Rom 15:5ff.).

Let us conclude. The experiences of St Paul, brought into theological focus and perspective while the Church was still taking its first steps, are a symbol, almost an anticipation, of so much which had to happen to the Church in her long course through the centuries. The apostle of the gentiles experienced periods of deep depression and affliction, and yet his generous heart accepted all the anxieties, afflictions and sufferings he had to endure. He wrote with pithy brevity: 'I am well content with these humiliations of mine, with the insults, the hardships, the persecutions, the times of difficulty I undergo for Christ' (2 Cor 12:10); he understood that he had even to die that his faithful might live: 'Death makes itself felt in us, and life in you' (ibid. 4:12), and with boundless generosity he exclaimed: 'For my own part, I will gladly spend and be spent on your souls' behalf, though you should love me too little for loving you too well' (ibid. 12:15). The Church follows the path traced out by the great apostle: though persecuted, afflicted, and oppressed, she continues tirelessly on her journey, doing good wherever she is, according to the word of the same apostle: 'Let us not be discouraged, then, over our acts of charity' (Gal 6:9). She meets internal weaknesses with constantly renewed reform, 'wholly intent', as the Holy Father says, 'to restore the splendour of greater purity and greater simplicity to her aspect', seeking again 'the features of her more fervent youth'[1]; she meets the difficulties which modern life causes the faithful with a more energetic apostolate, especially that of the laity of every class and age; the losses incurred through her children who abandon or neglect her she meets with magnificent missionary work which wins for Christ new peoples and nations; defections and divisions she is today meeting with an energetic movement for Church unity,

[1] John XXIII, *Discourse*, 13 November, 1960 in *A.A.S.* LIII (1960), p. 960.

seeking to draw all the baptized into the unity which Christ willed and prayed for.

In other words, the glaring contrast, often met with in this life on earth of the Church, between light and darkness, between sublimity and baseness, far from overcoming the Church, is for her a means of progress, a stimulus to greater humility, zeal and charity; and above all it is a means of her apostolate since, carrying in the steps of her Master the heavy cross of the weaknesses and sins of her children, she fills up the sufferings of Christ, according to the example of St Paul (cf. Col 1:24), for the building of the whole of his mystical Body. Today the Church is suffering a persecution of a severity unknown in all previous history. It is today, too, that with enlarged hearts, men are proclaiming their need of Christ and of his conquest for peace, for he, and he alone, is our hope and our salvation, the sole Saviour of humanity: 'This alone of all the names under heaven has been appointed to men as the one by which we must needs be saved' (Acts 4:12). For that reason the Church, with St Paul, repeats fearlessly: 'Christ must reign' (cf. 1 Cor 15:25). This is the sublime goal of the toilsome journey of the Church through the centuries and through the world: 'and when that subjection is complete, then the Son himself will become subject to the power that made all things his subjects, so that God may be all in all' (ibid. 15:28).

INDEX

Catholic Observers take part, 171, 188

statement of doctrine and purpose, 190-1

World Federation of Christian Students, 121-2

Zahrnt, H., 139n

Date D